DATE DUE

NOV 05	APR 2 2 2008	
APR 2 7		
OCT 3 0		
APR 04		
JUL 2 2		
DEC - 8		
APR 2 8		
MAR 2 9		
APR 2 0		
APR 1 7		
OCT 2 6		

Demco, Inc. 38-293

Race, Sex, and Policy Problems

Race, Sex, and Policy Problems

Edited by:

Marian Lief Palley
University of Delaware

Michael B. Preston
University of Illinois

Lexington Books
D.C. Heath and Company
Lexington, Massachusetts
Toronto

Library of Congress Cataloging in Publication Data

Main entry under title:

Race, sex, and policy problems.

1. Race discrimination—Law and legislation—United States—Addresses, essays, lectures. 2. Sex discrimination against women—Law and legislation—United States—Addresses, essays, lectures. 3. Abortion—Law and legislation—Israel—Addresses, essays, lectures, I. Palley, Marian Lief II. Preston, Michael B.
KF4755.A75R3   342'.73'087   79-11016
ISBN 0-669-01985-2

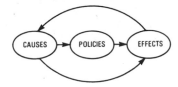

Policy Studies Organization Series

General Approaches to Policy Studies

Policy Studies in America and Elsewhere
　　edited by Stuart S. Nagel
Policy Studies and the Social Sciences
　　edited by Stuart S. Nagel
Methodology for Analyzing Public Policies
　　edited by Frank P. Scioli, Jr., and Thomas J. Cook
Urban Problems and Public Policy
　　edited by Robert L. Lineberry and Louis H. Masotti
Problems of Theory in Policy Analysis
　　edited by Philip M. Gregg
Using Social Research for Public Policy-Making
　　edited by Carol H. Weiss
Public Administration and Public Policy
　　edited by H. George Frederickson and Charles Wise
Policy Analysis and Deductive Reasoning
　　edited by Gordon Tullock and Richard Wagner
Legislative Reform
　　edited by Leroy N. Rieselbach
Teaching Policy Studies
　　edited by William D. Coplin
Paths to Political Reform
　　edited by William J. Crotty
Determinants of Public Policy
　　edited by Thomas Dye and Virginia Gray

Specific Policy Problems

Analyzing Poverty Policy
　　edited by Dorothy Buckton James
Crime and Criminal Justice
　　edited by John A. Gardiner and Michael Mulkey
Civil Liberties
　　edited by Stephen L. Wasby
Foreign Policy Analysis
　　edited by Richard L. Merritt

To
Mary and Howard

Contents

List of Figure and Tables

Introduction

It has been proposed that social movements are one of the "antistructures" generated by the process of institutionalization. The rise of a social movement "... is thus a sign that the old order is being challenged, having lost its sacredness as it becomes irrelevant to peoples' needs."[1] Members of such movements indicate their dissatisfaction and grievances with the status quo.[2] These movements indicate that new ideas and hopes are emerging and thus "demand attention, ... because they provide valuable clues, articulated in cries of anguish and declarations of hope, about the direction which future change will take."[3]

In the context of contemporary movements for equal rights for nonwhites and women as they are examined in this book, a social movement is defined as "a conscious, collective, organized attempt to bring about or resist large-scale change in the social order ..."[4] by a variety of means. It will be shown that the articulated demands of the civil rights movement and women's rights movement increasingly have been accepted as reasonable societal norms and expectations by many women and men. In fact, since the early days of these movements, much of the criticism of U.S. society raised by the first contemporary civil rights advocates and more recently women's righters has been accepted by the majority in the United States. At present, at least the rhetoric of support for equal rights for nonwhites and women is articulated by the U.S. majority regardless of age, religion, or social class. The positions of the vanguard of these movements have been accepted into the mainstream of U.S. thought (even if not totally in action) as the movements have made more and more people aware of the social, economic, and political inequality experienced by nonwhites and women. This acceptance does not mean, however, that the goals of either the civil rights movements or the women's rights movements have been fully achieved. In the pages that follow, it will be demonstrated that despite some very tangible policy gains for nonwhites and women, equality for these groups with white men is still a futuristic goal.[5]

When the idea for this book was conceived, the question arose as to how the materials could best be organized. Two alternatives seemed reasonable: the articles could be divided such that all the materials on nonwhites were in one section and all the articles discussing women were in another section; or, the materials could be integrated into functional categories. The latter method for organizing this collection was selected because it appeared that despite some of the differences in both the life conditions and the experiences of women and nonwhites in trying to influence the policy process in the United States, there are enough similarities in the contemporary experiences of these two population cohorts to suggest joint presentation and discussion.

Numerous books and articles of high quality have appeared which discuss the development of both women's and civil rights organizations. Also, considerable research has been generated on the unequal conditions that affect minorities in the United States. In this book different sets of questions are examined. More specifically, the questions raised relate to the stage after organization. That is, once the momentum for organization has been generated, what policies are addressed by the newly formed groups? How successful are these groups in influencing the outputs of the system? And, what are the impacts of selected policy decisions on the members of these organized groups?

The book has been divided into six sections. The first set of articles considers the role of individuals and groups in influencing policy. Anne Costain, Michael Preston, and Toni-Michelle Travis have contributed chapters addressing these relationships. Next, Cheryl Swanson and H. Brinton Milward, Kenneth Meier, M. Margaret Conway, and Maurice Woodard and Edward R. Jackson have each looked at executive orders and administrative regulations in promoting equality for racial minorities and women. Leslie Goldstein, Charles Bullock and Joseph Stewart, Jr., and Howard Palley have examined the effect of different judicial decisions on women and racial minorities. The section on judicial impacts is followed by a section on the impacts of legislative enactments on women and minorities. Donald McCrone and Richard Hardy, and Sarah Slavin Schramm have written articles for this part of the book. Policy impacts in the states are examined by Cal Clark, Janet Clark, and Jose Garcia, Susan Welch with Diane Levitt Gottheil, Glen Broach, and Marianne Githens and Jewel Prestage. Finally, in order to provide a perspective from another society, Yael Yishai has provided an analysis of abortion policy in Israel.

The Policy Studies Organization gratefully thanks the University of Delaware for its aid to the symposium on which this book is based. However, no one other than the individual authors is responsible for the ideas advocated here.

Notes

1. John Wilson, *Introduction to Social Movements* (New York: Basic Books, 1973), p. 4.

2. Anthony Oberscholl, *Social Conflict and Social Movements* (Englewood Cliffs, N.J.: Prentice-Hall, 1973), pp. 118-119.

3. Wilson, *Introduction to Social Movements,* pp. 4-5.

4. Ibid., p. 8.

5. For a discussion of some of the recent successes and the successful political strategies used by women in the policy arena, see Joyce Gelb and Marian Lief Palley, "Women and Interest Group Politics: A Comparative Analysis of Federal Decision-Making," *Journal of Politics,* May, 1979.

Part I
The Role of Individuals and Interest Groups in Influencing Policies

1

Eliminating Sex Discrimination in Education: Lobbying for Implementation of Title IX

Anne N. Costain

An increasingly common way for the federal government to handle demands generated by disadvantaged groups is that Congress passes legislation responding to the grievances of the group, and then the bureaucracy delays implementation of this legislation for prolonged periods. This has the effect of forcing the group to fight its most difficult political battles in bureaucratic agencies, out of the public eye. This deprives the group of the media attention and publicity which normally surround congressional lobbying campaigns and may even push a group to use disorderly tactics in an effort to recapture public attention.[1] Yet, if the group fails to fight within the corridors of the bureaucracy, the result may be legislation with no political effect.[2]

Congress has relatively little to lose in this process. It is on record with early support for the group's demands. Bureaucratic intransigence can be blamed for any subsequent failures in policy implementation.

This strategy of delay is similarly a rational one for bureaucratic agencies. The agency has the time to calculate what political costs it is likely to incur by making a serious effort to enforce this new legislation. By closely monitoring the behavior of groups supporting and opposing this legislation during the period of delay, agencies may weigh the long-term impact of adding the bill's supporters to the agency's existing clientele. Should the groups which stand to benefit from strong bureaucratic enforcement be unable or unwilling to maintain pressure on the agency, this may convince the agency that it can expect little ongoing support from these groups in future battles with Congress, the administration, or opponents of the legislation who might organize to attack the agency on this or other issues. Implementation of the legislation in this eventuality will be half-hearted and inadequate. If the group should prove itself politically skilled and a valuable ally for future bureaucratic struggles, the opposite result may be predicted.[3]

Government delays in implementing Title IX of the 1972 Education Amend-

This research was carried out under a grant from the Florence Eagleton Grants program sponsored by the Center for the American Woman and Politics of the Eagleton Institute of Politics, Rutgers University. Washington interviews were conducted while the author was a Visiting Scholar at the Brookings Institution. The study itself is based on interviews with members of Congress, their staff assistants, and members of the Education Task Force conducted while the lobbying described was in progress.

3

ments Act[4] seem to follow this pattern of deliberate and calculated inaction. The Department of Health, Education, and Welfare (HEW) was given responsibility in July 1972 for implementing a far-reaching set of objectives aimed at eliminating most forms of sexual discrimination in the U.S. educational system. Title IX prohibits most educational programs that receive federal funds from excluding individuals on the basis of sex, denying them the full benefits of the program, or subjecting them to discrimination within the program. Similarly, employment policies in these educational programs must treat individuals fairly without regard to their sex. Not until July 1975 were regulations put into effect to begin to reach these objectives. The interim period was one of mobilization by both proponents and opponents of Title IX. A series of struggles tested the political strength and endurance of each side. HEW played an almost neutral role, waiting to gauge for itself what political course would best serve its interests.

This study traces part of the lobbying process, focusing on how groups supporting Title IX sought to gain forceful implementation of Title IX. This lobbying had two dimensions. The first was to pressure HEW to issue strong regulations to implement Title IX and subsequently to convince Congress to allow these regulations to go into effect without weakening modifications. The second and somewhat separate phase of this struggle revolved around the Casey Amendment, legislation before Congress which would modify the original language of Title IX and limit the scope of the antidiscrimination provisions.[5] Supporters of Title IX had to protect the language of the title at the same time as they were called on to fight for adequate administrative regulations. This particular examination of Title IX implementation focuses on the efforts to win and protect strong administrative regulations. Since moves to amend laws after they are in effect are relatively common in the legislative process, it is the administrative portion of the battle over Title IX, the effort to have its provisions put into effect, which best illustrates the unusual difficulties faced by Title IX supporters. New interests like those pushing for an end to sexual discrimination in education must get legislation through Congress; block congressional efforts to amend or negate this legislation through subsequent bills; stimulate a skeptical, if not unfriendly, bureaucracy to act; and, in the case of educational policy, thwart congressional efforts to delay enforcement further through concurrent resolution rejecting agency regulations.[6] This analysis will concentrate on the latter two aspects of this process.

Legislative History of Title IX

Initial passage of Title IX in Congress did little to prepare groups supporting its provisions for future political battles. The title itself was a product of the work and legislative skill of Representative Edith Green (D-Ore.) and Senator Birch Bayh (D-Ind.) supported by little or no independent lobbying.[7] Although this title to the omnibus Education Amendments Act contained sweeping prohibitions against discrimination based on sex in most federally financed education programs, it passed both houses of Congress without receiving much attention either in committee or in Congress as a whole. Its implications for reforming U.S. educational institutions were almost completely overshadowed by the storm surrounding the then more politically salient issue of court-ordered busing.[8]

With scant evidence in the legislative record of either strong political support for this title or organized lobbying on its behalf, HEW took no public action for more than a year after Title IX became law. Ironically, HEW was finally pushed from this posture of inaction by a congressional amendment sponsored by opponents of Title IX. In 1974 Senator John Tower (R-Tex.) responded to rumors that Title IX might require school athletic programs to treat students equally regardless of sex, by introducing an amendment to the 1974 Education Amendments Act exempting sports from Title IX's provisions. Senator Walter Mondale (D-Minn.) in a compromise with Tower agreed not to oppose Tower's amendment if Tower would add a requirement that HEW must also publish regulations implementing Title IX within thirty days after the passage of the 1974 Education Amendments. Senator Tower agreed to this addition.[9] When the Tower amendment came out of the joint House-Senate conference, the original athletic provision of Tower's amendment was considerably altered, but the Mondale addition remained intact.

Prodded by this legislative action, HEW issued its first set of regulations implementing Title IX on June 20, 1974.[10] Following a newly enacted procedure for promulgating administrative regulations for education acts, these regulations were subject to congressional veto. The proposed rules were open for public comment for thirty days after their issuance. After this period of public comment, HEW could make any desired revisions and send the final regulations to Congress. Congress might then, if it chose, reject the regulations by concurrent resolution. If no concurrent resolution were passed, the regulations would go into effect automatically forty-five days after they had been issued.

Pro- And Anti-Title IX Lobbies

The issuance of the June 1974 HEW regulations combined with the prospect that Congress might reject the regulations, delaying still further the implementation of Title IX, spurred pro-Title IX groups to organize. By late fall of 1974, a small number of group representatives had started assembling periodically to share information and coordinate responses to administrative and congressional action of Title IX. Although the core group which began meeting to discuss Title IX consisted primarily of representatives of educational organizations, including the American Council on Education and the American Association of University

Women, the group expanded considerably through the spring of 1975 to include women's groups, public interest and student associations, as well as education groups.[11] This coalition in support of Title IX, which became known as the Education Task Force, combined lobbying groups like the National Student Lobby and Women's Lobby, research-oriented organizations like the Project on Equal Education Rights (PEER) and the Project on the Status and Education of Women, and mass-membership groups like the National Student Association and the League of Women Voters. This allowed the Education Task Force to apply pressure through a variety of different channels.

Lobbying against Title IX centered on the National Collegiate Athletic Association (NCAA) and the American Football Coaches Association, with its close ties to President Gerald Ford. During the period following the release of HEW's first set of Title IX regulations, these groups were successful in stimulating large flows of mail to HEW, to President Ford, and to Congress, criticizing the possible impact of Title IX on college athletic programs.

Pressuring HEW

HEW delayed for almost a year in submitting its revised Title IX regulations to Congress. Despite the opportunity that the absence of final HEW regulations provided for the pro-Title IX coalition to solidify its support, recruit new members, and collect data, the continued delay was frustrating to most of its members. Members of the Education Task Force were experiencing great difficulty in their efforts to maintain contact with the officials at HEW who were responsible for revising the regulations. Several organizational representatives who tried hard to work with officials in the department mentioned in separate interviews that HEW was not willing to view women or the Education Task Force as a constituency. When the revised Title IX regulations were completed, the Education Task Force was not informed of the weakening of regulations which had occurred. In fact, there was a concerted effort to limit the number within the bureaucracy who had access to the revised document before its release to Congress on June 4, 1975.

The attention of Education Task Force members turned understandably to the White House and Congress. The White House, like HEW, was not interested in cultivating a supportive women's rights constituency. After considerable political maneuvering by the Education Task Force and sympathetic congressional offices, with an assist from Vice President Rockefeller's staff, a meeting was finally scheduled at the White House with Richard Parsons of the Domestic Council. Women's groups had heard unofficially that HEW has submitted a revised version of the regulations to the President for approval in March of that year. In their meeting on May 13, pro-Title IX groups hoped to learn more about the content of these revised regulations as well as communicating their concerns about Title IX to the White House. Their scheduled meeting with Richard Parsons was useful in two respects. First, the views of the participating groups were presented. Second, the White House was alerted to the existence of an active, well-informed, broad-based coalition monitoring Title IX enforcement. The pro-Title IX groups did not learn as much from the White House. No clear administration position on Title IX regulations was communicated. In addition, Parsons, although undoubtedly in possession of the revised regulations, did not indicate what types of changes HEW had made. As several women noted bitterly in describing this meeting, they had to work all spring to talk with Richard Parsons while during the same period college football coaches opposed to Title IX got a well-publicized meeting with President Gerald Ford to express their views.[12]

The Congressional Battle

Overt actions taken by Congress prior to HEW's issuance of its revised regulations seemed to indicate greater responsiveness to anti-Title IX than to pro-Title IX groups. On December 31, 1974 an amendment to Title IX exempting social fraternities and sororities, Boy Scouts, Girl Scouts, YMCA, YWCA, Camp Fire Girls, and other voluntary youth organizations from coverage by law was signed by President Ford as part of the White House Library Conference Act. This amendment had been introduced by Senator Birch Bayh, one of the architects of Title IX, in an effort to prevent opposition to the inclusion of these organizations from being used as a wedge to amend Title IX even more seriously. In the House, Representative Robert Casey (D-Tex.) successfully added a surprise amendment to the education appropriations bill, exempting Boy Scouts, Girl Scouts, YMCA, YWCA, Camp Fire Girls, Boys Clubs, Girls Clubs, physical education classes, sororities and fraternities, whether honorary, service, or social, from the sex discrimination provisions of Title IX. Although this amendment for the most part repeated organizations already exempted by the Bayh amendment, it also went further by including honorary associations and all physical education classes. This amendment passed easily in the House, 253 to 145,[13] but had not been acted on by the Senate. Such legislative action seemed likely to encourage further congressional moves to limit Title IX.

Some critical events were also taking place in Congress behind the scenes. Representative James O'Hara (D-Mich.), an opponent of affirmative action programs, was planning hearings on the revised Title IX regulations. Education Task Force members had been alerted to Representative O'Hara's hostility to government action in support of equal opportunity by his Special Subcommittee on Education's September 1974 hearings on civil rights compliance and federal funding of institutions of higher education. If O'Hara's turned out to be the only legislative hearings on Title IX regulations, the possibility that strong enforcement provisions would be upheld by Congress was diminished.

Individual Education Task Force members and supporters of Title IX in Congress began a concerted effort to persuade the chair of another subcommittee to hold hearings on Title IX regulations. Representatives Augustus Hawkins (D-Calif.) and Donald Edwards (D-Calif.) were approached about hearings on the House side. On the Senate side, early contact was made with Senators Harrison Williams (D-N.J.) and Walter Mondale (D-Minn.).

Education Task Force members recognized that an alternate forum alone would not be enough to thwart O'Hara. The Education Task Force would need additional allies to win the fight on regulations. Coordinated efforts were made to attract the support of black civil rights groups. Since women's and civil rights groups were already working together to defeat proposed new consolidated procedural regulations to enforce civil rights laws, such linkages were not difficult to establish.

On June 4, 1975 the final HEW regulations were sent from the White House to Congress. The next day Senator Jesse Helms (R-N.C.) introduced a concurrent resolution to disapprove the Title IX regulations in their entirety. A similar resolution was soon introduced in the House by Representative James Martin (R-N.C.). Although these resolutions of total disapproval were buried in committee, plans for hearings by O'Hara's Subcommittee on Postsecondary Education were accelerated. The hearings had originally been announced for June 23. Instead they began a week earlier on June 17.

When the final schedule for the Title IX hearings was released, as the Education Task Force feared, it contained a large number of opponents of Title IX, including the NCAA and the American Football Coaches Association. Representatives of several Education Task Force groups who had been assured that they would be able to present testimony had been dropped from the list of testifiers.

Although O'Hara's hearings on Title IX were rushed through before the Education Task Force had adequate time to organize a large-scale lobbying effort in Congress, some of their behind-the-scenes work was starting to pay off. Representative Augustus Hawkins had requested and been given joint jurisdiction over the Title IX regulations with Representative O'Hara. Although Hawkins at the time did not plan to hold hearings on Title IX in his Equal Opportunity subcommittee, he had been persuaded by supporters of Title IX to retain some leverage over the regulations. The linkage between Title IX's enforcement provisions and those of Title VI of the 1964 Civil Rights Act was of particular concern. In addition, Hawkins, like other blacks in Congress, feared that the precedent established by allowing Congress to make wholesale revisions in agency procedures through concurrent resolution was a potentially dangerous one for civil rights enforcement.

With this background, O'Hara's subcommittee hearings opened on June 17.

The first testifiers were representatives of the American Football Coaches Association. This initial focus on the athletic provisions of the regulations dominated the hearings. Although testimony for and against the regulations was offered by a variety of individual and institutional representatives, discussion of the impact of Title IX on athletic programs was the only aspect of the regulations which was thoroughly covered in the hearings.[14]

A concurrent resolution drafted by O'Hara passed the subcommittee by a comfortable margin. This resolution eliminated (1) the institutional self-evaluation procedure, (2) the establishment of a grievance process, and (3) the need for educational institutions to claim a religious exemption from HEW. The subcommittee also passed a bill submitted by Representative O'Hara amending Title IX. This bill removed revenue-producing sports from coverage under Title IX as well as preventing Title IX from being used to integrate physical education programs. This bill, combined with the concurrent resolution, threatened to leave Title IX with little effect.

Representative Hawkins asked the full Education and Labor committee to give his subcommittee an opportunity to examine O'Hara's concurrent resolution before a full committee vote was held on it. Over O'Hara's objections, the Education and Labor committee voted to refer the resolution to Hawkins' Equal Opportunity subcommittee. Then, Representatives Lloyd Meeds (D-Wash.) and John Brademas (D-Ind.) began to raise questions about O'Hara's bill. What exactly were revenue sports? What effect would this bill have? Over O'Hara's by now heated objections, the bill was voted back to O'Hara's subcommittee for further hearings.

Representative Hawkins held one day of hearings and recommended rejection of the concurrent resolution. O'Hara did not bother to schedule more hearings in his subcommittee before the Title IX regulations went into effect.

Conclusion

The relatively new and untested lobby supporting women's rights has won a significant victory by getting Title IX implemented. Yet, this case illustrates the heavy burden placed on new lobbies to demonstrate their worth as potential clientele groups for federal agencies. In some respects this is more difficult than the public, and often relatively short-term, effort necessary to gain initial congressional passage of bills. Yet, without this added effort the fruits of legislative victory may be lost in the process of administrative rule making.

Pro-Title IX groups in this case controlled the outcome through their ability to sustain a multiyear struggle on behalf of their objectives. They did this by monitoring HEW's progress in writing regulations, pressuring the White House, and finally conducting an extensive behind-the-scenes campaign in Congress to protect the final regulations from weakening or delay.

The ability to conclude this effort successfully is testimony both to the importance of ongoing national lobbying in support of women's rights and to the significance of political alliances. Lobbying on behalf of Title IX was successful in large part because the supportive group could combine the pressures of women's, student, civil rights, and education groups. This combination of traditional HEW clientele groups with new untested groups proved too potent for HEW to offend by writing inadaquate regulations on Title IX. Similarly, the congressional threat to delay or modify HEW regulations still further was defeated by this same coalitional effort. In evaluating the potential impact of relatively untested lobbies, their success in becoming feared or valued clientele groups within the federal bureaucracy can be key in determining whether their legislative victories will result in lasting political influence.

Notes

1. An example of this method of handling the problems of disadvantaged groups is the case of HEW's implementation of regulations to provide equal rights for the handicapped. Almost three years elapsed between congressional passage of section 504 of the 1973 Rehabilitation Act and HEW's completion of administrative regulations. In the end HEW released the regulations only after sit-ins and demonstrations by the handicapped at HEW offices throughout the United States. Joseph D. Whitaker, "Handicapped Gather at HEW to Agitate for Rights Enforcement," *The Washington Post,* April 6, 1977, p. B8.

2. This type of outcome may be an example of "symbolic politics" as described by Murray Edelman, *The Symbolic Uses of Politics* (Urbana: University of Illinois Press, 1967).

3. As Francis Rourke observes, "Administrative agencies were forced to develop their own basis of political support, negotiating alliances in and out of government with a variety of groups that could be used to advance bureaucratic objectives or to assist an agency in fending off attack." Francis Rourke, *Bureaucracy, Politics and Public Policy,* 2d ed. (Boston: Little, Brown, 1976), p. 43. For a more complete discussion of this practice see pp. 42-59 in the same source.

4. Title IX of the Education Amendments of 1972: Prohibition of Sex Discrimination, P.L. 92-318, enacted June 23, 1972. *U.S. Code,* Title 20, sec. 1681.

5. U.S. Congress, "Amendment Offered by Mr. Casey of Texas," *Congressional Record,* April 16, 1975, pp. H2845-7.

6. See amendments to sec. 431 of the General Education Provisions Act contained in P.L. 93-380, sec. 509.

7. Most groups lobbying for women's rights in Washington in 1971 and 1972 were concentrating all their efforts on passing the Equal Rights Amendment (ERA). Legislation such as Title IX of the 1972 Education Amendments

Act seemed somewhat superfluous to those convinced that the ERA would rapidly be added to the constitution.

8. What discussion there was of Title IX shows little comprehension of the purposes or impact of this title. See U.S. Congress, "Higher Education Act of 1971," *Congressional Record,* November 4, 1971, pp. H39248-61.

9. U.S. Congress, "Provision Relating to Sex Discrimination," *Congressional Record,* May 20, 1974, S8488-9.

10. Department of Health, Education, and Welfare, "Education Programs and Activities Receiving or Benefiting from Federal Financial Assistance, Nondiscrimination on the Basis of Sex," *Federal Register,* vol. 39, no. 120, part II, pp. 22228-40.

11. Groups represented on the Education Task Force include the Federation of Organizations for Professional Women; Council on National Priorities; American Alliance for Health, Physical Education and Recreation; League of Women Voters; Cooperative College Registry; Intercollegiate Association for Women Students; Project on the Status and Education of Women of the Association of American Colleges; National Association of State Universities and Land Grant Colleges; Women's Lobby; National Student Lobby; Education Commission of the State Equal Rights for Women in Education; National Student Association; Project on Equal Education Rights; Women's Legal Defense Fund; National Council of Jewish Women; Resource Center on Sex Roles in Education; National Association for Women Deans, Administrators and Conselors; American Association of University Women; Teacher Rights; National Education Association; National Association for Girls and Women in Sports; ACLU Women's Rights Project; Association for Intercollegiate Athletics for Women; American Association of University Professors; Women's Equity Action League; Women's Rights Project; American Association of School Administrators; American Council on Education; Business and Professional Women's Federation; and National Organization for Women.

12. Eric Wentworth, "Sex Rule Bill Inquiry Backed," *The Washington Post,* July 29, 1975, p. A4.

13. U.S. Congress, "Amendment Offered by Mr. Casey of Texas," *Congressional Record,* April 16, 1975, pp. H2845-7.

14. U.S. Congress, House, Committee on Education and Labor, *Sex Discrimination Regulations. Hearings before the Subcommittee on Post-secondary Education of the Committee on Education and Labor,* 94th Cong., 1st sess., 1975.

2

The Impact of Collective Bargaining on Minorities in the Public Sector: Some Policy Implications

Michael B. Preston

Minority employment in the public sector has increased remarkably since the early 1960s. Indeed, the number of minorities employed by all levels of government in 1970 was 1.6 million, an increase of 90 percent over the preceding decade, while the number employed by the federal government rose by one-third between 1962 and 1972.[1] Of all federal employees 15 percent are black, although the proportion of blacks in high-level posts is much smaller. About two-thirds of all black government employees work at the state and local levels, and since 1960 the number of these workers has doubled. The result, then, is that minority employment as a proportion of total government employment has risen from 12.4 percent in 1965 to 14.7 percent in 1974.[2]

Parallel to the growth of minority employment in the public sector has been the growth of collective bargaining by public employees. Minority employees are thus subject to the conditions of collective-bargaining agreements negotiated by public unions. The past and present history of union discrimination against minorities—in both the public and the private sectors—raises the issue of the possible impact of collective bargaining on equal job opportunities for members of these groups.

There is no general agreement regarding the effect of collective bargaining on minorities, but the question has generated sharply conflicting views among leading black intellectuals. On one end of the spectrum, some observers, such as Sir W. Arthur Lewis, professor of economics at Princeton University, regard unionism as one of the worst evils besetting black workers in U.S. society.[3] This point of view focuses on restrictive practices by unions, often codified in labor-management agreements, which either prevent blacks from obtaining jobs or consign black workers to the lowest paid and most menial jobs in some of the nation's major industries. Those who hold this view argue strongly against the holding of monopoly by unions, which is usually effected through the use of referral systems, union shop agreements, and other union security arrangements.

The other end of the spectrum of opinion is perhaps best represented by

This is an extended version of a paper prepared for a minisymposium in the *Public Administration Review,* entitled "The Municipal Civil Service under Pressure," ed. Wilbur Rich, to appear. I would like to thank Stephanie Cole, Valerie Mudra, and Tony Halmos for their assistance in helping me to develop this chapter.

Bayard Rustin, executive director of the A. Philip Randolph Institute and a long-time labor organizer and civil rights activist.[4] Rustin believes that unionism is the best hope for black workers to gain a foothold in the U.S. economy. The major basis for this belief is a faith in trade unionism as a protector of wage standards and improved working conditions. Although proponents of this point of view are mindful of the discriminatory practices of some unions, they think that these practices can best be changed by working within the institutional framework of the labor movement, rather than by weakening union bargaining power through challenges to the union shop and other union measures.

The truth regarding the impact of unionism on minority groups[5] probably lies somewhere between the two extremes. There is no doubt that some unions have severely limited black occupational advancement by enforcing racially restrictive membership policies. Such unions, however, are confined to a relatively narrow group of industries—construction, for example—and even within those industries blacks have often found alternative routes to employment around the union's restrictive practices. Likewise, union policies on uniform work standards that protect blacks from wage discrimination are common and nearly universal among national and international master union contracts.

The effects of past discrimination by unions against minorities have caused government authorities and civil rights groups to be wary of collective bargaining by public unions. Since the passage of the Civil Rights Act of 1964,[6] including Title VII of that act, the elements of the collective-bargaining process which tend to perpetuate job discrimination have received close attention. Some of the most important litigation under Title VII has been directed against collective-bargaining arrangements which unlawfully restrict the employment opportunities of minorities and women. The court proceedings have helped reconcile the conflict which sometimes exists between the right of unions and management to engage in the joint determination of employment standards under the national labor policy, on the one hand, and the right of minorities and women to enjoy equal job opportunities under the national equal employment policy, on the other. That litigation, however, leaves open many important questions of public policy related to minority groups.

To a large extent the benefits to be gained by minorities from the collective-bargaining process will depend on the influence of minority groups in the process that has been called "intra-organizational bargaining"[7]—the process that precedes collective bargaining with the employer. It is this question—the importance to minorities of gaining greater influence in the intraorganizational bargaining process and the methods by which this can be achieved—that is the focus of this chapter.

First, however, it is necessary to review the current collective-bargaining situation in the public sector and the position of minority employees in that sector. We focus on the public sector because black employment in federal, state, and local government has increased considerably in the last fifteen years, as shown earlier in this chapter. More important, while the Civil Service Commission has been responsible, albeit belatedly, for the recent increase in the recruitment of minorities, new collective-bargaining agreements negotiated by public employee unions could alter this situation.

Public Sector Unionism and Minority Employment

Over the years the public sector has employed increasingly greater proportions of the total workforce, and at present federal, state, and local governments employ nearly 19 percent of the civilian workforce.[8]

In 1962 forty-one unions or employee associations had 1.225 million members in the public sector as a whole.[9] This represented 7 percent of the total trade union membership in the United States in that year. By 1972 eighty-six unions or employee associations had 4.52 million members in the public sector— 19.5 percent of the total trade union membership in that year.[10] The breakdown is shown in table 2-1.

Although it began in the 1880s, unionization of workers in the public sector was slow to gather force. For example, the organization of police did not really begin until 1915, when the Fraternal Order of Police was formed for the purpose of achieving civil service protection and better pension plans for police officers. In 1937 the American Federation of State, County, and Municipal Employees (AFSCME) chartered a police local. By 1946 it had thirty-six locals composed entirely of police and another thirty-three locals in which police officers were members. In 1953 a number of independent local associations of police came together in a loose confederation—the International Conference of Police Associations (ICPA). Most firefighters belong to one union, the International Associa-

Table 2-1
Public Sector Unions, 1972

Sector	Number of Unions	Number of Members (in thousands)	Percentage of Total Trade Union and Association Membership
Federal	51	1,394	6.0
State	44	814	3.5
Local	29	2,312	10.0
Total	86[a]	4,520	19.5

Source: U.S. Department of Labor, *Directory of National Unions and Employee Associations* (Washington: Government Printing Office, 1974).

[a]These numbers are not additive because a number of unions organize in more than one sector.

Table 2-2
State and Local Government Employee Membership in Unions and
Associations, 1969–1970

Organization	Membership (in thousands)
Union	
American Federation of State, County, and Municipal Employees	441
International Association of Fire Fighters	132
Service Employees International Union	124
Laborers' International Union of North America	24
International Brotherhood of Teamsters	57
Others	50
Total	828
Association	
Fraternal Order of Police	80
International Conference of Police Associations	142
State associations	618
Local associations	300
American Nurses' Association	40
Total	1,180
Total of unions and associations	2,008

Source: Jack Stieber, *Public Employee Unionism: Structure, Growth, Policy* (Washington: Brookings Institution, 1973), table 1.1, p. 12. Reprinted with permission.

tion of Firefighters (IAFF), formed in 1918 and affiliated with the American Federation of Labor (AFL). In addition to the police and firefighters' unions, the dominant organizations in the nonfederal public sector are AFSCME, the Service Employees International Union (SEIU), and, with an even larger total membership, the independent state and local employee associations.[11] The breakdown of union and association membership in 1969-1970 can be seen in table 2-2.

In a study of public sector unionism, Stieber found that outside the federal sector and excluding teachers and transit workers, in 1970 the 2 million union and association members constituted 38 percent of all full-time state and local employees. Unions alone were found to have enrolled about 16 percent of all full-time employees, excluding teachers and transit workers in state and local governments. Whether the 38 percent represented by both unions and associations (or some in-between figure) is the appropriate measure of employee organization depends on the degree to which the employee associations fill the collective-bargaining role.

Although there are some fifty-one unions in the federal sector, six major unions organize the bulk of the nonpostal federal employees, representing a total of 1.2 million workers, or 59 percent of all nonpostal federal employees (66

Table 2–3
Major Unions in the Federal Sector, 1976

Organization	Blue-Collar Membership	White-Collar Membership
American Federation of Government Employees	205,496	484,533
National Federation of Federal Employees	32,674	103,397
National Treasury Employees Union	502	83,366
National Association of Government Employees	33,484	44,394
Metal Trades Council	55,382	3,247
International Association of Machinists	29,392	3,467

Source: U.S. Civil Service Commission, *Spotlight on Labor Relations* (Washington: Government Printing Office, 1976).

percent of postal and nonpostal employees together are represented by unions). The percentage of white-collar federal workers represented by unions has reached 51 percent, while 84 percent of blue-collar workers belong to unions.[12] Current membership of the six major unions in the federal sector can be seen in table 2-3.

Not unexpectedly, this increase in unionization has been accompanied by an increase in collective bargaining in the public sector. Most states and localities have approved collective bargaining for their employees. At the federal level, an executive order issued by President Kennedy in 1962 permitted collective bargaining by federal employees for the first time.

At the same time as the growth in unionization and the spread of collective bargaining in the public sector, federal legislation over the past fifteen years has opened up employment opportunities for racial minorities in federal, state, and

Table 2–4
Minority Employment as a Proportion of Total Government Employment, 1965–1974

Year	Percentage
1965	12.4
1970	14.0
1971	14.1
1972	14.6
1973	15.0
1974	14.7

Source: U.S. Department of Commerce, Bureau of the Census, *Statistical Abstract of the United States,* 1975, table 580.

Table 2-5
Federal Civilian Employment, 1966–1974

Year	Total Employees	Total Minority Employees[a]	Percentage
1966	2,303,906	442,374	19.2[b]
1967	2,621,939	496,672	18.9
1968	2,621,939	496,672	18.9
1969	2,601,611	501,397	19.3
1970	2,571,504	505,035	19.6
1971	2,573,770	502,752	19.5
1972	2,542,067	509,307	20.0
1973[c]	2,520,354	515,129	20.4
1974[c]	2,433,485	510,061	21.0

Note: Unless otherwise indicated, all data are taken from U.S. Civil Service Commission reports, 1966 to 1972.
[a]Blacks, Spanish-surnamed, Orientals, and Native Americans.
[b]91.2 percent of employees identified.
[c]U.S. Civil Service Commission, *Civil Service News,* June 11, 1975.

local governments.[13] The growth of minority employment in the public sector is shown in table 2-4, while minority employment in the federal government is shown in table 2-5.

As a result of the increase of minority employment in the public sector, one of the major issues associated with the growth of public employee unionism is the impact that collective bargaining has upon equal job opportunities. This impact has varied across occupations. It is possible to analyze the possible impact of collective bargaining on minority groups in the public sector by examining two distinctive types of public employee unions: legal-formal and pluralistic. (The former refers to public employee unions in which qualifications are normally specified by formal government authorities, while the latter refers to unions that normally demand some type of educational credential for entrance and promotion. Pluralistic unions, on the other hand, have less restrictive entrance and promotion qualifications as well as a more diverse clientele.)

Legal-Formal Type

The legal-formal type of public employee unions is exemplified by teachers', firefighters', and police unions. The record of these unions has not been good with respect to minority hiring. History has shown the exclusionary practices of these highly organized civil service unions. Frances Fox Piven has stated the case this way:

Obviously, elaborate entrance and promotion requirements now limit access by Blacks to municipal jobs. Indeed one can almost measure their strength of public employee associations in different cities by their success in securing such requirements, and in keeping minorities out. In New York, where municipal workers are numerous and well-organized, 90% of the teachers are white; in Detroit, Philadelphia and Chicago, where municipal employees are not well organized, 25% to 40% of the teachers are Black.[14]

On close examination, it may be a bit unfair to characterize the low proportion of blacks in the New York City teacher corps as due to union policy; this is more nearly due to the reliance on formal examinations as selection and promotion devices and on the tenure system, which the union has undoubtedly supported but which it did not invent. That is to say, the reliance on formal requirements (such as credentials and entrance examinations) and the discriminatory attitude of most management personnel were early obstacles to minority employment.

If the *formal* requirements for teachers have restricted minority employment, the rigid *legal* entrance requirements for the police and firefighters' unions are even more detrimental to minorities.[15] For example, the results of past and present discrimination by the firefighters' union are vividly illustrated by a survey of minority employment in four Illinois cities. In Chicago, blacks constitute 33 percent of the total population but only 4.9 percent of the firefighters. In Peoria, the black population is 12 percent, but only 2 percent of the city's firefighters are black. The black population of Champaign is 10.4 percent, but only 3.8 percent of the firefighters are black. Finally, in Urbana, the black population is 10.9 percent, but blacks constitute only 2.4 percent of that city's firefighters.[16]

A 1970 survey of blacks on the police forces of various cities has shown that while the extent of discrimination is high, it is not as severe as in the fire services. Thus in that year, in Atlanta, for example, with a black population of 51 percent, 10 percent of the police force were black. In Chicago, 33 percent of the population were black, but only 16 percent of the police were black. In New York, with a black population of 21 percent, 9 percent of the police were black, while in Washington, D.C., where 71 percent of the population were black, only 37 percent of the police were black. The police forces of other major cities display similar characteristics.[17] There is no question, then, that the legal-formal type of unions have discriminated, and still do so, against minorities.

Pluralistic Type

The second type of union in the public sector can be characterized as pluralistic. This type of union is usually more newly established in the public sector, has more minority employees, and is more egalitarian in its policies than is the legal-formal type. Pluralistic unions would include, for example, the community and building service occupations and sanitation workers, all of which are located in the state and local government sectors. These occupations are normally recruited by the unions listed in the first part of table 2-2, particularly AFSCME. Minority membership will be directly related to the functional and occupational distribution and the geographic location of the public employees represented by a union. In the central cities, where blacks hold most of—and sometimes almost all—the low-skilled jobs in public works, sanitation, street maintenance, and hospitals, most local unions are predominantly black. It has been estimated that about one-third of AFSCME membership is black, with further membership by other minority group members.[18]

While the pluralist type of union is more egalitarian in the recruitment of blacks, most of these unions are concentrated in agencies serving largely black clienteles, such as welfare, manpower, neighborhood health centers, and community relations offices.[19] Stated differently, while these unions are less discriminatory, the jobs are lower in status and income.

The Impact of Collective Bargaining on Minorities

The only true representation that minorities receive through the collective-bargaining process is in the area of wage benefits. Blacks and other minorities in a particular work group will be able to achieve the same wage increases as other workers, since the union involved must bargain for all workers. But on other issues, such as layoff practices, promotions, referrals, and grievances, minority representation is inadequate. First, seldom are minorities able to elect members of their own group to leadership positions within the union, because very rarely are they present in that union in sufficiently large numbers to ensure a victory in a union election. Second, when votes are taken of a union's membership, minorities are unable to stop policies that may harm them, nor are they usually able to add amendments to the negotiable issues which are presented to management. The result is a vicious circle—minorities cannot take power because of their small numbers, and their small numbers allow the other members to get their way through control over policy decisions.

Some writers have argued from this that the concept of unionization itself is harmful to minorities. This argument is difficult to sustain. Various empirical research has shown that (1) blacks are more likely to join unions than whites and (2) blacks in unions are paid more than those who are not union members.[20] The problem for minorities is not the concept of unionization itself but rather the methods and inequitable policies employed by many unions that keep unionization and collective bargaining from being as great a benefit to minorities as it is to white employees. For example, in Hartford, Connecticut, the AFSCME local refused to provide three black policemen with legal counsel in a grievance against the city, while giving such aid to three white policemen in a federal suit charging Hartford police with discrimination against minorities. Thus past discriminatory policies and practices by both union and management have effectively limited the number of minorities in most legal-formal unions. In the pluralistic unions, although specific exclusionary policies are rare, the number of blacks in the areas of employment covered by those unions is often not a majority of the total employment, thus restricting the roles of blacks in those unions as well.

The current position of blacks in unions is best considered with reference to the different types of collective bargaining highlighted by Walton and McKersie.[21] One type which they discuss is intraorganizational bargaining. Both parties at the bargaining table do not represent monolithic positions; that is, there is no single, unified view of the demands that should be made by the union or management's response to those demands. On the union side—of most concern here—almost invariably meetings of members will be held to formulate bargaining policy before negotiations begin. At this point, the absence (at least in most cases) of a majority of blacks among the union's total membership will weaken their position in intraorganizational bargaining. Apart from blacks there are often other minority groups of union members with special needs and interests. While the latter are sometimes in the same weak position as blacks—the most common case is that of craft workers in an industrial union—their position is very different.

Craft workers are in a strong position by virtue of the type of job they hold. Craft members of unions are often able to close a whole plant without support from the semiskilled or unskilled members of the union. The unions have recognized this by giving the craft workers rights of veto over contract determination. This is the case in both the rubber and the automobile industries.

In comparison, blacks are rarely in such skilled jobs, more usually holding jobs requiring low levels of skill or none at all. They are, therefore, in a numerical minority and are not in a position to assert any significant influence over the form of the contract beyond their numbers, as skilled craft workers can. Therefore, they are in a very weak position in intraorganizational bargaining. On the management side, there will be little or no pressure to improve the position of black employees, partly because of long-standing general discriminatory attitudes in society as a whole, but more specifically because the management will sense, usually rightly, that the advancement of minority employees relative to others will be a low priority for the union and therefore of little value as a response by management in the bargaining session itself. Therefore, for any real advance of the position of minorities in collective bargaining to occur, the change has to take place on the union side. Not only should the union alter its own internal policies with regard to minorities, but it also has to raise their needs to a more significant level at the bargaining table. Past union practices make this alternative unlikely.

In this context, it is necessary to consider the alternatives available to minorities to bring about fair representation.

Policy Alternatives

The right to bargain collectively and unionize will continue to grow. This is especially true for unions involved in representing employees of local governments. By the end of the 1970s, most state and local associations will probably merge or affiliate with unions. The power of unions will grow as their membership grows, with the AFL-CIO affiliates dominating the labor relations field.[22] All the public employee unions will continue to demand a part in deciding merit policies, even in the face of the fiscal crises faced by cities like New York. Indeed, the fiscal crises and the high unemployment rates that exist in cities have provoked a reassessment by minorities of seniority systems and layoff policies of public employee unions.

Under these circumstances, what policy alternatives seem to offer the optimum solution to fair representation of minorities in public employee unions? Over the last few years six alternatives have been suggested. We shall briefly discuss and analyze these options as feasible solutions to the problem of fair representation.

1. *Form separate unions.* This alternative is likely to be rejected because separate minority unions would be too small to obtain bargaining rights. In most states, once a union is recognized as the agent representing a group, it has exclusive recognition. In practically all instances, the predominantly white unions hold this position. Without exclusive recognition, separate unions are powerless.
2. *Form separate locals within existing unions.* This alternative is unlikely to be effective because such locals would be able to deal with only discrimination by the union leadership, and not other sources.
3. *Work within the union.* This is possible, but not feasible, because the minority is not large enough or "strategically located" to exert influence—and almost all union decisions are taken by a straight majority vote. Thus in this and other instances, the democratic electoral process works against minority interests.
4. *Community pressure.* Such pressure is helpful if it is exerted in the kind of dispute that can arouse community sympathy. Otherwise community pressure is likely to be useful only for morale boosting, although this could be important at times.

5. *Form a separate association.* This is a good strategy, but usually it is more symbolic than substantive. However, the symbolic function may lead to cohesion and solidarity in the face of discouraging events. This may lead, in turn, to substantive development, that is, the ability to speak collectively and bring legal suits in the name of the association.[23] Thus, the formation of a separate association—while remaining in the union—allows these groups to use their ties with the large minority population to provide political backing for demands.

6. *Legal action.* This is, and has been, the most effective strategy. Action can be taken under federal or state laws, civil rights legislation, or constitutional provision (where appropriate) to secure fair representation or redress against unfair hiring and promotion policies.

The most often used and most effective alternatives seem to be a combination of 5 and 6. Separate associations act as grievance boards and morale-boosting devices; they tend to give minorities in these unions a feeling of cohesion while at the same time demonstrating to potential recruits that they will not be without some form of support. Most associations go beyond the symbolic; they threaten the majority with legal action where discriminatory actions (such as promotion, transfer, and layoff policies) exist within the union. They also threaten to bring suits against unions that restrict the entrance of new minority recruits. While legal action is slow and uncertain, it is at present the most effective tactic.

Conclusion

In the legal-formal type of public employee unions, where jobs are diminishing and salaries are high, minority employees face two major problems: (1) the need to find ways to reduce the discriminatory recruitment policies of both management and unions which limit the number of minority employees, and (2) the need to eradicate discrimination in promotion and layoff policies toward existing personnel. In the more egalitarian, pluralistic-type unions, which are newer, expanding faster, and with less rigid entrance requirements, the emphasis needs to be less on recruitment and more on reducing barriers to promotion and developing an equitable layoff policy.

It would seem that the best way to attack the legal-formal system is by using options 5 and 6—to alter the rigid formal-legal entrance requirements attached to union jobs. The lowering of these barriers would lead to increased black employment and membership in unions, which, in turn, would give blacks greater strength of numbers and a more equal chance to affect the unions' future collective-bargaining stance.

Meanwhile, or course, pressure should be exerted on unions to voluntarily appoint some black representatives to the bargaining unit or to a subcommittee that screens the issues to be submitted for arbitration. Also, the general development in society as a whole leading to reductions in discrimination is bound to ease this particular problem, as well as others.

There is some evidence that strategies 3 and 4 will work under certain conditions. Examples are the strikes by minority employees in Memphis and Cleveland. In these cases, black employees won the right to be represented in the collective-bargaining process and have their grievances resolved. In the Memphis strike, blacks made up the majority of members and were thus able (with community and national union support) to gain control of the union and to force management (the city of Memphis) to recognize them as legitimate bargaining agents. The price for success in the Memphis case was extremely high (Martin Luther King, Jr., was assassinated in the process of negotiations). In Cleveland, on the other hand, blacks were able to successfully force an end to some discriminatory policies of white city administrators and to gain not only economic justice but status and dignity as well.[24]

It may well be that the options listed will not apply to many of the pluralistic unions, where blacks are well represented. In most other cases, it would be fair to argue that minority grievances and needs in the collective-bargaining process will be protected only where they are of equal strength (or nearly so) or where the use of legal action, or the threat of it, forces unions and management to alter their traditional ways. When and if some safeguards are built into the collective-bargaining process that ensure minorities fair representation, the concept of unionization will then become as beneficial to minority group members as it is to white union employees.

Notes

1. U.S. Department of Commerce, Bureau of the Census, *General Social and Economic Characteristics,* series PC(1), table 93, June 1972, and *Industrial Characteristics,* series PC(21-7F), June 1967, p. 135.

2. U.S. Department of Commerce, Bureau of the Census, *Statistical Abstract of the United States* (Washington: Government Printing Office, 1975), table 580.

3. W. Arthur Lewis, quoted in *The New York Times,* May 11, 1969.

4. Bayard Rustin, *The Failure of Black Separatism* (reprint: A. Philip Randolph Institute, January 1970).

5. The terms *minority groups* and *blacks* will be used interchangeably in this chpater since blacks constitute an overwhelming majority of the minority group members in the United States. And while it is apparent that some of these same problems concern women, I have decided not to include them in this chapter for the sake of brevity. For an overview on the problems of women, see

Marian Lief Palley, "Women and the Study of Public Policy," *Policy Studies Journal* 4 (Spring 1976): 288.

6. Congressional Quarterly Service, *Revolution in Civil Rights,* 3d ed. (Washington 1967).

7. Richard E. Walton and Robert B. McKersie, *A Behavioral Theory of Labor Negotiations* (New York: McGraw-Hill, 1965).

8. U.S. Department of Commerce, Bureau of the Census, *Statistical Abstract of the United States* (Washington: Government Printing Office, 1975), table 579.

9. U.S. Department of Labor, *Directory of National Unions and Employee Associations* (Washington: Government Printing Office, 1974).

10. Ibid.

11. Jack Stieber, *Public Employee Unionism* (Washington: Brookings Institution, 1973), p. 12.

12. U.S. Civil Service Commission, *Spotlight on Labor Relations* (Washington: Government Printing Office, 1976).

13. Sar A. Levitan et al., *Still a Dream: The Changing Status of Blacks Since 1960* (Cambridge, Mass.: Harvard University Press, 1975), p. 164.

14. Frances Fox Piven, "Militant Civil Servants in New York City," *Transaction* 7, November 1969. Published by permission of *Transaction.* Copyright © 1969, by Transaction, Inc. It should be noted that black teachers in the New York City schools have gradually increased since Piven's article in 1969:

Year		Number of Teachers	
	Total	Number of Blacks	Percentage of Blacks
1970	56,675	4,601	7.7
1971	55,734	4,572	8.2
1972	55,166	4,845	8.8
1973	56,168	4,989	8.9
1974	55,415	5,299	9.6
1975	48,424	4,888	10.0
1976	47,239	4,781	10.1
1977	49,767	5,285	10.6

See: Board of Education of the City of New York, Office of Educational Statistics (New York, August 14, 1978).

15. Herbert Hill, "The Racial Practices of Organized Labor," in *The Contemporary Record,* ed. Julius Jacobsen (Garden City, N.J.: Doubleday, 1968), pp. 286–353. See also Stieber, *Public Employee Unionism,* p. 65.

16. Michael B. Preston, "Representative Bureaucracy and Minority Employment in Illinois" (unpublished paper, Institute of Government and Public Affairs, University of Illinois, 1976).

17. William B. Gould, "Labor Relations and Race Relations," in *Public Workers and Public Unions,* ed. Sam Zargoria (New York: Prentice-Hall, 1973), p. 143.

18. Stieber, *Public Employee Unionism,* pp. 25-36.

19. Preston, "Representative Bureaucracy." See also Levitan et al., *Still a Dream,* p. 165.

20. See, for example, James H. Scoville, "Influences of Unionization in the U.S. in 1966," *Industrial Relations,* October 1971, pp. 354-61. See also Levitan, *Still a Dream,* pp. 168-72.

21. Walton and McKersie, *A Behavioral Theory of Labor Negotiations.*

22. Stieber, *Public Employee Unionism,* pp. 212-15.

23. Hervey A. Juris and Peter Feuille, *Police Unionism* (Lexington, Mass.: D.C. Heath, 1973), pp. 165-76. On the effectiveness of pressure by these associations, see p. 173 in that work.

24. James E. Blackwell and Marie R. Haug, "The Strike of Cleveland Water Works Employees," in *Racial Conflicts and Negotiations,* eds. W. Ellison Chalmers and Gerald W. Cormick (Ann Arbor: University of Michigan, 1976), pp. 109-50. See also pp. 71-74 in that work.

3

Black Women in the Continuing Struggle for Equality

Toni-Michelle C. Travis

The civil rights movement and the women's liberation movement of the 1960s present two models for black women to follow in continuing their fight for equality. In the civil rights movment black racial identity was a unifying force in recruiting followers, as well as the underlying issue to all demands for equal rights. Black men and women easily identified with the various types of discrimination they had experienced because of their race. For blacks the opposition was clear-cut. In an effort to achieve full and equal citizenship the movement sought to strip away the barriers of segregation and discrimination created by white people in the United States. The movement welcomed men and women of any race who supported these views and thereby created a broad base of support. During the course of the civil rights movement the focus changed from trying to solve the political problems of being black to the economic problems of being black. Blacks no longer asked only for the opportunity to vote. They also wanted better jobs, with the opportunity to improve their standard of living.

In the women's liberation movement class status brought the women together. The women united because their complaints stemmed from experiencing similar problems based on their economic status. In the beginning stages of the women's movement the opposition was vaguely defined as white chauvinistic males. Gradually the movement focused on employment problems and securing passage of the Equal Rights Amendment. In this case there is a shift from specifically middle-class issues to issues that should interest all classes of women. As the issues were redefined, the membership expanded, but the majority of members were still middle-class white females. Few men supported the women's movement because they were worried about the extent and degree to which the movement would diminish their status and position of power in U.S. society. Black women have joined, but their support came primarily from the ranks of middle-class blacks who identified with the educational and occupational experiences of the white members. The benefits of the women's liberation movement have been political and economic in terms of employment opportunities and promotions for women.

The problem is, What is the future course for black women to take? In order to reach a conclusion, the role of race and class consciousness must be assessed in the two movements, along with the goals and benefits from the perspective of the black woman.

The Montgomery, Alabama, bus boycott of 1955, which provides a convenient date for marking the beginning of the civil rights movement, differed from previous political acts on the part of blacks. Here blacks were initiating, rather than merely responding to a government decision or an election result. Previous political events such as the Scottsboro trial of 1931, Adam Clayton Powell's election to Congress in 1941, and the 1954 Supreme Court decision in the *Brown* v. *Board of Education of Topeka* suit, which appeared to be a remote legal pronouncement, affected the black population. However, none of these political events raised the political and racial consciousness of the black community to the extent that it made a prolonged and unified response. Although blacks had been denied political rights in the South, which created a low level of political consciousness, racial consciousness was always at a high level among blacks because of their segregated status in Southern society. In this situation Mrs. Rosa Parks' sense of racial consciousness caused her to respond openly against segregation, an extremely dangerous practice for a lone black to attempt, when she refused to give up her seat to a white person on a public bus. This single act created a spark sufficient to trigger and sustain a citywide boycott of the bus company. This political and economic protest by black citizens in Montgomery encouraged others throughout the country, who felt that they had been struggling in isolation, to intensify their fight for equality. Mrs. Parks' individual protest grew into a collective protest at the local and later the national level.

For Southern blacks politics consisted of exclusion from a political system. Blacks could not participate in party politics, vote, or run for public office, except in rare cases. Only after the success of the Montgomery bus boycott was becoming clear did blacks begin to understand the potential force of their new political consciousness. As they became encouraged to try to change their political situation, blacks developed a feeling of unity which fostered a positive sense of racial identity.

Blacks assessed their resources in the face of the formidable opposition which controlled the political parties, financial institutions, press, police, state legislatures, and courts in the Southern states. The only resources were numbers of people and organizational experience, which came primarily from participation in church activities. Money was not plentiful because the low income of most Southern blacks did not provide for any disposable income for contributions.

Articulating a clearly defined goal is crucial to the success of a movement, although goals may shift over time in response to membership support or actions on the part of the political system. The focus of the Southern front of the civil rights movement was to secure voting rights and end segregation in public accommodations. In the later stages of the movement the goal did not remain clear as factions variously sought integration or the implementation of the black power philosophy as their primary goal. Basically, blacks were continuing their fight to exercise the rights they were granted as citizens. There was no attempt to acquire new rights or privileges, only to make full use of those rights which were technically available but not granted in practice. Because blacks had been such a powerless group in the South they realized that they must carefully plan each demonstration. Targets for direct action confrontations were chosen on the basis of their ability to effectively use the media to demonstrate problems of glaring racial injustice in specific Southern communities. Black strategists led by Dr. Martin Luther King, Jr., felt that blacks would most effectively present their case by mobilizing large numbers of nonviolent people who would confront the easily antagonized Southerners. By using a combination of peaceful activities such as marches, sit-ins, pray-ins, and boycotts Dr. King was able to command the attention of the media and eventually the federal government.

Confrontations were skillfully orchestrated around an underlying religious theme. Effective use was made of elevating the issues of the movement to moral issues which were aimed at embarrassing white Christians.[1] Television helped depict the Christian theme of suffering when a crucial march was timed to coincide with the period from Good Friday to Easter Sunday. Children were even recruited for participation in some of the more dramatic demonstrations in order to gain sympathy and support for the nonviolent, seemingly helpless blacks.

Television, as it recorded the deaths of civil rights workers, made the public aware of the violence habitually perpetrated by Southern whites, even against nonviolent blacks. The medium of television provided a dramatic state whereby the viewer was drawn into the scope of the conflict[2] through the use of easily recognized symbols. One could see on the nightly news the battle of good versus evil, Christian, brotherly love versus inane hatred, and the spontaneous eruption of physical force versus organized, nonviolent, passive resistance. With such universal values at issue it was easy to appeal to a cross section of the U.S. population: men and women, the black and white citizens, lay and religious community leaders, and all age groups.

The civil rights movement successfully raised the consciousness of the nation, making everyone aware of the political, economic, and social consequences of being black in the United States. Changes began to take place in race relations as the South began to desegregate public facilities. Desegregation throughout society affected every aspect of life and eventually made it possible for blacks to apply for jobs which had been previously closed to them.

A new sense of racial consciousness and pride was created across class lines in the black community. Blacks realized that it took a united effort on the part of black men and women to create sufficient political pressure to bring about such sweeping changes in U.S. society.

The civil rights movement benefited all blacks, but black women gained organizational experience from their participation which could later be utilized in electoral or nonelectoral politics, including launching their own movement. Minimally black women gained the ability to use public facilities, to vote throughout the South, to participate in party politics, and to run for political office.

Now let's focus on the women's liberation movement and how it began. In the 1960s three separate but related events seemed to initiate the women's movement. These events, as noted by Jo Freeman in *The Politics of Women's Liberation*,[3] include President Kennedy's establishment of the President's Commission on the Status of Women and subsequent commissions in each state, the publication of Betty Friedan's *The Feminine Mystique,* and the addition of the word *sex* to Title VII of the Civil Rights Act of 1964 prohibiting discrimination in employment. These events brought women together, made them aware that they were still denied their rights, and made them aware that male congressmen considered sexual equality a joking matter.[4]

Friedan's book contended that American women were confronted with a problem called the feminine mystique, which placed the highest value and the only commitment for women on fulfillment of their femininity.[5] Women supposedly had trouble because they tried to be like men, rather than accepting their own nature. Friedan stated that the problem confronting women "is not sexual, but one of identity—a stunting or evasion of growth which is perpetuated by the feminine mystique."[6] The feminine mystique had limited woman to only two choices, "'being a woman' or risking the pains of human growth."[7] Although Friedan's statements were intended to cover the problems of all women, in reality they had limited applicability to the past or present situation of black women.

What is the solution to the feminine mystique? Friedan answered simply: Say no to the housewife image, reject the feminine mystique by asserting your identity and self as an individual.[8] The key to escaping from the confining role of the feminine mystique was education. Therefore, Friedan advocated that part-time educational facilities be made available to women so that they could continue their education in a life plan, rather than just in a four-year college curriculum.[9]

Men were to define their identity by their work, while women were expected to have their identity defined by sex. Friedan points out that historically "the work that a man had to do to eat, to stay alive, to meet the physical necessities of his environment, dictated his identity."[10] Women were to restructure their lives by using their education to take a salaried job, which would give them a sense of identity. Time-consuming volunteer activities did not adequately provide this sense of identity derived from work. It is clear that Friedan's solutions had little relationship to the problems faced by black women who learned early in life that they had to accept the pains of growth by taking a paying job out of necessity.

Unlike the civil rights movement the start of the women's movement in the

1960s cannot be dated from the occurrence of a dramatic event which sparked a mass response. The beginning of the women's liberation movement is a coming together of like-minded women, Betty Friedan and others, who felt that they were being treated unfairly by society. However, their complaints differed from those of the civil rights movement. These twentieth-century women had not been prohibited from exercising their right to obtain an education, hold a paying job, and assert their own identity; they just had not exhibited a high enough level of political consciousness to act before this time.

Racial consciousness is not a factor in unifying members of the women's liberation movement, who are members of the dominant cultural group. However, a sense of middle-class consciousness coupled with feelings of relative deprivation are the motivating forces in the case of these women. Relative deprivation, as described by Runciman, fits the situation of college-educated white women who were usually exclusively housewives, or one of the few professional women in their work situation.

> We can roughly say that A is relatively deprived of X when (1) he does not have X, (2) he sees some other person or persons, which may include himself at some previous or expected time, as having X (whether or not this is or will be in fact the case), (3) he wants X, and (4) he sees it as feasible that he should have X.[11]

In analyzing the increase in strain that led up to the current women's movement, Jo Freeman warns us

> to pay particular attention to the changing circumstances of middle-class women in order to show that while their absolute deprivation may have been lower than that of other women, relative deprivation increased significantly—and did so in a time when the justifying myth of male precedence was being slowly eroded.[12]

Resources available to the women included access to media and organizational skills, rather than overwhelming numbers. As educated women, they were well aware of the importance of utilizing printed and electronic media to further their cause. Although media resources were within easy reach, especially to the New York chapter of the National Organization of Women (NOW), the women found it difficult to attract serious media coverage. The staging of dramatic confrontations, a new, attention-getting tactic during the civil rights movement, had lost its media appeal. Organizational skills were a resource many women carried over from work in the civil rights movement.

From Friedan's book it was difficult to tell what the long-range goal should be for women, beyond the immediate assertion of a new identity which rejected the traditional wife and mother role. Uncertain goals and a lack of agreement between the older and younger women in the movement on how to proceed quickly caused the movement to split into two distinctive groups.[13] Therefore, the women's movement did not appear as a cohesive unit because there was no ideological focus to pinpoint one social problem. To the public, NOW appeared to be a New York City-based organization composed of women who worked in one of the most urban, culturally permissive cities in the world. What could these women complain about? When the media sought an answer, they were presented with issues such as bra burning, in contrast to the weighty moral issues of the civil rights movement. The issues of the women's liberation movement were not successfully expressed dramatically in moralistic terms of good versus evil, where the women could make themselves appear as sacrificial martyrs.[14]

The women's movement certainly increased awareness of the economic and social situation of white women among the U.S. population. Day care centers and abortion clinics were started in many states because of the efforts of women. Job categories traditionally only open to men began to hire women. In other instances law suits were brought in cases of employment discrimination.

Over time the movement focused on the overarching goal of securing passage of the Equal Rights Amendment, which helped unite the various factions of the movement. Women's organizations even sought to bring economic sanctions against those states which have not ratified the Equal Rights Amendment by having conventions withdraw from these states. However, the battle to secure passage for the ERA amendment continues.

A look at black and white women in terms of their family structure, race, and class situation helps explain how black women interpret the civil rights and women's liberation movements. Black and white women view U.S. society from totally different perspectives based on their historically different experiences. For black women race has been the determining fact for every aspect of life. The fact that one is black controls family structure, the potential for earning power, and ultimately class status. Black families which are often headed by a female have come under considerable scrutiny and attack. However, recent studies[15] since the Moynihan Report[16] in 1965 show that what may be a functional, normal family unit among blacks might be considered a deviant, disorganized family structure when judged by criteria for examining white family structures. Of prime importance is the difference in the female role in black and white culture. The black female expects to be a working wife and is aware that she may be the principal or only wage earner in a family. A Bureau of the Census report on women statistically supports the image of the working wife in black families:

> For more than two decades the labor force participation rate for black women has been higher than that for white women. . . . In 1974, 49 percent of black women were in civilian labor force, compared with 45 percent of white women. In every age group, except 16 to 19 and 20 to

24, black women were more likely than their white counterparts to be in the labor force. Also, a somewhat larger proportion of black women than white women who worked during 1974 worked year round full time.[17]

At least four routes are open to black women who continue the fight for equality:

1. Black women can join the women's liberation movement in significant numbers.
2. Black women can build a viable, nationwide black women's liberation organization.
3. Black women can join black men in an organization to fight for the rights of black women.
4. A new civil rights movement can develop composed of black and white supporters which focuses on the grievances of black women.

The likelihood of black women following each of these courses of action will be examined.

The first possibility would be for black women to join white women in the women's liberation movement. Since the women's movement is composed primarily of middle-class white women, it is unlikely that they can expect to receive serious support from black women until they broaden their base of support among white women. The rural female, the Midwestern homemaker, the Southern and Plains farm wife is still not convinced that she has problems and grievances in common with her white urban sister.

Census Bureau reports on black and white women point out significant differences in life situations. Black women are more urban than white females and are more often in the lower economic categories and head single-parent households than white women. The percentage of black women in metropolitan areas in 1974 was 75.7, while for white women the percentage was 67.5. The ratio of black to white women was 1.12 in metropolitan areas and 2.27 in central cities.[18] In looking at the percentage of black families with female heads as a percentage of all families below the poverty level in 1974, the figures are 66.9 percent for blacks and 37.2 percent for white females.[19] These figures indicate widespread differences in family structure and economic level.

Historically, the demands of black and white women have been different. White females are making demands about freedom from housework, suburban boredom, and participation in unfulfilling community work—in essence, freedom from minor annoyances in their privileged lives. Black women have been concerned with issues of survival and demands of equal opportunity, which they share with black men.[20]

For a viable women's movement to exist across racial lines, black women must be shown that they have the same class-based interests as white women. White women, in turn, must realize the relationship between sexism and racism in U.S. society.[21] Although race has been the overriding issue for black women, rather than class, this does not rule out the possibility of black and white women coming together if class-based issues become more salient to both groups. This would be based on the assumption that more black women attain middle- and upper-class income status. For example, black and white professional women might find that their interests center on the need for more flexible educational programs, fair promotion procedures, and equity in credit and financial transactions. For women in the middle income range the demands might be equal pay for equal work, opening up new job opportunities for women, and a chance to move from a clerical to a managerial position. Those in unskilled jobs as service workers might desire the establishment of more abortion clinics, better health care and day care facilities, and assistance in finding a job which will remove them from the welfare rolls.

The formation of a viable, nationwide black women's movement is a possibility based on racial identity, but there are major problems in uniting black women across class lines. Black women view their struggle to gain equality primarily in racial terms because race has been the dominant, more constant barrier to their advancement, rather than sex. However, this analysis hypothesizes that as more black women attain middle-class status, because they hold managerial and professional jobs, their consciousness of discrimination based on sex and class status will rise sharply, causing them to identify more with the situation of working white women. Racial group identification will not disappear, but the thrust of discrimination will shift from race to class status.

Black women are well aware of the potential divisiveness that could result in the black community if a movement were to develop among black women. A nationwide black women's organization might only serve to hinder job opportunities and economic advancement for black men, creating a situation which would be detrimental to the black family. Black women are keenly aware of the educational and occupational opportunities they have had in the past, in contrast with the limited opportunities available to the black male. A serious split could develop among blacks if black women significantly outdistance black men in the white-collar job market.

A new movement could develop uniting black men and women to fight problems which specifically affect black women. The problem is, Who would be the leaders in such a movement? The employment situation for the black male creates uncertainty, insecurity, and the inability to plan for the future as a wage earner or the head of household. If the potential friction between black men and women is minimized, it would be necessary to let the men assume the leadership positions. But it is unlikely that capable women who could assume leadership positions will forget how black women were forced into a subordinate role by black men in the latter days of the civil rights movement. In a recent interview on the women's movement, Margo Jefferson observed that black men began to take the attitude:

> We will have our manhood or we will level the earth in the attempt. We will demand that our women fall into some unholy combination of medieval African: You will be childbearers and, in some cases, goddesses— and just medieval, period.[22]

Black men and women agree that the main issue is discrimination, which still exists in most sectors of U.S. society. As a consequence, barriers remain in education, employment, and housing. There are problems in agreeing on specific tactics to follow and the type of benefits that would be sought. Better-paying jobs and more adequate housing, important symbols of upward mobility, would certainly benefit blacks individually and as family members.

There are major obstacles in trying to organize a new civil rights movement because of the current climate of race relations in the United States. Since the South has allowed blacks into the political system and desegregated public accommodations, it is more difficult to pinpoint glaring examples of racism. Because the South can no longer be singled out for its racial policy it has become difficult to focus on another limited geographic area. This causes the public to view current racial problems as isolated instances of racism, rather than a pervading social condition. Although school busing may be a national issue, it gets only intermittent media attention until tensions flare in specific cities such as Louisville, Kentucky, or Boston. Any future movements for the benefit of blacks would need a unified effort on the part of black men and women, as well as strong support from whites in powerful positions. Therefore, a new movement based on black racial identification will probably not receive sufficient support from a cross section of the population to sustain itself.

Television remains a powerful medium for publicizing social movements, but the dramatic techniques of the 1960s have lost their effectiveness. A racial situation may be reported on the television, but it is not the lead story. Part of the dramatic effectiveness of the civil rights movement of the 1960s was that the public consciousness had been raised by a moral issue. Moral issues remain— human rights issues such as international terrorism, imprisonment of political prisoners, racism in Africa, but not the continuing racism in the United States.

In order for future movements to be successful, whether based on racial or class interests, they must be able to raise the political consciousness of the American people to a level of activity. However, coordinated activity toward a clearly defined goal is only one condition necessary for a successful national movement. There must also be a broad base of support, across class lines and racial groups. The use of new tactics, which effectively utilize the media, while bringing pressure to bear economically or politically on society will propel the movement forward. Given these conditions, the most likely coalition to develop would be across racial lines joining black and white women in a movement which focuses on the role of women in families and the status of women in jobs in all sectors of the economy.

Notes

1. Charles P. Henry, "An Event Oriented Approach to Black Politics," Ph.D. dissertation, University of Chicago, 1974.

2. See E.E. Schattschneider, *The Semi-Sovereign People* (New York: Holt, Rinehart and Winston, 1960).

3. Jo Freeman, *The Politics of Women's Liberation* (New York: David McKay Company, 1975), pp. 52–53.

4. Ibid.

5. Betty Friedan, *The Feminine Mystique* (New York: Dell Publishing Company, 1963), p. 37.

6. Ibid., p. 69.

7. Ibid., p. 305.

8. Ibid., p. 330.

9. Ibid., p. 356.

10. Ibid., p. 321.

11. Freeman, *The Politics of Women's Liberation,* p. 17 quoting W.G. Runciman, *Relative Deprivation and Social Justice* (Berkeley: University of California Press, 1966), p. 10.

12. Freeman, *The Politics of Women's Liberation,* p. 17.

13. Ibid., p. 81.

14. For a discussion of the drama of resistance and confrontation see Orrin Klapp, "Dramatic Encounters," in Joseph Gusfield, ed., *Protest, Reform, and Revolt* (New York: Wiley, 1970), pp. 377–393.

15. See Andrew Billingsley, *Black Families in White America* (Englewood Cliffs, N.J. Prentice-Hall, Spectrum Books, 1968); Joyce Ladner, *Tomorrow's Tomorrow* (Garden City, N.Y.: Doubleday, Anchor Books, 1971); John H. Scanzoni, *The Black Family in Modern Society* (Chicago: University of Chicago Press, Phoenix Books, 1977).

16. Daniel Patrick Moynihan, "The Negro Family: The Case for National Action," cited by Lee Rainwater and William Yancey, *The Moynihan Report and the Politics of Controversy* (Cambridge, Mass.: M.I.T. Press, 1967).

17. U.S. Department of Commerce, Bureau of the Census, *A Statistical Portrait of Women in the United States,* Special Studies series P-23, no. 58, 1976, p. 60.

18. Ibid., p. 66.

19. Ibid., p. 75.

20. See Ladner, *Tomorrow's Tomorrow,* and Linda La Rue, "The Black Movement and Women's Liberation," *The Black Scholar,* May 1970, p. 36.

21. Ibid. Also see Shulamith Firestone, *The Dialectic of Sex* (New York: Bantam Books, 1972).

22. Stephen Singular, "Moving On," *The New York Times Magazine,* April 30, 1978, p. 28.

Part II
The Impact of Executive Orders and Administrative Regulations

4

The Impact of Organizational Structure, Technology, and Professionalism on the Policy of Affirmative Action

Cheryl Swanson and
H. Brinton Milward

Introduction

While there is a great deal of controversy over the federal government's policy of affirmative action, national political leaders have continued to support the concept. Following the institutionalization of affirmative action we can legitimately raise questions about the implementation of that policy. Minority and women's groups have been highly critical of efforts to implement affirmative action programs, yet very little systematic research has been done to evaluate their impact. This research proposes to remedy this situation by using a theoretical model derived from the literature on organizational-environmental interaction to assess the implementation of federally mandated affirmative action *problem* programs.

The central proposition to be tested is that when faced with demands to comply with affirmative action policies, organizations will attempt to address these demands by hiring greater numbers of minorities and women in high-level positions. At the same time, they will try to minimize the impact of change on the organization by employing minority and female employees in organizational subunits which are isolated from the central or core activities of the organization. While the central focus of the research is the motivation to exclude minorities and women from the core activities of the organization, a number of additional variables are analyzed which may be significant in evaluating the distribution of minorities and women in organizations.

Environmentally Induced Change and Organizational Adaptation

On one hand, since public organizations are dependent on their environments for human and financial resources, they must be sensitive to externally induced

41

change such as affirmative action to ensure their growth and survival. On the other hand, organizations do not passively accept demands for change, and in many cases they may view these demands as threatening to the ongoing operations of the organizations.[1] Therefore, from one perspective organizational effectiveness is dependent on the ability to adapt to changes in the environment and to structure change to the organization's advantage.

Most of the literature on organizational-environmental interaction deals with the external adaptation of the organization to its environment. In this case organizations create boundary-spanning units such as personnel, public relations, or community affairs departments which interact with the environment for the purpose of buffering or protecting the technical core of the organization from environmental uncertainty or disturbance. The concept of the technical core as developed by Thompson refers to the central productive center of an organization where products or services are produced as the desired outputs of the management of the organization (or, in the case of public organizations, the desired output of legislative bodies).[2]

An example of external adaptation may occur where a subgroup of the population demands a change in the manner in which services are produced and delivered. Organizational participants may resist these demands on the grounds that that the present mode of production and delivery is the most efficient and effective one. To protect the production unit from demands for change, organizations may create a special unit to placate the dissatisfied citizenry, and if the unit is successful, citizens' demands will be satisfied or muted without bringing about any significant change in the ongoing operations of the organization.[3]

In the case of personnel, buffering activities may focus on supplying organizations with human resources in such a way as to limit uncertainty and increase predictability. This often requires a great deal of organizational effort.[4] For example, through a system of testing and educational certification, the civil service systems found in most government jurisdictions often effectively screen out those who deviate from desired patterns.[5] Wamsley and Zald note that the same motivation explains the manner in which most civil service systems recruit higher-level officials.

> An assumption that public organizations merely tap into civil service pools for [higher officials] is totally unwarranted. [Higher-level] recruitment and socialization now appear to have definite patterns that vary from one organization to another. It is not too hazardous a hypothesis that organizations will find some means of being more selective about recruiting and training their [higher officials] than is required by civil service. If they are legally required to be open about recruitment, they will institute an intensive socialization program.[6]

A similar phenomenon has been observed in organizations with distinct recruitment cultures. Whether it is the State Department preferring Ivy League graduates or the Forest Service preferring products of forestry schools at land grant universities, organizations will prefer to hire people from a source that is familiar and who have been socialized to accept the dominant values of the organization.

How does this affect women and minorities? Since women and minorities have been limited in their opportunities to acquire this type of socialization, we hypothesize that they will often be viewed as uncertain, nonhomogeneous resources and, as a result, less attractive candidates for recruitment into the organization. Herbert elaborates on this point by noting that one of the reasons that women and minorities have had such a difficult time being recruited into higher-level positions is the belief both among women's and minority organizations and in the management cadre of public organizations that positions held by these subgroups were and are made possible by the direct or indirect efforts of women's and minority organizations.[7] Because of this, they are expected to be spokesmen for their respective groups. While this is useful to management (if they want the black perspective on any decision, all they have to do is ask), it also makes them suspect in management's eyes as they value higher-level employees who are first and foremost loyal to the organization.

While affirmative action programs are designed to correct this kind of recruitment bias, there is no reason to believe that the process of buffering occurs only at the contact point where the organization meets the environment (external buffering). We believe that an internal buffering process continues to operate within the organization with respect to personnel. Thus, if organizations are forced to hire high-level officials whom they view as nonhomogeneous, they will attempt to minimize their impact on the internal functioning of organizations. One strategy for achieving this goal may be to cluster minority and female employees into "elephant burial grounds" which are isolated from the core activities of the organization. The "elephant burial grounds" may have no meaningful work to do and may overlap with other organizational subunits. They may, in fact, be completely redundant, but because public organizations are monopolies, there are no market constraints and the added cost of complying with affirmative action is simply passed on to the taxpayers. Management may not even make a pretext of demanding that these "elephant burial grounds" perform their functions because the purpose of having them is strictly to satisfy external demands.

Thus, in attempting to comply with demands to hire greater numbers of minorities and women, internally generated needs and demands may take precedence over those generated external to the organization. Organizations may develop strategies that channel newly hired minorities and women into directions that are perceived to confer the lowest costs and the greatest benefits on the organization. In the light of the previous discussion, one of these strategies is to protect the technical core of the organization from nonhomogeneous human resources. The following hypothesis is offered to test this assumption.

Hypothesis 1: In federative organizations, women and minorities who hold administrative, technical, and professional (ATP) positions will tend to be clustered in organizational subunits which provide services external to the organization rather than those which can be characterized as performing management and control functions. [8]

It should be noted that hypothesis 1 refers to federative organizations. The organization under examination, a county government, is a federative organization because it represents a comglomeration of functions with no single or cohesive purpose or mission.[9] Given this description of a federative organization, it becomes necessary to reformulate the concept of the technical core.

Since federative organizations perform very diverse kinds of functions, "consensus on the attainment of its whole collection of heterogeneous goals may be low and it is likely to be located exclusively in the organization's central leadership and bureaucracy."[10] These administrative units control resources and communications which are critical in holding together a multifunctional organization. Thus, for our purposes internal management and control functions constitute the technical core. This administrative technology is the one technology that is standard throughout a federative organization. Since it can be inferred that units which perform management and control functions are some of the most powerful in the organization, the exclusion of women and minorities from these units has important policy implications.

While organizations will tend to protect central control units from stress associated with change, a number of other factors may be significant in assessing the implementation of affirmative action policies. Additional variables included in the analysis are professionalism, cooptation strategies, and organization slack.

Professionalism, Recruitment Culture, and Organizational Exclusion

The education of individuals for public service is often of a professional nature. The public service in the United States at all levels is increasingly being professionalized in regard to the general professions—law, medicine, and engineering— but also with government-created professions such as public administration, social work, and planning.[11]

With professionalism has come the practice of franchising the selection process to professional institutions. These institutions may also choose people with a predisposition to accept professional norms and values. This franchising means that recruitment is a two-step process. First, the applicant must be certified by a professional school or program. Second, the organization recruits from only those who are so certified. At the same time, the relationship between the profession and the organization becomes reciprocal. In an organizational sense this means that professionals demand a certain amount of autonomy from their employing institutions.

Each of these professions develops an "institutionalized thought structure" which justifies the generally accepted practices of the profession and also justifies the professionals' approach to dealing with problems in their sphere of competence.[12] The institutional thought structure of a profession and its relative autonomy may make professionally dominated organizations or organizational subunits extremely resistant to penetration by women and minorities, since these subgroups have had little role in participation in or the definition of the organizational cultures of our society.

The characteristics of professionalism that have been discussed so far are relevant to the concept of organizational response to change. Palumbo and Styskal observe that "professionals tend to look at things in terms of their own occupational biases . . ." and will resist demands for change that either run contrary to professional norms and values or tend to decrease their power within the organization.[13] It is suggested that professionals will resist policies to hire greater numbers of women and minorities because (1) the administration of affirmative action policies by central personnel units conflicts with the orientation of professionals to exercise control over their domains and (2) professionals may view the policy of employing greater numbers of women and minorities as conflicting with credentialing requirements. Because minorities and women have previously been denied certain educational opportunities, professionals might perceive these groups as being less qualified than other applicants in the employment pool or less willing to accept the dominant norms and values of the profession. Given the foregoing discussion, we would expect to find the following.

Hypothesis 2: A greater proportion of ATP women and minorities will be employed in organizational subunits characterized by a lesser degree of professionalism than in more professionally oriented subunits.

Denying employment to women and minorities in more professional subunits may have a significant impact on these subpopulations since, like management and control units, more professional divisions are likely to confer a greater degree of status, power, and prestige on their participants.

Cooptation and a Representative Government

Organizations may find it desirable to recruit minorities and women when it is necessary to establish orderly and reliable mechanisms for reaching a target population.[14] Thus, administrative convenience in linking organizations to clients may be the reason that the areas of housing, welfare, and health have a higher proportion of blacks in high-level positions than transportation or agriculture.[15]

The U.S. Civil Rights Commission found examples of this in an employment study.[16] They discovered that blacks were being type-cast for certain positions such as staff jobs for human relations councils, civil rights commissions, or assistants to ranking administrators. The jobs have high status and command high salaries, but the jobs focus almost exclusively on minority group problems. Police departments have used this strategy in staffing rape investigation units with female detectives. They have also attempted to recruit minorities for patrol duty in predominantly nonwhite areas of the city.

Therefore, the type of clientele served by an organizational subunit must be considered in examining the placement of women and minorities. Personnel officers and other administrators with hiring responsibilities may see the placement of women or minorities in certain organizational subunits as an opportunity to enhance client support. This would be the case particularly in units where a large proportion of the clientele is either women or minorities. The clientele would be expected to give greater support to agencies that are staffed with employees who because of their race or gender are perceived as representing clientele interests.[17] Given these assumptions, the following employment pattern would be expected.

Hypothesis 3: Greater proportions of ATP women and minorities will be found in organizational subunits that have a large minority and/or female clientele.

Again, the strategy of placing minorities and women into units on the basis of clientele characteristics is significant for the interests of these subpopulations. Since client-based subunits are not part of the central management and control centers of the organization, minorities and women are effectively channeled away from the most important decision-making centers. Selznick notes that

> In general, the use of formal cooptation by a leadership does not envision the transfer of actual power. The forms of participation are emphasized but action is channeled so as to fulfill the administrative functions while preserving the focus of significant decision in the hands of the initiating group.[18]

Thus, while client satisfaction is an extremely important consideration, employment on the basis of client characteristics serves to exclude these subgroups from important positions in the organization, and with respect to minorities it also serves to perpetuate existing patterns of segregation.

Organizational Slack

The previously mentioned hypotheses relate to certain organizational needs and strategies that organizations employ to meet these needs which, in turn, may affect the employment patterns of women and minorities within an organization. However, it is also possible that certain other factors may influence the employment distribution of women and minorities independently of the motivations described. We believe that turnover rate is one of the factors and should be included in research of this nature.[19]

In attempting to meet affirmative action requirements agencies may be constrained by limited resources. If new positions cannot be created to accommodate demands for the employment of more women and minorities, their employment may depend on vacancies in existing positions. Thus it is plausible that organizational subunits that are normally resistant to change (that is, those that exhibit a high degree of professionalism or perform management and control functions) may employ greater proportions of women and minorities than those that are characteristically less resistant to change (units that are less professional or perform external service functions). This could be the case if the former types of subunits have high turnover rates and the latter types have very few vacancies over a long period.

Hypothesis 4: There will be a greater proportion of ATP women and minorities in organizational subunits with high turnover rates.

The employment of women and minorities according to turnover rates may also be significant in terms of the welfare of these particular groups of people. It is difficult to draw any conclusions about the desirability of working in various departments, agencies, and programs, but it is highly possible that units with the highest turnover rates are for various reasons also the ones which offer employees relatively fewer advantages.

Data Base and Measurement of Organizational Variables

Employment data on ATP women and minorities were obtained for the county government of Jackson County, Missouri, for the year 1976. As indicated earlier, the Jackson County government is designated as the organizational unit under study; and various separately administered departments, agencies, or programs within the country government are designated as subunits of the organization. Jackson County lists forty-three subunits in its reporting of employment data by race and sex. Three subunits do not contain administrative, professional, or technical positions, and a description of classification codes was not available for two subunits. In addition, complete data on organizational characteristics were not available for all subunits. As a result, the number of employees will vary depending on the type of organizational trait being examined. One of the departments for which complete data were not available—Juvenile Court Services —employs a large number of ATP employees of which a substantial proportion are women and minorities. Given these data problems, it is difficult to make comparisons among agency characteristics to determine which ones are most descriptive of employment patterns among women and minorities.[20]

The organizational subunits under investigation were dichotomized into internal management and control and external service units, more professional and less professional units, service units with hetergeneous clientele and those which service large proportions of women and/or minorities, and units with high turnover versus those with low turnover rates.

Examples of divisions performing internal control functions include data processing, budgeting, and records. External service units include departments such as public works and health and welfare.

Professionalism is often manifested in certain behaviors or in the possession of certain skills and attitudes. Since these are difficult to measure, education is often used as an indicator of professionalism and is the one selected for this analysis. The median education for all ATP employees was computed on the basis of the minimum educational requirements for each position as outlined in Jackson County's pay and job classification plan. The average education for all ATP positions in each subunit was then computed. Those subunits which were above the median were classified as high in professionalism and those falling below the median were designated as exhibiting a lower degree of professionalism.

It should be noted that educational levels are measured for administrative and technical positions as well as for positions which have traditionally been defined as professional such as those relating to law and medicine. All ATP positions are included in the measurement of education because of the trend in recent years toward the professionalization of many types of jobs which do not fall within any narrow technical definition of professionalism. For example, public administrators now describe themselves as professionals, and many law enforcement officials support a move toward professionalization even though in the latter case there has traditionally been no formal education or certification process associated with the job.[21] What all the "new professionals" have in common is a concern with achieving a more professional status. To accomplish this goal, the new professions have attempted to gain more control over job certification, and this has often resulted in an increase in the number and kinds of requirements that an individual must meet before he or she is considered to be qualified for a particular position. Given these considerations, a broader operational definition of professionalism seems appropriate.

External service units were divided into those which service a mixed clien-

tele according to race and sex, for example, public works or parks and recreation, and those which service a high proportion of minorities or women, for
example, health, welfare, and corrections.

Finally, organizational subunits were classified as either high or low in turn-
over according to their relationship to the median turnover rate for all subunits.
Turnover data were available for a one-year period from November 1975 to
December 1976.

Research Findings

In terms of total employment minorities do fairly well. According to the 1970
census, Jackson County's black population is 17.3 percent of the total and
minorities comprise 25.2 percent of all ATP employees. Women are represented
in ATP positions at a somewhat higher proportion (28.8 percent), but on the
other hand, they represent 52.7 percent of the total Jackson County population.
While the total figures are quite impressive for nonwhites, the policy implications of this research are that considerations other than total employment figures
should be examined in evaluating whether affirmative action goals are being met.

Table 4-1 shows the relationship between an employee's race and sex and
employment in organizational subunits by functional type. It is interesting to
note that the hypothesis is supported for minorities but not for female employees. A greater proportion of all nonwhite as opposed to all white ATP
employees is located in subunits that perform external service functions. The
relationship between race and employment by type of subunit is significant at
the .001 level. The Yules Q statistic is fairly high at .52.[22]

In the case of women, the employment pattern is the reverse of that predicted. A greater proportion of the female rather than the male ATP workforce
is employed in internal control units, although the relationship between sex and
employment by type of subunit does not appear to be a significant one. One of
the reasons why women are better represented in central control units is a
result of the opportunities available to them in the Assessment Division. Women
comprise almost 34 percent of this division of 77 employees. The position held
by most of the women is that of assessor, a job which requires real estate experience. Because of the nature of real estate work in the private sector (many
positions consist of part-time jobs that are often considered to be supplemental
to the main source of family income), there is probably a fairly large pool of
female employees with the requisite experience for this type of position. Another explanation for the disparity between women and minorities is that
women as a group may be perceived as holding values which conform more
closely to those of the organization.

The relationship between employee race and sex and employment of organizational subunits by degree of professionalism is shown in table 4-2. The find-

Table 4-1
Relationship between Employee Race and Sex and Employment in Organizational Subunits by Functional Type

Employee Characteristics	Employment in Organizational Subunit											
	Internal Control Function			External Function			Total		Chi Square	Significance Level	Yules Q
	N	R%[a]	C%	N	R%	C%	N	%			
Race											
White	136	28.3	88.3	344	71.7	70.5	480	100.0	18.7	.001	.52
Nonwhite	18	11.1	11.7	144	88.9	29.7	162	100.0			
Sex											
Male	106	23.2	65.8	351	76.8	71.9	457	100.0	.41	.70	-.07
Female	48	25.9	31.2	137	74.0	28.1	185	99.9			

[a]The data analyses for all tables are based on row percentages. Column percentages provide the reader with additional information on the proportion of the total workforce that consists of minorities and women within each type of organizational subunit.

Table 4-2
Relationship between Employee Race and Sex and Employment in Organizational Subunits by Degree of Professionalism

	Employment in Organizational Subunit									Chi Significance		
Employee Characteristics	More Professional			Less Professional			Total			Square	Level	Yules Q
	N	R%	C%	N	R%	C%	N	%				
Race												
White	69	21.1	82.1	258	78.9	88.6	327	100.0		1.40	.30	−.26
Nonwhite	15	31.2	17.8	33	68.8	11.3	48	100.0				
Sex												
Male	64	20.9	76.2	242	79.1	83.2	306	100.0		1.65	.20	−.21
Female	20	29.0	23.8	49	71.0	16.8	69	100.0				

ings are the reverse of what was predicted. A higher percentage of the nonwhite and women employees are found in more professional subunits, although the relationships are certainly not very strong and are significant at only the .30 and .20 levels, respectively. At any rate, professionally dominated subunits do not seem to be any more highly resistant to employing women and minorities than their less professional counterparts.

One of the reasons for this finding may be that women and minorities in the applicant pool in Jackson County compete fairly well in terms of credentialing requirements. To the extent that credentialing is important to professionals, the race or sex of the applicant may not be a significant consideration. In less professional departments where credentialing requirements receive less weight, the race or gender of an employee may be a more important variable in the selection process.

According to table 4-3, the relationship between an employee's race and employment patterns by type of clientele served is significant at the .01 level. The Yules Q statistic is fairly strong at .68. It was not possible to test the relationship between employee sex and type of clientele served because only two subunits were identified which serve a predominantly female clientele, and these subunits employed only eight individuals. However, given the distribution of employment by sex in these subunits, the hypotheses would tend not to be confirmed with respect to women. One subunit employed no women, and the second employs three women for a total of 38 percent.

The final relationship under examination is that between employee sex and race and employment patterns in subunits according to turnover rates. Table 4-4 indicates that subunits with higher turnover rates do not employ a significantly greater proportion of ATP women and minorities than more stable divisions. Indeed, the relationship is the reverse of that expected for female employees.

In summary, there is some support that an individual's race will determine where he or she is employed in that organization. Organizations do seem to employ more minorities in subunits that perform external service functions, and the character of an agency's clientele also describes employment patterns for ATP minorities. Women are not likely to be represented in external service units as opposed to those which are part of the technical core of the organization, suggesting that women may be assimilated more easily into units performing management and control functions. However, as noted earlier, it is necessary to look more closely at the type of positions held by women in these particular units.

The hypotheses with respect to professionalism and turnover were not supported by the data. However, several Jackson County officials commented to us that in comparison to other organizations with which they had experience, Jackson County as a unit ranks relatively low in professionalism. Also, since the turnover data were only for a one-year period, we would hesitate to draw any firm conclusions in terms of its relationship to employment patterns. At any

Table 4-3
Relationship between Employee Race and Employment in Organizational Subunits by Nature of Clientele

| | Employment in Organizational Subunits | | | | | | | | | |
| Employee Characteristics | Heterogeneous Clientele Population | | | Clientele Predominantly Nonwhite | | | Total | | Chi Square | Significance Level | Yules Q |
	N	R%	C%	N	R%	C%	N	%			
Race											
White	74	22.0	91.4	262	78.0	66.4	336	100.0	18.9	.001	.68
Nonwhite	7	5.0	8.6	132	95.0	33.5	139	100.0			

Table 4-4
Relationship between Employee Race and Sex and Employment in Organizational Subunits by Degree of Turnover

| | Employment in Organizational Subunit | | | | | | | | | |
| Employee Characteristics | High Turnover | | | Low Turnover | | | Total | | Chi Square | Significance Level | Yules Q |
	N	R%	C%	N	R%	C%	N	%			
Race											
White	109	36.4	85.8	190	63.5	88.4	299	99.9	.25	.70	-.11
Nonwhite	18	41.9	14.2	25	58.1	11.6	43	100.0			
Sex											
Male	109	38.1	85.8	177	61.9	82.3	286	100.0	.48	.50	.13
Female	18	32.1	14.2	38	67.8	17.7	56	99.9			

rate, these initial findings would seem to warrant additional research using a more complete and comparative data base.

Conclusions and Policy Implications

In this chapter we have dealt theoretically and empirically with how public organizations are expected to react to increased pressure to assimilate larger numbers of minority and women employees at higher levels than ever before. Given our theoretical perspective, it was expected that in general organizations will respond to demands for change by the least change capable of neutralizing or meeting the intrusive process. A number of hypotheses were offered for which the predicted response was similar—minimal compliance with the demand for change with internally defined organizational needs taking precedence over externally induced demands. The findings on minority employment were suggestive of this particular response to demands for change.

In terms of policy implications, we suggest that current approaches to compliance have been and can still be effective at an early stage in affirmative action efforts. This is especially true when organizations have only recently been actively engaged in discrimination against women and minorities. It is also useful as a gross technique to monitor the aggregate behavior of a large number of organizations. However, as students of organizational behavior, we have come to believe that compliance agencies need to focus on finer and more precise measures to monitor organizations after the initial affirmative action plan has been adopted and efforts at compliance have been made. This second-stage effort could be like an audit by the Internal Revenue Service. Only a small proportion of the taxpayers are audited, but the threat of the audit acts as an incentive to comply with the tax law. Likewise, affirmative action audits would rely not on regulation per se but on creating an incentive structure that utilizes what is known about how organizations and people in them behave. The threat of answering questions on the distribution of employees within organizations may deter subtle patterns of discrimination. If organizations act to avoid uncertainty and minimize the effect of the environment on the technical core, the threat of an audit such as we propose might tip the balance of uncertainty in favor of compliance with both the letter and the spirit of the law. This research will hopefully serve as a step toward developing such a second-stage affirmative action capability.

Notes

1. James D. Thompson, *Organizations in Action* (New York: McGraw-Hill, 1967); P.R. Lawrence and J. W. Lorsch, *Organizations and Environment* (Homewood, Ill.: Richard D. Irwin, 1969); F.E. Emery and E.L. Trist, "The

Causal Future of Organizational Environments," *Human Relations* 19 (1965): 21-31.

2. Thompson, *Organizations in Action.*

3. John J. Kirlin, "The Impact of Increasing Lower-Status Clientele upon City Governmental Structure: A Model from Organization Theory," *Urban Affairs Quarterly* 8(1973): 317-343.

4. Charles Perrow, *Organizational Analysis* (Belmont, Calif.: Brooks-Cole, 1970).

5. H. Brinton Milward, "Politics, Personnel and Public Policy," *Public Administration Review,* forthcoming.

6. G.L. Wamsley and M.N. Zald, *The Political Economy of Public Organizations* (Lexington, Mass.: D.C. Heath, Lexington Books, 1973), p. 70.

7. Adam W. Herbert, "The Minority Administrator: Problems, Prospects, and Challenges," *Public Administration Review* 34(1974): 556-563.

8. It should be noted that the research hypotheses focus on employees who hold administrative, technical, and professional positions. These positions are the top three employment categories in the Equal Employment Opportunity Commission's broad classification of job types. Previous efforts to describe employment patterns by race and sex have generally shown that women and minorities hold a disproportionate share of low-paying jobs that require little formal education. For our purposes it is desirable to control as much as possible for differences in skills and educational attainment that affect where individuals are placed in an organization.

9. For a more detailed description of a federative organization, see Milward and Swanson, "The Effect of Uncertainty on Public Organizations," *Administration and Society* (forthcoming).

10. Lawrence B. Mohr, "The Concept of Organizational Goal," *American Political Science Review* 67(1973): 470-481.

11. Frederick C. Mosher, *Democracy and the Public Service* (New York: Oxford University Press, 1968).

12. R.L. Warren, S.M. Rose, and A.F. Bergunder, *The Structure of Urban Reform* (Lexington, Mass.: D.C. Heath, Lexington Books, 1974).

13. D.J. Palumbo and R.A. Styskal, "Professionalism and Receptivity to Change," *American Journal of Political Science* 18(1974): 385.

14. Phillip Selznick, "Cooptation," in Merlin B. Brinkerhoff and Phillip R. Kung, ed., *Complex Organizations and Their Environments* (Dubuque, Iowa: William C. Brown, 1972).

15. Herbert, "The Minority Administrator: Problems, Prospects, and Challenges."

16. U.S. Commission on Civil Rights, *For All the People . . . By All the People* (Washington: Government Printing Office, 1969).

17. Norton Long, "Bureaucracy and Constitutionalism," *American Political Science Review* 46(1952): 808-818.

18. Selznick, "Cooptation," p. 143.

19. John J. Kirlin, "The Impact of Increasing Lower-Status Clientele upon City Governmental Structures: A Model from Organization Theory."

20. In spite of some problems with the data, it should be noted that data of sufficient detail to test the hypotheses under consideration are extremely difficult to obtain. We are grateful to the Jackson County officials who gave us access to their employment data.

21. James Q. Wilson, *Varieties of Police Behavior* (Cambridge, Mass.: Harvard University Press, 1968).

22. It should be noted that a high percentage of the total ATP minority workforce (68.6 percent) is located in one department classified as performing external functions—Juvenile Court Services.

5 Affirmative Action: Constraints and Policy Impact

Kenneth J. Meier

Much research in U.S. state politics has related public policy outputs to environmental factors. This research has centered on the relative impact of political and economic variables on state expenditure levels. Dawson and Robinson first added political variables to the relationship between state economic constraints and spending in functional areas.[1] Dye continued the research, underscoring the conclusion that economic factors were the better predictors of state spending policies.[2] Since these early studies, state policy analysis has diverged in several different directions. Lineberry and Fowler applied the correlational analysis to city governments.[3] Through the use of factor analysis, Sharkanshy and Hofferbert found that political factors had a significant impact on policy.[4] Fry and Winters, Sullivan, and Booms and Halldorson have related income redistribution to economic and political variables.[5] On a nonexpenditure level Walker has related state characteristics to policy innovations, finding a strong political impact on public policy.[6] Ecological analysis of state policies has, in short, proved to be a fruitful area of research.

Within the heritage of these earlier studies, this chapter investigates three questions about affirmative action. First, the success of affirmative action programs in achieving racial representation in the states is related to economic, political, and administrative/labor pool factors theoretically supportive of affirmative action. The study of economic, political, and administrative/labor pool constraints on affirmative action allows inferences about a controversial policy to be made as the policy is being implemented. The study relates standard arguments about affirmative action and racial representation through statistical analysis to determine which factors facilitate or hinder the success of these programs.[7] Second, then this chapter relates one policy variable, racial representation, to other policy variables to determine if affirmative action has any impact on other policies. Two theories, representative bureaucracy and agency socialization, yield conflicting predictions as to whether the recruitment of minorities will alter administrative policy outputs. Third, the chapter presents additional data on the recently raised issue of the impact of elite behavior on public policy.[8] Administrative elites, as implementers of public policy, are the final actor (before feedback) in the policy process. Previous studies have considered only preimplementation elite behavior.[9]

The Dependent Variable: Racial Representation

Under the merit system, employee racial backgrounds were assumed to be irrelevant, and therefore little data were collected on the racial composition of the
public service. With the more recent pressure of affirmative action and the
emphasis on goals and quotas,[10] however, some measures of both total minority
employment and minority employment at different levels of the state bureaucracies have become available. From 1970 to 1972 the Civil Service Commission
collected racial employment data in selected state and local grant-aided agencies.
Since participation in these surveys was not universal, the data were of question-
able accuracy. In 1973 the Equal Employment Opportunity Commission began
collecting these data, and participation in the survey was mandatory for state
and local governments. To date, only 1975 data are publicly available; these
data form the basis for all minority employment variables used in this study.[11]

Minority representation can be divided into two different dimensions. The
first dimension is simply the minority employment in the government bureaucracy, or, as Sigelman terms it, "minority penetration."[12] *Minority penetration*
is operationalized as the ratio of the percentage of state and local employees
who are minorities to the percentage of the state population that are minorities.
The minority penetration ratios ranged from .23 to 1.57 with a mean of .86
(indicating that the average state underrepresents minorities by 14 percent in its
bureaucracy). Racial representation, however, deals not only with access to
government employment but also with eliminating discrimination after minorities have been hired. By hiring maintenance and staff personnel with little
authority, states can achieve a high percentage of minority employment without
affecting the normal operating procedures of the bureaucracy. The position
which the minority administrator occupies in the agency is also important. To
tap this dimension, a second measure, minority stratification, was created.
Minority stratification is the Gini index of inequality which contrasts the minority employment at the same level.[13] The distribution measures for 1975 ranged
from -1.54 to .50 with a mean of .25. Since it is possible that minorities might
be in better positions than whites in certain state bureaucracies, the Gini index
at times is less than 0, the lower limit which signifies a perfectly equal distribution. The distinctiveness of these two aspects of affirmative action is under-
scored by the low product moment correlation between them ($r = +.22$).

Independent-Variable Clusters

Economic

State policy analysis has a long tradition of incorporating economic variables.[14]
A developmental theory is usually used to relate economic variables to public

policy. As the state becomes more urban, wealthy, and so forth economic constraints on public policy diminish. As economic constraints diminish, the state can spend more money delivering services, especially social welfare services, to the people. This chapter uses Dye's four economic constraints taken from the 1970 U.S. census—urbanization (percentage of the population living in urban areas), median family income, median education, and the percentage of industrial employment—as economic variables.[15]

Political Factors

Political variables include some summary measures of the state's politics and some minority-specific variables. Indices of party cohesion, party competition, interest group strength, power of the governor, and responsiveness to general public opinion and to opinion on civil rights were used as political variables.[16] Political variables are usually related to policy outcomes either by V.O. Key's competition hypothesis or by a political development theory.[17] As politics becomes more competitive, parties have to appeal to diverse groups to be elected. As a result, two-party competitive states will exert more effort in social welfare areas because the parties compete to provide services for large blocs of voters.

The development thesis argues that as states become more politically sophisticated (that is, develop alternative methods of interest aggregation, reduce constraints on the executive, and so on), they will become more responsive to a broader segment of the population. As a result, politically developed states should support more extensive social welfare policies.

Administrative/Labor Pool Factors

Three possible administrative/labor pool factors have theoretical linkages to the success of affirmative action. The strength of the merit system, operationalized as the percentage of employees covered by the merit system, should hinder affirmative action.[18] Second, labor pool factors such as the level of minority education, minority income, the size of the bureaucracy (and thus turnover), competition for minorities by private business, the size of the minority population, and the average administrative salary all can be related to employment of minorities.[19] Finally, federal policy designed to increase minority employment should vary in effectiveness with the leverage that the federal government has. As indicators of this leverage, this chapter uses the per capita federal aid and the percentage of state revenue which the state receives from the federal government.

Economic Constraints[20]

The economic development hypothesis predicts that as a state develops, discrimination will be forced out of the bureaucracy in favor of more equal treatment. Discrimination will moderate because the larger economic pie provides for minority opportunities that are not at the expense of nonminorities and because economic development will spawn a minority middle class better able to articulate minority demands. Minorities in the more developed states should fare better both in total employment and in terms of relative position in the bureaucracy. According to table 5-1, the hypothesis holds only between minority penetration and education and median family income. Successful minority penetration occurs generally in *rural*, nonindustrial states with high education and income levels. In short, the Midwestern and New England states, those with the fewest minorities, do the best proportionally because their goals are relatively low.[21] In terms of minority stratification, the pattern holds for education and

Table 5-1
**Simple Correlations between Minority Employment
and Environmental Variables**

Environmental Variable	Minority Penetration	Minority Stratification
Economic		
Urbanization	−.11	.07
Family income	.26	.31
Median education	.38	.40
Percentage of industrial employment	−.43	−.15
Political		
Responsiveness to public opinion	−.14	.00
Party cohesion	.30	−.15
Interest group strength	−.04	.38
Hofferbert party competition index	−.29	.22
Power of the governor	.24	.11
Responsiveness of civil rights	.05	.22
Administrative/Labor Pool		
Strength of the merit system	−.02	−.04
Size of the bureaucracy	−.14	.19
Average administrative salary	.13	−.28
Per capita federal aid	−.29	.18
Minority population percentage	−.05	.50
Percent revenue−federal sources	.33	.39
Private sector minority employment	.20	−.34
Median minority education level	−.24	−.54
Median minority income	.47	−.29
Growth in state bureaucracy	.15	.23

income. Minorities achieve higher organization positions in nonindustrial states where the income and education levels are high.

Political Influences

Racial representation can be hypothetically related to several political variables. Party competition should force parties to compete for minority votes and offer programs to secure minority representation in the government bureaucracy. The other political variables are related to minority employment more directly. Since in many states the governor reflects a more urban clientele than the state legislature, success in affirmative action should be related to the power of the governor. Party cohesion is needed to pass antidiscrimination measures. Cohesion and representation should, therefore, be positively correlated while interest group strength, a divisive force, should be negatively related to affirmative action. Finally, as the demand for affirmative action grows, success in minority employment should be related to the state's responsiveness to public opinion.

As table 5-1 reveals, minority penetration is related to party cohesion, the competitiveness of the parties, and the power of the governor. All other relationships were not confirmed by the data. Minorities fare best in public employment where parties are cohesive, where the parties are *not* competitive, and where governors have strong formal powers. Although the party competition hypothesis was not confirmed, an explanation may be available. Since parties are only one of many means of aggregating interests, competitive parties may not be necessary to successfully press affirmative action programs. In this instance, the governor may provide the focal point for minority interest aggregation.

Minority stratification in the bureaucracy, on the other hand, is related to a variety of political variables. Minorities achieve best results where interest groups are strong, parties are competitive, the state is responsive to public opinion on civil rights, and the parties are not cohesive. Key's traditional hypothesis concerning party competition and government responsiveness holds only for minority stratification.

Administrative/Labor Pool Correlates

Since many minority group members have argued that the merit system discriminates against minorities with its unnecessarily high entrance standards and since the Civil Service Commission would argue to the contrary that merit principles aid minorities through nondiscrimination,[22] the results of table 5-1 are surprising. The strength of a state's merit system is unrelated to either minority penetration or minority stratification.

Several hypotheses concerning minority employment and the other administrative variables are plausible. Minority penetration should be higher where the bureaucracy is large so that more employment opportunities exist, where the administrative salaries are higher so that the state can bid competitively for minority personnel, and where the percentage of minorities in the population is large and well educated so that a qualified labor pool exists. Affirmative action should also be successful where minority incomes are low so that public employment is an attractive alternative and where private sector minority employment is low, indicating that public employment is not at a competitive advantage.

In terms of these hypotheses, minority penetration varies in its relationship to administrative factors. Although states with higher administrative salaries do attract more minority personnel to the bureaucracy, minority penetration is positively correlated with minority income levels, inversely correlated with minority education levels, and inversely correlated with the size of the bureaucracy. These statistics again indicate that impressive minority employment percentages are probably achieved in small states with few minorities who are relatively prosperous economically.

Minority stratification shows more congruence with the major hypothesis. Minority personnel achieve leadership positions in those states where the bureaucracy is large, where the minority group membership is a large percentage of the population, and where the bureaucracy is growing. They also do well, contrary to prediction, where minority education levels are low and salaries are low. Successful affirmative action at all levels of the bureaucracy, then, appears to be a function of the number of minority personnel available, the number of opportunities for public employment, and the desirability of government employment.

Minority penetration and stratification should be positively related to both per capita federal aid and the percentage of the state's revenue that comes from federal sources. Both figures should indicate the leverage that the federal government can use to encourage affirmative action in the state. Minority penetration is positively related to the percentage of federal funds and negatively related to the per capita federal aid. On the other hand, the distribution of minority employment is positively related to per capita federal aid and the percentage of federal funds. Federal financial controls appear to have a large potential impact on minority hiring, especially at higher levels.

The Relative Impact of Economics, Politics, and Administration

The simple correlations presented in table 5-1 oversimplify the relationship between the independent variables and affirmative action success. None of these relationships occur in a vacuum, although the results do underscore the contention that minority penetration and minority stratification are two different phenomena. The true impact of each varible can be assessed only when the impact of all other variables is controlled. To compare the relative impact of all the environmental variables, the four best predictors[23] in each cluster of independent variable were selected. The four political factors are party competition, power of the governor, party cohesion, and interest group strength. The four administrative factors include size of the state bureaucracy, size of the minority population, minority income, and the average administrative salary. The same number of variables was chosen in each area so that the predictive ability of each cluster, as well as of each variable, could be compared. If certain clusters contained more variables than others, then the reduction in degrees of freedom would give that cluster a predictive edge, all other things being equal.[24]

Table 5-2 presents the multiple correlation coefficients between the three independent-variable clusters and the minority employment measures. Using the correlations, the economic and administrative/labor pool clusters appear to have equal influence on minority penetration in the state bureaucracy with the political factors a distant third. The comparisons are misleading, however, since much of the variance explained by one cluster of variables can also be explained by the other clusters. To determine the relative impact of each cluster of variables, a variant of block recursive causal modeling is used.[25] The direct impact of each cluster of variables is measured by the variation that cluster explains in minority employment after the other two clusters have explained all the variance they can. Direct impact, then, is equivalent to additions to R^2.[26] The total correlation between all the variables and minority employment can be partitioned into the variance explained solely by each cluster and the shared variance (see table 5-3).

Table 5-3 reveals that economic variables are the best predictor of minority penetration when other clusters are controlled (.24), predicting better than political factors (.01) and administrative/labor pool factors (.22). The results should not be taken to imply that political factors are unimportant in affirmative action; they are important. Their *direct* impact, however, is less than the relative direct impact of economic and administrative factors.

Table 5-2
Impact of Economic, Political, and Administrative Factors on Minority Employment—Correlations

	Economic Factors	Political Factors	Administrative Factors
Minority penetration	.70	.45	.68
Minority stratification	.48	.48	.56

Table 5-3
Direct Impact of Environmental Clusters on Minority Employment

	Minority Penetration	Minority Stratification
Economic variables	.24	.04
Political variables	.01	.20
Administrative variables	.22	.19
Shared variance	.27	.17

The distinction between minority penetration and minority stratification is nowhere as apparent as in the relationship to the three variable clusters. Table 5-2 reveals the correlations between the independent-variable clusters and minority stratification. Although both economic and political factors are related to the Gini distribution of minorities in the bureaucracy, administrative variables have a stronger relationship with minority stratification. Table 5-3 shows, however, that political factors play a major role with administrative/labor pool factors in determining minority stratification. The direct impact of political factors (.20) and administrative/labor pool factors (.19) is much stronger than the economic impact (.04).

Before some design possibilities for successful affirmative action programs are suggested, the model's total predictive ability and the relative contribution of each independent variable should be noted. Table 5-4 presents both sets of data. The twelve environmental variables explain 74 percent of the variance in minority penetration. The most important variables related to minority penetration are median family income, industrial employment, size of the minority population, minority income, and size of the state bureaucracy. All five are either administrative or economic variables.

Minority stratification, as expected, shows strikingly different results although the model's predictive efficacy is almost as high ($R^2 = .60$). Of the economic variables only median education level and family income are major factors. All the political factors except party competition are strongly related to the distribution of minority employment. The remaining major influences are administrative—the size of the bureaucracy, average administrative salary, and the characteristics of the minority labor pool (size).

The data suggest that designing administrative arrangements to achieve affirmative action success will produce poor results in raising the level of minority penetration. Any success in this area, to the extent that manipulation is possible, is likely to be attained through long-run methods (that is, economic development or higher minority incomes). The stratification of minorities in the bureaucracy, on the other hand, does not appear to be as constrained by economic

Table 5-4
Direct Impact of Twelve Selected Environmental Variables on Racial Representation—Path Coefficients

Environmental Variable	Minority Penetration	Minority Stratification
Urbanization	-.16	.07
Median family income	-.25	-.28
Median education	.18	.23
Industrial employment	-.52	-.13
Party cohesion	-.07	-.33
Interest group strength	-.13	-.42
Party competition	-.04	.01
Gubernatorial power	.06	-.38
Average administrative salary	.00	.47
Minority population percentage	-.23	-.38
Minority median income	.69	.14
Size of the bureaucracy	-.24	-.26
	$R^2 = .74$	$R^2 = .60$

factors. Given a small labor pool of qualified minorities, the best results are achieved in small bureaus that pay relatively well. One possible explanation is that large bureaucracies tend to develop professionalized criteria for promotions and thus may be less responsive to minority demands for equity.[27] Smaller bureaucracies without these obstacles can permit more rapid promotions. Higher administrative salaries, on the other hand, are directly related to how attractive civil service positions are to minorities. The current economic situation for state government makes the salary inducement a feasible alternative. As states continue to run budget surpluses, administrative salaries will benefit; and, as a result, minority hiring at upper levels will continue to improve.

If the economic, political, and administrative/labor pool factors are interpreted as constraints on affirmative action programs, can an agency-run affirmative action program have any impact? Although the high predictive level of the environmental constraints ($R^2 = .74, .60$) indicates major constraints on administrative activities to improve minority representation, some optimism is possible. Twenty-six percent of the variance in minority penetration and 40 percent of the variance in minority stratification are not explained by these constraints. In all probability such factors as administrative commitment to affirmative action, type of affirmative action program, and other controllable variables account for much of this unexplained variation. We need a study on the variation in state affirmative action activities to determine how effective different types of programs can be, given the economic, political, and administrative/labor pool constraints on them.

The Policy Impact of Affirmative Action

The correlates of minority representation would be the terminus of this research were it not for the theory of representative bureaucracy. The theory of representative bureaucracy was developed by Kingsley, imported to the United States by Levitan, extended by Long and Van Riper, and applied to affirmative action by Krislov.[28] The proponents of the theory argue that the social origins of bureaucrat exert a great deal of influence on the bureaucrat's attitudes and thus his/her policy behavior. A representative bureaucracy, then, should lead to policies responsive to the general public.[29]

Following the reasoning of that theory, Lovell argues that recruiting minorities to the bureaucracy will infuse people into the bureaucracy who hold divergent values.[30] Since the value premises a person holds when making decisions are partial determinants of the decision's outcome,[31] bureaucracies representative of minority groups should make policy more responsive to the wishes of the minority groups. The theory assumes that the administrators have the discretion to act and that racial characteristics are a strong influence on behavior.

The theory of representative bureaucracy has not gone without challenge. Numerous case studies have demonstrated the impact which agency affiliation has on policy preferences.[32] Agencies socialize their employees by structuring incentive systems, through personnel procedures and several other methods.[33] Agency socialization presents a challenge to representative bureaucracy because the forces of agency socialization may well outweigh those of social origins. Meier and Nigro compared the impact of social origins and agency affiliation on U.S. federal civil servants' attitudes and found that agency affiliation far outweighed the impact of origins.[34] These two theories provide the opportunity for a critical test, with representative bureaucracy predicting that affirmative action has policy implications and agency socialization predicting that it does not. This test goes beyond that of Meier and Nigro in that it deals in policy rather than just policy attitudes.[35]

If minority representation has an impact on policy decisions, bureaucracies more representative of the minority population should administer policies more responsive to those minorities. Since this question cannot be answered directly with the data at hand, some indicators must be derived. This analysis assumes that minorities have an interest in increased social service expenditures but no interest in highway hardware expenditures. A more representative bureaucracy, therefore, should advocate more funds to be spent on social services. Since the budget process is based to some extent on administrative advocacy,[36] this pressure should be translated into policy outcomes.

Because the relationship between representation and policy outcomes might be spurious, external factors likely to influence both must be controlled. Economic variables are strong influences on both racial representation and policy outputs and, therefore, must be controlled in a policy assessment of minority representation. The impact of minority representation, then, will be measured by the variance in policy outputs which minority representation explains after economic factors have been controlled.[37]

The first cluster of policy variables to be examined is the per capita expenditure levels for education, highways, welfare, health, and police.[38] From the economic and political position of most minorities we could hypothesize that a representative bureaucracy should result in higher expenditure levels for education and welfare and lower expenditure levels for highways, health, and police.[39]

Table 5-5 shows the policy impact of minority representation. Minority penetration does not have a significant impact on any of the five expenditure levels. In fact, the relationships are in the predicted direction only two out of five times. Minority stratification has, as would be expected, a greater impact on public policy. Stratification accounts for 2.9 percent additional variance in education expenditures and 7.3 percent additional variance in health care expenditure. The education relationship, however, is in the wrong direction. State bureaucracies with more minorities actually spend less on education. The other four relationships are in the correct direction.

Since state policies include not only the level of expenditures but also the distribution of the state budget among various functional categories, the percentage of the budget spent on health, education, highways, and welfare was also related to minority employment. Minority penetration percentages contribute 2.5 percent additional variance to the explanation of education expenditures, and the relationship is in the hypothesized direction. For the three other policy areas the results are inconclusive. Minority stratification, on the other hand, has its greatest impact on welfare spending (3.7 percent) with little impact on health, education, or highway expenditures. The relationship between minority stratification and welfare is in the correct direction. Representative bureaucracies (in terms of stratification) spend more on welfare.

In an attempt to simplify the myriad dimensions of state policy, Sharkansky and Hofferbert developed factor score measures of state policy. They found two distinct dimensions of policy—welfare/education policy and highway/natural resources policy.[40] These factors have the advantage of combining diverse policy decisions into dimensions directly relevant to this study. When these two factors are related to minority penetration, the relationships, although in the correct direction, are not statistically significant. On the other hand, minority stratification has a significant impact on welfare/education and an insignificant impact on highways/natural resources. For both aspects of racial representation the relationships with the factor scores indicate that bureaucracies with successful affirmative action programs exist in states that spend more for social services and less for hardware items.

A final policy area subject to minority pressures and thus likely to be influenced by the presence of minority administrators is income redistribution. Both Fry and Winters and Booms and Halldorson have developed indicators of the

Table 5-5
Policy Impact of Minority Employment, Controlling for Economic Level of
the State

Policy Area	Variance Explained by Economic Factors	Direction of Predicted Relation-ship	Minority Penetration		Minority Stratification	
			Percentage of Variance Added	Direction	Percentage of Variance Added	Direction
Education level	49	+	.4	+	2.9[a]	–
Highway level	56	–	.1	–	1.1	–
Welfare level	22	+	.6	–	1.7	+
Health level	13	–	1.4	+	7.3[a]	–
Police level	31	–	.4	+	.1	–
Highway percentage	62	–	.1	–	.9	–
Welfare percentage	16	+	.2	–	3.7[a]	+
Education percentage	6	+	5.3[a]	+	1.6	–
Health percentage	17	–	1.5	–	1.6	–
Welfare/ education factor	70	+	.3	+	2.3[a]	+
Highway/ resources factor	8	–	.3	–	1.8	–
Redistribution– Fry	15	+	0	+	1.6	+
Redistribution– Booms	50	+	.7	+	0	–

[a]Significant at the .05 level.

degree to which state policy redistributes income.[41] Although minority penetration and minority stratification are both positively related to income redistribution, in all four cases the results are not statistically significant.

The data demonstrate that the policy implications of affirmative action are
somewhat ambiguous.[42] For minority penetration, the relationship is in the
correct direction nine of thirteen times, but only one of the correct relationships

is significant. The minority stratification measure fares better. Ten of the thirteen relationships are in the correct direction, but only three are statistically significant. Although the evidence is slight, minority stratification appears to have greater relevance for public policy than does minority penetration.

This evidence is more consistent with the theory of agency socialization than representative bureaucracy. Although most impacts are in the correct direction, the relationships are small, indicating that the policy preferences of minorities are being tempered by the socialization process.

Before one concludes that agencies can resocialize the policy preferences of minority employees, three qualifications should be noted. First, the measure of public policy is so crude that we cannot expect large relationships. Just finding relationships in the correct direction may be all that can be hoped. Second, this analysis assumed that the interests of minority administrators will coincide with the interests of the minority population. The two groups may not hold the same preferences. For example, the minority administrator may perceive that the current welfare system is detrimental to members of his or her minority group and thus hold different attitudes concerning welfare spending than the remainder of the minority group. Another example would be opposition to educational expenditures where the distribution of educational funding discriminates against poor or minority districts. Third, high-level minority administrators might be in nonpolicy positions or have occupied their positions for too short a period to have an impact. Minority administrators are often placed in staff positions, particularly those that deal with affirmative action programs. In short, public policy variations as the result of affirmative action might be too complex to be tapped accurately by the available measures.

Conclusion

This study of the policy constraints and implications of affirmative action has revealed that two dimensions of racial representation—minority penetration and minority stratification—not only are theoretically distinct but also lead to different empirical results. The major constraints on penetration of state bureaucracies by minorities are the state's economic and administrative/labor pool characteristics. Political variables add explanation, but they are clearly minor compared to the other factors. The stratification of minorities within the bureaucracy, however, is most constrained by administrative/labor pool factors and political characteristics.

More important than the correlates of affirmative action success, this study investigated the policy implications of a minority representation. The penetration and stratification of public sector minority employment are positively related to state policies which benefit minority citizens. Despite this positive relationships, most of these correlations are not statistically or substantively significant. Usually minority employment explains less than 1 percent of the variance in public policy. These findings are consistent with the hypothesis that agencies resocialize their employees to be agency advocates no matter what their background.

Together these findings have implications for future policy making. Clearly bureaucratic systems can be designed so that the possibilities for successful affirmative action programs, at least in the long run, are maximized. Under the correct conditions, improving the salary schedules of state bureaucracies will attract more minority personnel. Further, long-term payoffs can be expected from programs designed to improve the education and income of minority groups since minority income levels were highly related to affirmative action success even with multiple controls.

Finally, the fact that minority representation does not lead to responsiveness in terms of different policy outputs does not mean we should reject our goals of affirmative action. The arguments for affirmative action based on equity or maximum use of human resources were always stronger arguments. Representative bureaucracies remain an admirable goal. But neither should we be surprised that making the bureaucracy more racially representative will have little impact on the policies it administers.

Notes

1. Richard E. Dawson and James A. Robinson, "Interparty Competition, Economic Variables, and Welfare Policies in the American States," *Journal of Politics* 25 (May 1963): 298–311.

2. Thomas R. Dye, *Politics, Economics and the Public* (Chicago: Rand McNally, 1966).

3. Robert L. Lineberry and Edmund P. Fowler, "Reformism and Public Policies in American Cities," *American Political Science Review* 61 (September 1967): 701–716.

4. Ira Sharkansky and Richard I. Hofferbert, "Dimensions of State Politics, Economics, and Public Policy," *American Political Science Review* 63 (September 1969): 867–879.

5. Brian R. Fry and Richard F. Winters, "The Politics of Redistribution," *American Political Science Review* 64 (June 1970): 508–522; Bernard H. Booms and James R. Halldorson, "The Politics of Redistribution," *American Political Science Review* 67 (September 1973): 924–933; John L. Sullivan, "A Note on Redistributive Analysis," *American Political Science Review* 66 (December 1972): 1301–1305.

6. Jack L. Walker, "The Diffusion of Innovation among the American States," *American Political Science Review* 63 (September 1969): 880–899.

7. The variable of central concern in this chapter is racial representation or

minority employment, not affirmative action. The operationalizations introduced later are two different indicators of representation; affirmative action is a process, and no indicators of the process are used in the analysis. Occasionally the terms *success in affirmative action* and *racial representation* are used interchangeably although they will always mean racial representation. Since an equitable degree of racial representation can result from a successful affirmative action program, both terms will be retained. This chapter deals with the influences affecting minority representation in state bureaucracies and the impact that representation has on other policies. Clearly these issues are also central to the broad issue of affirmative action.

8. Richard I. Hofferbert, *The Study of Public Policy* (New York: Bobbs-Merrill, 1974).

9. Dye, *Politics, Economics and the Public;* Hofferbert, *The Study of Public Policy.*

10. David H. Rosenbloom, "The Civil Service Commission's Decision to Authorize the Use of Goals and Time Tables in the Federal Equal Employment Opportunity Program," *Western Political Quarterly* 26 (June 1973): 236–251.

11. Alaska and Hawaii were deleted from this analysis. Hawaii was deleted because the majority of the state is nonwhite, thus making affirmative action a process which differs greatly from that in the mainland states. Alaska was deleted because large federal expenditures distort the policy levels of the state. The extreme values for variables in these states would distort the analysis by inflating the size of the correlation coefficients.

12. For purposes of this study minority groups include blacks, Spanish Americans, Native Americans, and Orientals. The definition is taken directly from the U.S. Civil Service Commission. The terms *minority penetration* and *minority stratification* were taken directly from Lee Sigelman, "State and Local Employment of Spanish Americans in the Southwest," *Public Service* 2, no. 1 (November 1974): 1–5.

13. The EEOC survey lists employment by salary level. The Gini coefficients were calculated by entering the lower salary levels first under the assumption that discrimination is more likely to be present at the top of the organization. To facilitate comparison, the Gini index values were reversed in the regression equations so that high numbers were equivalent to successful affirmative action.

14. Dawson and Robinson, "Interparty Competition"; Dye, *Politics, Economics and the Public.*

15. Dye, *Politics, Economics and the Public.*

16. The political variables come from the following sources: party cohesion, Austin Ranney, "Parties in State Politics," in Herbert Jones and Kenneth N. Vines, *Politics in the American States* (Boston: Little, Brown, 1965), pp. 61–100; party competition, Hofferbert, *The Study of Public Policy;* interest group strength, Harmon Zeigler, "Interest Groups in the States," in Jacob and Vines, *Politics in the American States,* pp. 101–150; gubernatorial power, Joseph A.

Schlesinger, "The Politics of the Executive," in Jacob and Vines, *Politics in the American States,* pp. 207-238; responsiveness measures, Richard L. Sutton, "The States and the People," *Polity* 3 (Summer 1972): 451-476; and Anne H. Hopkins, "Opinion Publics and Support for Public Policy in the American States," *American Journal of Political Science* 18 (February 1974): 167-177.

17. V.O. Key, *Southern Politics* (New York: Random House, 1949).

18. Merit systems generally use criteria of education and experience as indicators of merit at the administrative level. Since these criteria are racially maldistributed, a strong merit system would underrepresent minorities.

19. Some of the administrative factors such as size of the minority population could also be used as political factors as well as labor pool factors.

20. In this and the following two sections affirmative action success will be related to exogenous environmental variables by simple correlations. Since many other variables condition the relationship between affirmative action and the environmental variables and since more complex relationships will be examined later, these findings should be considered only illustrative.

21. Minorities probably fare better in such states because the states contain few minorities. Without a critical mass of minorities, discrimination in employment has no economic justification.

22. Bernard Rosen, "Affirmative Action Produces Equal Employment Opportunity for All," *Public Administration Review* 34 (May/June 1974): 237-240.

23. The four best predictors were selected on the basis of the magnitude of the standardized regression coefficients (path coefficients) when all the variables from a single cluster (for example, the cluster of administrative/labor pool variables) were used to predict affirmative action.

24. Sullivan, "A Note on Redistributive Analysis."

25. John L. Sullivan, "Multiple Indicators and Complex Causal Models," in H.M. Blalock, Jr., *Causal Models in the Social Sciences* (Chicago: Aldine, 1971).

26. For a discussion of this technique see David R. Morgan and Michael R. Fitzgerald, "When Push Comes to Shove: Desegregating American Schools since 1968," Paper presented at the 1978 annual meeting of the Midwest Political Science Association, Chicago, April 20-22.

27. Small bureaucracies might also be more successful because they can recruit a small number of minorities and register a larger percentage gain than can a larger state bureaucracy with the same size input.

28. J. Donald Kingsley, *Representative Bureaucracy* (Yellow Springs, Ohio: Antioch Press, 1944); David M. Levitan, "The Responsibility of Administrative Officials in a Democratic Society," *Political Science Quarterly* 61 (1946): 562-598; Norton E. Long, "Bureaucracy and Constitutionalism," *American Political Science Review* 46 (December 1952): 808-818; Paul P. Van Riper, *History of the United States Civil Service* (New York: Harper & Row, 1958); Samuel

Krislov, *Representative Bureaucracy* (Englewood Cliffs, N.J.: Prentice-Hall, 1974).

29. For a comprehensive critique of the theory see Kenneth J. Meier and Lloyd G. Nigro, "Representative Bureaucracy and Policy Preferences: A Study in the Attitudes of Federal Executives," *Public Administration Review* 36 (July/August 1976): 458-470. They contend that little is known about the relationship between social origins and socialization experiences, that upward mobility and agency socialization must be considered, that attitudes are better indicators of representativeness than social origins, and that individual bureaus rather than the entire bureaucracy must be examined.

30. Catherine Lovell, "Three Key Issues in Affirmative Action," *Public Administration Review* 34 (May/June 1974): 235-237.

31. Herbert Simon, *Administrative Behavior* (New York: Free Press, 1976).

32. Morris Janowitz, *The Professional Soldier* (New York: Free Press, 1960); Herbert Kaufman, *The Forest Ranger* (Baltimore, Md.: Johns Hopkins Press, 1960); Sidney Baldwin, *Politics and Poverty* (Chapel Hill: University of North Carolina Press, 1968).

33. Simon, *Administrative Behavior.*

34. Meier and Nigro, "Representative Bureaucracy and Policy Preferences."

35. The perceptive reader will note that this chapter does not test the agency socialization hypothesis. It only derives the prediction that racial representativeness will have no impact on policy as representative bureaucracy predicts.

36. Aaron Wildavsky, *The Politics of the Budgetary Process* (Boston: Little, Brown, 1974).

37. Although the population rather than a sample is used in this analysis, measures of significance were used to determine impact. This procedure, although not meaningful in a statistical sense, will focus attention on *nontrivial* relationships. That is, statistical significance is used as a test to find substantively significant results. Since administrative inputs into the policy process are the last in a "funnel of causality" and administrative impacts are only one of many elite influences, we should not expect large impacts.

38. The analysis uses state and local per capita expenditures. Using only state expenditures would distort the analysis since states vary in the degree to which they use local governments as instruments to implement policy.

39. The relationship for health expenditures must be clarified. Since health care is primarily a middle-class issue, the analysis assumed that minority populations would perceive that the benefits of health care go primarily to others.

40. Sharkansky and Hofferbert, "Dimensions of State Politics."

41. Fry and Winters, "The Politics of Redistribution"; Booms and Halldorson, "The Politics of Redistribution."

42. The author also investigated the policy impact of affirmative action for

women. Since women do not consistently share political attitudes to the degree
that minorities do, the results were not included in this study since no direction
of policy impact could be hypothesized. The results reveal that only for educational expenditures did the distribution of women in the bureaucracy have an
impact. In that instance the states with successful affirmative action programs
spent less money on education.

6

Discrimination and the Law: The Equal Credit Opportunity Act

M. Margaret Conway

A continuing attack on unfair credit practices is underway in the United States. The first blow in this legislative campaign was struck in 1968 with the passage of the Truth in Lending Act, and several additional laws have continued the campaign. This chapter focuses on the Equal Credit Opportunity Act of 1974 and the 1976 amendments to the act. The Equal Credit Opportunity Act (ECOA) prohibited discrimination on the basis of the sex or marital status of a credit applicant in evaluating the applicant's creditworthiness. Amendments enacted in 1976, which became effective in March 1977, extended the act's coverage to prohibit discrimination against any applicant on the basis of race, color, religion, national origin, age,[1] or because all or part of the applicant's income is derived from a public assistance program.[2] Amendments passed in 1976 also increased enforcement mechanisms available under the act.

Several questions are considered in this chapter. What were the patterns of discrimination which led to the perceived need for the law? Is the coverage provided by the law adequate? What are the remedies provided by the law and the regulations issued under it, and what are the administrative arrangements for enforcement of the law and regulations? Are these effective in obtaining goals sought through the passage of the act and its amendments?

The Problem and the Initial Solution

The attack on discrimination in credit practices had several origins. The National Commission on Consumer Credit detailed in its 1972 report several types of discrimination against women by credit-granting institutions and businesses. These include:

1. More frequent denial of mortgage loans to single women than to single men
2. Denial of credit to a married woman in her own name
3. Requiring a woman who has married to reapply for credit after marriage, usually in her husband's name

---

The research assistance of Nancy A. Campbell in collecting materials for the preparation of this chapter is appreciated and acknowledged.

4. Unwillingness to count at full value a wife's income when a married couple
    applies for credit
5. Denial of credit to a widowed or divorced woman, who frequently had not
    established a credit history of her own[3]

The Congressional Joint Economic Committee, in hearings held in 1973,
collected evidence of discrimination against both women and the elderly in the
granting of credit. Testimony before the committee established that credit was
terminated for many older citizens upon retirement because they had become
"unemployed." Elderly citizens who applied after retirment often were denied
credit simply because they were not working, regardless of whether their income
was adequate to repay any debt incurred.[4]

Several bills introduced in the House and Senate during the 93d Congress
sought to remove these discriminatory patterns. The Consumer Affairs Subcommittee of the House Committee on Banking, Currency, and Housing held
extensive hearings on a comprehensive anti-credit discrimination bill. However,
a nongermane Senate rider added the Equal Credit Opportunity Act of 1974 to a
House bill dealing with Truth in Lending Act amendments which had originated
in another House subcommittee.[5] The House conferees accepted this amendment which focused on credit discrimination only on the basis of sex and marital
status, ignoring discrimination on the basis of age, race, national origin, and
other now prohibited grounds, in order to enact legislation prior to adjournment
of the 93d Congress. The Federal Reserve Board was delegated responsibility
for drafting regulations to carry out the provisions of the act, with enforcement
powers distributed among a dozen different federal agencies charged with
regulatory responsibility for various types of credit-granting businesses and
institutions.

If a credit applicant believes discrimination has occurred in the decision
made on his or her application, the applicant can, or course, complain to the
creditor and request consideration. Under the 1974 Equal Credit Opportunity
Act, several other courses of action became available. One is the filing of a suit
by the applicant against the creditor. The applicant, if the suit is won, can receive actual damages plus up to $10,000 in punitive damages, as well as court
costs and a reasonable attorney's fee.[6] Yet another alternative, where a pattern
of discrimination exists, is to join others in filing a class action suit. The 1974
act limited damages in a class action suit to $100,000 or 1 percent of the credi-
tor's net worth, whichever is less. Any person believing discrimination on a prohibited basis has occurred in the denial of a credit application may also file a
complaint with the appropriate federal government enforcement agency, which
may then use the complaint record as a basis for its enforcement investigations.

The ECOA accomplished several important objectives in the drive toward
ending credit discrimination. Neither sex nor marital status may be used in
evaluating creditworthiness. A spouse's income may not be discounted in evalu-

ating creditworthiness. Alimony, child support, and separate maintenance payments are considered in evaluating creditworthiness only if the applicant wants such payments considered. However, a number of problems remain unsolved, and controversy surrounded the regulations drafted by the Federal Reserve Board to carry out the ECOA.

Deficiencies in the Original Law and Regulations

The hasty enactment of the ECOA may have contributed to the deficiencies of the law as perceived by consumer advocates. These deficiencies included the coverage of the law, remedies available and the procedures for obtaining them, administrative enforcement procedures, and the act's compatibility with state laws.[7] Failure to include the elderly as a protected class particularly created discontent with the ECOA.[8] Less obvious but equally significant shortcomings included the failure to preempt certain types of state laws limiting married women's ability to contract, the absence of any coordinating body to ensure uniform enforcement of the act by the dozen federal agencies having administrative responsibilities, the failure to authorize the U.S. Attorney General to investigate or bring suit in credit discrimination cases, and the too short (one-year) statute of limitations for filing of civil suits for actual and punitive damages by credit discrimination victims.

The drafting of regulations by the Federal Reserve Board involved intensive lobbying by both credit-granting and consumer groups. The initial draft regulations (Regulation B), issued in April 1975, contained a number of provisions which were strongly proconsumer. A revised draft of Regulation B, issued in September 1975, contained a number of modifications favored by creditors. The final draft, issued in October 1975, represented from the perspective of consumer interests only a limited improvement over the September draft.

Regulation B, as finally issued by the Federal Reserve Board, threatened to seriously impair the effectiveness of the ECOA.[9] In order to ensure that credit applicants obtain fair treatment, those denied credit or an extension of credit need to be apprised of the reasons for the credit termination or denial. The original draft of Regulation B required that a clear and meaningful statement be provided for the applicant when credit is denied or terminated. The final draft required only that a suitable statement be made available if the credit applicant requested it; furthermore, the statement did not have to be in writing. In addition, the regulations provided no specific time period for notifying the applicant of the action on the credit application. Regulation B merely required that the applicant be informed within a "reasonable time."

Consumer interest advocates and several members of Congress criticized these provisions as permitting discriminatory practices to persist, since an applicant might obtain neither a timely response nor a clear understanding of the reasons for an adverse action on the credit application. Furthermore, the absence of a written statement of reasons for the adverse action could inhibit filing of a suit against the creditor or pursuing administrative remedies.

Several other problems became apparent. Did credit discrimination victims have the right to recover damages under both state and federal laws, where state credit discrimination laws were in effect? Did use of a state administrative agency foreclose an applicant from using a federal administrative agency to seek a remedy? How could class action suits be encouraged without bankrupting small business or limiting the general availability of credit?

In summary, several aspects both of the Equal Credit Opportunity Act of 1974 and of the regulations drafted by the Federal Reserve Board to carry out the law dissatisfied consumer representatives and many members of Congress. As a consequence, both House and Senate banking committees considered legislation in the 94th Congress to extend the coverage of the law and to improve its enforcement mechanisms.

The Second Round of Attacks on Credit Discrimination

In hearings held on extension of the act's coverage, Jeffery M. Bucher, a member of the Board of Governors of the Federal Reserve Board (FRB), argued that coverage should not be extended until sufficient time for experience with actual effects and administrative enforcement of the law had elapsed. Furthermore, the FRB's representative argued for a two-year lead time between passage of any amendments and their effective date in order to permit adequate time for drafting revised regulations and securing comments on them from various interests.[10] Congress was not persuaded by these arguments and substantially amended the ECOA, with the amendments becoming effective March 23, 1977, one year after final passage.

The amendments enacted in 1976 extend the coverage of the ECOA to prohibit discrimination against a credit applicant on the basis of race, color, national origin, age (provided that the applicant has the capacity to contract), the applicant's receipt of all or part of his or her income from public assistance, or the applicant's exercise of rights under the Consumer Credit Protection Act.

Prohibitions against discrimination on the basis of age or receipt of public assistance income have generated considerable controversey. Under the law, inquiry about an applicant's age or whether his or her income derives from public assistance does not constitute a discriminatory act if the inquiry seeks to ascertain the amount and probable continuance of the applicant's income level, credit history, or other information considered pertinent under Regulation B. However, age may be used in a credit scoring system only as long as a negative value is not assigned to an elderly applicant's age. In effect, younger applicants may be given a lower score than older applicants; this would not, under the provisions of the law, constitute discrimination. (Studies by various creditors indicate that credit risk decreases with increasing age.) The prohibition against discrimination against public assistance recipients protects several different types of applicants from arbitrary denial of access to credit. These include families receiving aid to dependent children, social security recipients, veterans receiving disability payments, and credit applicants receiving state or federal assistance available to the handicapped.

Dissatisfaction with the enforcement procedures provided in the 1974 act resulted, after considerable debate, in stronger enforcement mechanisms being provided by the 1976 amendments. One is the authorization of the filing of civil suits by the Attorney General. These suits may originate from investigations instigated by the Attorney General or as a result of referrals from an agency charged with enforcing the ECOA's provisions. Furthermore, the statute of limitations for the filing of a suit is extended from one to two years. The Senate Banking, Currency, and Urban Affairs Committee report argues that a credit applicant who requests a government agency to investigate an alleged act of discrimination might not receive a response to the complaint within the one-year period established in the 1974 act. In addition, publicity surrounding the report from a government investigation might cause some individuals denied credit on prohibited grounds to become aware of their rights under the law; an extension of the time limits for filing suits facilitates their recovery of damages for the discriminatory act of a creditor.

The problem of encouraging class action suits, while at the same time protecting small businessmen from financial disaster, led to several alternative proposals for changing the maximum damages obtainable in class action suits. The 1974 act provided for a maximum of $100,000 or 1 percent of net worth, whichever is less. Since an individual could recover a maximum of $10,000 in damages from an individual suit, the limit of $100,000 tended to discourage the filing of class action suits. The Senate committee recommended the alternative of a maximum of $500,000 or 1 percent of net worth, whichever is less. Some consumer advocates and members of Congress urged maximum damages of $50,000 or 1 percent of net worth, whichever is larger. They argued that this would be a very strong deterrant for larger businesses, for whom 1 percent of net worth constitutes a very considerable figure. As finally enacted, the maximum damages awardable in a class action suit are $500,000 or 1 percent of net worth, whichever is less.

The 1976 amendments to the act also attacked the problems of the timely notification of credit applicants and the provision of reasons for an adverse action. Creditors must now notify applicants within thirty days of the action taken on their application for credit.[11] Furthermore, a creditor must provide a written statement of the reasons for an adverse action on an application. The creditor can include a written statement, which can be in the form of a checklist, in the letter informing the applicant of the adverse action, or the creditor may indicate in the letter informing the applicant of the adverse action that a written statement of the reasons for the action will be provided to the applicant upon request.

Various creditor groups argued vigorously against this requirement of notification of reasons for adverse action during both the legislative process and the initial drafting of Regulation B after enactment of the ECOA in 1974. The cost of notifying applicants of an adverse action was one principal ground for the opposition. Sears, Roebuck and Company estimated that each notification would cost a minimum of $5. However, the company assumed that an individually composed and typed letter would be used, rather than a form letter.[12] In its revisions of Regulation B to incorporate the 1976 amendments, the Federal Reserve Board provided a set of sample forms, including a checklist of reasons for denial, which might be used by creditors to inform applicants of the basis for the adverse action. Creditors also criticized the provision of adverse-action reasons on the grounds that such information might offend applicants and therefore result in loss of future business from the offended potential customers. Supporters of the requirement that creditors provide reasons for any adverse action argue that it is helpful to applicants denied credit, perhaps leading either to correction of faulty records which may inappropriately result in the credit denial or termination or to actions on the applicants' part which would enable the applicant to secure credit in the future. To facilitate the protection of consumer credit applicants' rights, the Federal Reserve Board in the revised Regulation B also increased the time from fifteen to twenty-five months after the date that a creditor has notified an applicant of the action taken that the creditor must retain the application in its original form, or a record of it.

Another set of problems receiving congressional attention was the confusion over the relationship of the ECOA to state laws on credit discrimination, the rights of credit applicants to use both federal and state antidiscrimination enforcement procedures, and the rights of credit discrimination victims to relief under both state and federal law.

The ECOA requires that state laws concerning credit discrimination be compatible with federal law. A credit applicant discriminated against on prohibited grounds can recover damages under federal or state law, but not both. However, a credit discrimination victim can pursue administrative remedies under both state and federal law. Furthermore, requesting administrative relief through a state agency does not prohibit seeking monetary damages under federal law.

Other Significant Provisions of the ECOA

Several other aspects of the ECOA are of particular significance to women. Among them is the requirement that women be able to establish a personal credit history through accounts listed by creditors in the spouse's name. Prior to the passage of the ECOA, credit accounts used by a married woman were usually in the husband's name, even if the wife was the principal wage earner in the family. After a divorce or the death of the husband, the woman was in the unfortunate situation of having no credit history of her own. Under the provisions of the ECOA, all credit account holders or applicants for new accounts must be notified, using a form specified in Regulation B, that an account may be listed in the name of both husband and wife, and credit account holders or applicants may request dual listing by signing the form which under Regulation B must be sent to them.

Since the enactment of the ECOA, a woman has the right to obtain credit in her own name, based on her own creditworthiness, without a cosigner, if a cosigner would not be required for a man applying for a similar type of credit. In this circumstance, the creditor may not ask any questions about the spouse. However, information about the spouse may be obtained if the spouse will use the account or will be contractually liable for the account or if the spouse's income will be relied on to repay any credit obtained. Information about the spouse also may be legally requested by a creditor in a community-property state or if alimony, child support, or separate maintenance payments from a spouse or former spouse will be relied on for repayment.

Other patterns of discrimination are also attacked by the ECOA and Regulation B of the Federal Reserve Board. Regulation B establishes a number of procedural requirements to be followed in the consideration of credit applications. Either a written or an oral statement which would discourage on a prohibited basis a reasonable person from making or pursuing a credit application is forbidden, although information about characteristics on which creditors may not discriminate may be requested under certain circumstances, as, for example, the regulations permitting inquiries about marital status in community-property states.

Other prohibitions are absolute. For example, creditors are forbidden to inquire about birth control practices or intentions concerning the bearing or rearing of children. However, a creditor may ask about the number and ages of dependent children, since the creditor might consider such information relevant to the existing financial obligations of a credit applicant and the applicant's ability to repay a loan.

Any credit rating system used by a creditor must be demonstrably and statistically sound and empirically derived. This is defined by Regulation B to be a system based on appropriate sampling of the creditor's applicant files, aimed at predicting creditworthiness with respect to minimizing bad debt and operating expenses "in accordance with the creditor's business judgement,"[13] which is validated by distinguishing between creditworthy and noncreditworthy applicants at a statistically significant rate. A system developed by another lender may be used provided it has been empirically validated. A system formulated prior to accumulation of sufficient cases for empirical validation must be validated as soon as sufficient lending experience is accumulated to permit validation.

Reports to accompany credit discrimination legislation issued by the House and the Senate banking committees make quite clear that the committess believe the the effects test developed in employment discrimination cases should be extended to use in credit discrimination cases. The Senate report states that enforcement agencies are free to look at the effects of creditors' practices as well as their motives and intentions.[14]

The effects test, formulated in *Griggs* v. *Duke Power Company*,[15] employs a three-step process. In credit discrimination cases, the following steps would be involved:

1. A plaintiff established a prima facie case which shows that a credit practice has a discriminatory effect on a protected class.
2. The defendant replies by showing that the practice has a "manifest relationship" to the credit decision process.
3. The plaintiff must show that there is an alternative practice which would have less discriminatory effect on the protected class and serve the creditor's legitimate needs equally well.

The use of the effects test makes possible an attack on credit practices which appear neutral but which are discriminatory in their effects. An individual or group must demonstrate membership in the protected group and injury from the practice, but a direct, causal relationship need not be established. Thus if women or the elderly or members of minority groups are more likely to be adversely affected by a credit practice, the effects test may be used.

Unsolved Problems of Credit Discrimination

While the ECOA represents substantial progress toward equal opportunity in access to credit, the goal of equal credit opportunity is not yet attained. Some critics have suggested that the exemption from some provisions of the ECOA granted for business, securities, and public utilities credit by Regulation B is counter to the aims of the legislation. In the 1976 Senate committee report accompanying proposed amendments to the ECOA, the committee states that Regulation B legitimately recognized that significant difference may exist between consumer and business credit. The bill therefore authorized the FRB to exempt certain types of business credit transactions where the act's provisions are considered "unnecessary."

For low-income women, denial of hospital care and denial or termination of utilities services have been a particular problem which in many cases can be attributed to the poor credit history of the spouse or ex-spouse. The ECOA requires that only the creditworthiness of the applicant for credit be considered; hence, a poor credit history of a spouse should not result in denial of credit to a low-income credit applicant. However, the failure of the ECOA to apply its preemption of state law provisions to public utilities may result in the utilities denying credit to women separated from their husbands.[16]

Another problem limiting the effectiveness of the ECOA may be the failure to preempt state "necessities" and "family expense" laws. State laws frequently provide that purchases made by one spouse to meet the needs of other members of the family are the legal responsibility of the other spouse. Family expense is similar in its assignment of provision for the needs of family members to either spouse, with both being responsible for the ensuing obligations. These laws may result in low-income women having a credit history which includes reponsibility for a husband's or ex-husband's bad debts. The ECOA does not preempt these state laws.[17]

An additional loophole in the effectiveness of the ECOA arises from its failure to preempt state laws of coverture. The common-law disability of coverture limits the legal right of married women to contract; creditors would logically not extend credit to one who lacks the capacity to contract and hence would not be legally bound to repay the debt.[18]

Further complications to the effectiveness of the ECOA are presented by property laws in community-property states. As has been pointed out, inquiries about the spouse's creditworthiness are permitted for lenders in community-property states. Both the ECOA and Regulation B exempt from their provisions a creditor who makes distinction on the basis of sex or marital status because of state property laws which directly or indirectly affect creditworthiness, and these are particularly relevant in community-property states.[19]

Proposals for further revision of the ECOA have focused on the law's coverage, with several bills being introduced in the House of Representatives during the 95th Congress to prohibit discrimination against any credit applicant on the basis of the geographic location of the applicant's residence or the applicant's occupation.[20] The proposed prohibition regarding geographic location of the residence is aimed at the practice of denying credit to anyone residing within a particular postal Zip code area or neighborhood, a practice which could be used to evade the law forbidding consideration of race, national origin, ethnicity, or religion in the evaluation of creditworthiness. Occupational discrimination might also be used in some cases as an evasion of the law prohibiting credit discrimination on other grounds.

While the goal of equal credit opportunity based solely on the creditworthiness of the applicant has not yet been fully attained, the Equal Credit Opportunity Act of 1974 and its 1976 amendments represent substantial progress toward that goal.

Several types of problems remain. One is the failure of the ECOA to preempt certain types of state laws which limit the access of women to credit. Another is the potential for evasion of the ECOA through discrimination against classes of borrowers, based on place of residence or occupation, who are not protected by the ECOA. The assignment of enforcement responsibility to a dozen federal agencies, without any formal coordinating mechanism, and the usual pattern of stronger representation of creditor than borrower interests on the regulatory boards or among high-level political appointees of the enforcement agencies create the potential for less than vigorous enforcement of the ECOA's provisions through administrative procedures. Careful, continued monitoring of the effectiveness of the ECOA by both Congress and consumer interests can contribute substantially to ensuring effectiveness in achieving the goals sought under this significant addition to this nation's equal rights policy.

Notes

1. Provided that the applicant has the legal capacity to contract. For the law as amended, see U.S.C. 15: 1691-1961e. For the Federal Reserve Board regulation implementing the law as amended, see Board of Governors of the Federal Reserve System, Regulation B (12 C.F.R. 202), effective March 23, 1977.

2. Applicants also may not be rejected because of their good-faith exercise of any right under the Consumer Protection Act.

3. U.S. National Commission on Consumer Finance, *Consumer Credit in the United States* (Washington: Government Printing Office, 1972), pp. 152–153.

4. *Hearings on the Economic Problems of Women before the Joint Economic Committee*, 93d Congress, 1st Sess., 1973.

5. Provisions of S. 2101 were added to H.R. 11221 by Sen. William Brock on June 13, 1974. After some revisions, the Senate amendments were accepted by House conferees, and the conference report was adopted by the House and Senate in October 1974.

6. Establishing the monetary value of the actual damages from credit discrimination may be difficult.

7. See, for example, Laurie D. Zelon, "Equal Credit: Promise or Reality," *Harvard Civil Rights–Civil Liberties Law Review* 11 (1976): 186-216. For a discussion of the political struggles involved in passage of the 1974 act and in drafting the regulations to carry it out, see Joyce Gelb and Marian Lief Palley, "Women and Interest Group Politics," *American Politics Quarterly* 5 (July 1977): 331-352.

8. See the comments of Rep. Frank Annunzio, Rep. Chalmers P. Wylie, and Rep. Leonore K. Sullivan, in *Hearings before the Subcommittee on Con-*

sumer Affairs of the House Committee on Banking, Currency, and Housing on H.R. 3386, 94th Cong., 1st Sess., 1975, pp. 9-16.

9. U.S. Board of Governors of the Federal Reserve System, "Regulation B," *Federal Reserve Bulletin* 61 (November 1975): 762-769.

10. *Hearings on H.R. 3386,* 94th Cong., 1st Sess., pp. 22-26.

11. A reasonably longer time may be specified by the Federal Reserve Board for some types of credit transactions.

12. *Hearings before the Committee on Banking, Housing, and Urban Affairs on the Equal Credit Opportunity Act Amendments and Consumer Leasing Act, 1975,* 94th Cong., 1st Sess., 1975, p. 402.

13. Regulation B, Sec. 202, 2ii.

14. Senate Report 589, 94th Cong., 2d Sess., p. 4; House Report 210, 94th Cong., 1st Sess., p. 5.

15. 401 U.S. 424, 1971.

16. Brook Baker and Elliot Taubman, "The Equal Credit Opportunity Act: The Effect of the Regulations on the Poor," *Clearinghouse Review* 9 (December 1975): 543-546.

17. Ibid.

18. For discussions of the problems which this engenders, see "The Impact of Michigan's Common-Law Disabilities of Coverture on Married Women's Access to Credit," *Michigan Law Review* 74 (November 1975): 76-105.

19. For discussions of the impact of the ECOA in community-property states, see Linda S. Hume, "A Suggested Analysis for Regulation of Equal Credit Opportunity," *Washington Law Review* 52 (1977): 335-367; John W. Cairns, "Equal Credit Opportunity Comes to Women: An Analysis of the Equal Credit Opportunity Act," *San Diego Law Review* 13 (1976): 960-977; Anne K. Bingaman, "Equal Management of Community Property and Equal Credit Opportunity," *Idaho Law Review* 13 (1977): 161-175; Judy Gray, "Credit for Women in California," *UCLA Law Review* 22 (1975): 873-902.

20. See, for example, H.R. 8451, 95th Cong., 1st Sess., 1977. Five other bills containing one or both extensions of coverage were also introduced.

7

Minorities and Policy Problems: An Overview as Seen by the U.S. Commission On Civil Rights

Maurice C. Woodard and
Edward R. Jackson

For the past twenty-one years, the U.S. Commission on Civil Rights (hereafter referred to as the Commission in many places) has methodically and systematically produced an absolutely astounding weatlh of data documenting a variety of forms of racial, ethnic, sex, religious, and age discrimination. The Commission, often unknown and equally often misunderstood, has sometimes noisily but more frequently quietly gone about its task of investigating, documenting, and reporting denials of equal protection under the laws. One of the more interesting but generally unknown results of the Commission's efforts is what might be called the Commission's "national civil rights agenda." The many problems identified by the Commission over the years (most of which remain unsolved) are, in fact, the major policy concerns of those who desire a society void of discrimination. The Commission has, intentionally or not, produced a national civil rights agenda.

Obviously, Congress did not intend the Commission to perform this task. The creation of the Commission resulted more from the quilt of the nation than from some preconceived notion about devising an affirmative plan of action to dismantle vestiges of discrimination. As one of the early works of the Commission noted, it was only a "manifestation of the belated response of a conscience-stricken people to the imperative need somehow to make good the promises of democracy in support of equal protection of the laws regardless of race, color, religion, or national origin."[1]

Originally established in 1957 by the Civil Rights Act of the same year as a "temporary, independent, bipartisan, Federal agency," the Commission's task was to "collect, study, and apprise information relating to civil rights throughout the country and to make appropriate recommendations to the President and Congress for corrective action."[2] Over the years, as the Commission became more and more independent, its activities became more and more adventuresome. As one speaker noted, the Commission has gone beyond merely reporting to the President and Congress; it has "prodded the Congress, nagged the President and aided the Courts."[3] It has, in addition, marked off a national civil rights agenda.

Elements of a National Agenda

In its twenty-one years of operation the Civil Rights Commission has developed a degree of political independence which has permitted it to take bold positions on major civil rights issues. This independence has resulted in part from the nature of the Commission's organizational structure and in part from the skills of the commissioners and the staff director. Commenting on the independence of the Commission, one writer noted:

> . . . by maintaining an independence and integrity the Commission has demonstrated a consequent willingness to approach civil rights problems honestly—even if its vision is limited and fallible. This is in itself of important political value. It ensures that among competing opinions, interests and pressures the existence of certain unpleasent facts will not be totally ignored. There is strength and stability in facts.[4]

Ignoring the traditional political dangers in taking firm stands on controversial civil rights issues, the Commission has outlined a rather extensive civil rights agenda. In this chapter attention is directed to five principal areas of the agenda: voting, housing, education, employment, and women's rights. In each case an effort is made to outline the major unresolved problems as seen by the Commission.

Voting Rights

One of the first problem areas which caught the attention of the Commission was the voting rights of minorities. This was only natural since for a long time the government has viewed the attainment of this right as a necessary prelude to the attainment of other rights.

In spite of all the attention that the right to vote has received from the government (including a host of laws such as the 15th Amendment; Civil Rights Acts of 1957, 1960, and 1964; and the Voting Rights Act of 1965), overt and covert voting discrimination remains a fact of life for many minorities. As the Commission and its fifty-one-state advisory committees noted:

> The right to vote and to participate in America's democratic political system are two of the basic tenets of our Constitution. Although the denial of these basic rights to minority citizens appears to be somewhat less blatant in 1977 than it was in the late 50's, threats of economic sanction, gerrymandering, and redistricting of minority communities prevent or hinder full compliance with the law.[5]

In a prior major report on voting rights issued in 1975, this same theme was expressed:

> For the minority citizen, the right to vote is still a precarious right. In conjunction with the persistence of discrimination, the persistence of vulnerability to economic and physical pressure shapes the minority citizen's response to the opportunity to participate. For many minority voters, entering a polling place is crossing into dangerous territory, where personal experience and the shared heritage of centuries tell them they do not belong.[6]

And in its last report on voting rights issued in 1978, the same theme emerges: "Despite the gains made by minorities and women in the political arena in 1977," said the Commission, "full participation remains an unattained goal."[7]

As in other areas examined in this chapter, the Commission has noted some of the major problem areas which must be solved. These problem areas must be addressed by the academic community as well as by government.

First, attention must be directed toward the uneven progress toward full enfranchisement of minorities in certain jurisdictions. Answers must be provided to the questions of why minority registration is so low in some locations and not others, and why minorities cannot get elected to "positions of real influence" in some jurisdictions where they do get elected to minor positions.

Attention must also be directed to the problems relating to the enforcement of major voting rights legislation. General questions pertaining to enforcement can be raised. Why has the Justice Department not developed an effective monitoring system to detect failures to submit proposed changes in voting laws, practices, and procedures as required by law?[8]

Why have federal examiners not been used extensively in recent years? In cases where examiners have been used, why has the Justice Department not ensured "that a substantial number of minorities serve as observers" and why has the public not been adequately informed of the presence and purpose of observers?[9]

The Commission urges that careful attention be paid to problems hampering voter registration. This would include such things as the failure of local jurisdictions to assist in an "affirmative, nonpartisan effort" to register individuals, more liberal registration laws, the establishment of more convenient registration places and a better system to inform the public of the time and place of registration, increased numbers of minorities serving as registrars or serving on the staffs of registrars, and elimination of the negative and discriminatory attitudes of many registration officials.

Many of the problems hampering voter registration also hamper voting in elections. Some of these include the location of voting places, the inadequacy of voting facilities, the failure to inform minorities of changes in voting places, the failure of election officials to provide assistance to illiterate persons and to American Indians and Hispanics who may have language difficulties, and the unequal treatment of minorities with regards to the use of absentee ballots. And, of course, there remains the age-old problems of the use of physical and economic threats to discourage registration and voting by minorities.

General problems directly relating to minorities running for office have been noted by the Commission, such as the requirements of excessive qualifying fees, lack of cooperation from local officials, the unequal treatment of poll watchers for minority candidates, the prevention of minority candidates from campaigning in white communities, the outright abolishing of public offices likely to be won by minority candidates, preventing winning minority candidates from taking office, and substituting appointment for election in filling certain offices.

Particular attention must be directed at the more grandiose skemes to dilute minority voting strength or to deny minorities their voting rights. This, of course, refers to the use of multimember districts (in place of single-member districts), racial gerrymandering, use of at-large elections, and the use of annexation, consolidation, and incorporation.

Needless to say, this is by no means a complete list of the problem areas relating to voting rights. It is but a partial agenda for research by the academic community and for action by the various layers of government.

Housing

Unlike the area of voting, equal opportunity in housing only recently began to receive any meaningful attention from the federal government. As a matter of fact, equal opportunity in housing was the last of the major civil rights public policy areas to receive substantial attention from the government.[10] To be sure, there has been a "federal presence in housing since the early 1930s," but that presence contributed to discrimination in housing as opposed to helping to destroy discrimination.[11] It was not until 1962 that the government began to make some efforts to abolish discrimination. In that year, President Kennedy issued an Executive Order prohibiting discrimination in housing with funds obtained via federally assisted programs. Title VI of the Civil Rights Act of 1964 addressed some aspects of housing discrimination. However, it was not until 1968 that the government made a conscious effort to come to grips with the ubiquity of this problem. In that year Congress enacted the Federal Fair Housing Law.

In 1973 the Commission noted that these laws had appreciably little impact on the various forms of housing discrimination. The Commission noted:

But these acts have not reversed the pattern of residential segregation. Between 1960 and 1970 residential segregation actually increased. Some minority group families are moving to the suburbs, but in far smaller numbers than white families. Many suburban black families merely exchange an inner-city ghetto for a suburban black enclave. That the housing laws have not had an impact in reversing the patterns of segregated housing underscores the complexity of the denial of equal housing opportunity to minority groups.[12]

More than two years later when the Commission issued its major report on equal opportunity in housing, the Commission found that very little had changed in the housing area. The Commission concluded in that report that "at this juncture in our Nation's history . . . , the Commission finds that the forces promoting discrimination in housing hold powerful, if less than universal, sway."[13] This view remains unchanged in 1978. In its State of Civil Rights Report—1977, the Commission pointed out:

Twenty-nine years ago Congress pledged a decent home and a suitable living environment as basic rights of every American family. In 1968 Congress declared that, as a matter of national policy, housing discrimination must end.

In 1977 these two promises remained unfulfilled for millions of minority and female-headed households. Rising housing costs, the markedly lower incomes and high levels of joblessness among minorities and female-headed households, and continuing discrimination in the housing marketplace stand as major obstacles to the achievement of equal housing opportunities in this Nation.[14]

The Commission has identified a number of specific areas which must be addressed in order to ensure equal opportunity in housing. These would include such practices as the outright refusal to rent or sell to minorities, "blockbusting," "racial steering," and "redlining." Although many of these and other such practices are already illegal, enforcement of the laws has been somewhat wanting. This, of course, leads directly into what the Commission believes to be one of the major obstacles to equal opportunity in housing—lack of federal enforcement. In its major report on the civil rights enforcement effort in 1974, the Commission noted that the enforcement actions taken by those federal agencies responsible for promoting equal housing opportunity "have generally been either superficial or incomplete and have had little impact on the country's serious housing discrimination problem."[15] That effort remained deficient in 1977.[16] Creative means must be devised to (1) uncover Fair Housing Law violations and (2) move effectively and efficiently to investigate and dispose of the substantial backlog of housing discrimination complaints.

Close attention must be given to the practice of "exclusionary zoning" by local jurisdictions which is effectively used to discriminate against minorities. Such zoning usually prohibits construction of higher-density, multifamily housing units, thus denying to many minorities the opportunity to purchase low- and moderate-priced housing.

The federal housing programs also require close scrutiny. Specifically, attention must be given to what the Commission calls the "shrinking" budget request for public housing, to the types of housing on which these public monies have been spent, and to the failure of the most recent of the housing programs—Section 235 homeownership housing program—to meet the housing needs of low-income U.S. families.[17]

The most recent additions to the body of federal laws relating to equal opportunity in housing are the Community Development Block Grant Program and the new Housing and Community Development Act of 1977. Considerable attention will have to be devoted to the success or failure of these programs in helping to ensure what Congress has called the right of every U.S. family to a decent home and a suitable living environment.

Education

Desegregation of public schools has been uneven since the landmark *Brown* v. *Board of Education* decision in 1954. The Commission, in a report entitled *Twenty Years after Brown: Equality of Educational Opportunity,* found that school desegregation was progressing well in the South. It had increased from less than 19 percent in 1968 to more than 46 percent in 1972.[18] Nevertheless, the preponderance of black youngsters still attended predominantly minority schools twenty years later. Minimal progress had occurred in the North during a similar period. The increase was less than 1 percent. In 1972 more than 71 percent of black pupils still attended predominantly minority schools. The Commission also noted with deep concern the continued displacement or demotion of black professionals in the desegregated school system and the high incidence of minority group expulsion. A 1976 Commission report documented the continued progression of desegregation in the nation. The comprehensive investigation revealed that desegregation in most communities had "gone peacefully and smoothly—for every Boston and Louisville there are dozens of other communities, which have received no headlines and attracted no television coverage, where desegregation is proceeding without major incident."[19]

The dearth of desegregation in metropolitan areas was brought to the attention of policymakers in a 1977 study.[20] Racial segregation was still the conventional pattern in the largest school system in the country because of the outmigration of whites and racially restrictive housing patterns. The report reads: "Children in metropolitan areas remain in racially isolated schools because of policies of racial containment to which government has contributed greatly."[21] The Commission recommends metropolitan school desegregation as a panacea to this recurring problem.

Bilingual-bicultural education for Mexican Americans and other linguistically and culturally different groups has been recommended by the Commission since 1971.[22] Progress to date has been negligible. It is felt that this program of instruction is the optimum method of improving learning for youngsters who experience language difficulty in schools. The Commission feels that learning will be made easier for pupils in a culturally diverse setting and facilitate the learning process for nonminority students.

Minority access to professional and graduate schools has been the focal point of increased controversy since 1977 as the Supreme Court considers *Regents of the University of California* v. *Bakke.* In this case, a white filed suit against the University of California medical school at Davis on the grounds that he was denied entry even though he had higher test scores than some minorities who were accepted. The University had set aside 16 out of 100 first-year slots for educationally and economically disadvantaged persons. Bakke contends that this special admission plan violated his 14th Amendment right to equal protection opportunity. The Commission strongly supports the affirmative action of the medical school and related race-conscious college admission programs that will compensate for the past exclusionary policies and increase the quantity of minority professionals.[23]

Employment

Political authorities have attempted to dismantle overt racial and sexual employment discrimination in a series of past legislative, judicial, and executive policies at the national level. The lack of enforcement of the foregoing policies, however, has received an inordinate amount of detailed investigation by the Commission. Many reports have shown that the designated federal departments and agencies have not effectively enforced policies of equal employment opportunity. The federal civil rights enforcement effort was found to be inadequate, devoid of leadership, and suffering from duplication, fragmentation, and inconsistent policies generally.

Data were marshaled by the Commission as early as 1969 to show that administrative units with civil rights responsibilities were not effectively implementing civil rights policies in general and equal employment in particular.[24] The nonenforcement of equal employment policies was the central motif in a 1974 study analyzing the equal employment opportunity activities of the Equal Employment Opportunity Commission, the Civil Service Commission, the Department of Labor, and the Equal Employment Coordinating Council.[25]

Calling the federal efforts to thwart discrimination "fundamentally inadequate," the Commission on Civil Rights identified a series of enforcement problems. First, most of the administrative units had inadequate personnel and resources to ferret out employment bigotry. Some agencies had so few resources that they could not scrutinize all their contractors even once in a period of twenty years. Second, federal employees were not offered the same personnel protection by the Civil Service Commission as those in the private sector under the aegis of the Equal Employment Opportunity Commission. The Civil Service Commission both formulated personnel policies for federal employees and evaluated their efficacy. Finally, the departments and agencies did not work in unison and often disagreed on matters of substantive and procedural policies. They disagreed on virtually all relevant personnel policies, such as the definition of employment discrimination, fringe benefits, testing and test validity, and the use of goals and timetables as a remedy. The Equal Employment Coordinating Council, created to promote consistency, has completely failed to achieve unity of corrective action. The Coordinating Council itself could agree on only a symbolic meaning of affirmative action.

Attempts to rectify many of the policy problems were documented by the Civil Rights Commission in a 1977 sequel to the above-mentioned report.[26] The Commission attributes this to the positive actions and concerns of President Carter and some of his recent appointees. The 1977 report asserts that the summer of 1977 "may go on record as the period of greatest activity by civil rights agencies and offices since the Government established mechanisms to combat employment discrimination."[27] Many of the new appointees were attempting to formulate a uniform set of selection guidelines and related personnel matters. Agencies were also engaging in critical self-audits, and many had proposed changes in their enforcement of equal employment opportunity programs. Finally, President Carter had articulated the need to consolidate the government's equal employment programs and efforts generally.

In the private sector, again the denial of equal employment opportunity was identified by the Civil Rights Commission. In a 1976 monograph, the Civil Commission examined the labor practices and policies of referral unions, which constitutes a large percentage of organized labor in this country. The Commission reported that referral unions adamantly maintained discriminatory practices which severely delimited the employment of minorities and women. Moreover, minorities and women were generally found in the traditional occupational categories when they were employed. Many referral unions did not have any minority or women members. Their paucity of membership stems from discriminatory practices. For example, the Civil Rights Commission asserts that blacks constituted between 0 and 1.6 percent of the membership in the building and trade unions. By 1972, the black presence was approximately 3.6 percent.[28]

Women and minorities were also employed in the traditional positions in the television industry. White male domination was the orthodoxy at the decision-making positions in the hierarchy. Moreover, stereotyped portrayal characterized television drama. Blacks are often casted in ghetto and comic roles exclusively. Finally, the Commission asserted the Federal Communications Commission was remiss in policing its licensees for their negative and restrictive personnel policies.[29]

Another chronic employment problem for minorities and women has been the discriminatory efforts of employment policies based solely on seniority. In a timely 1977 study of this recurring problem, the Commission on Civil Rights analyzed the overall effects of the 1974–1975 economic stagnation on programs to ensure equal job opportunities for women and members of minority groups. A disproportionate number of the foregoing groups were laid off during this period because they were only recently employed and had earned only a few years' seniority. The Commission contends that seniority erodes the policies of affirmative action as originally construed and frustrates the intent of Title VII of the Civil Rights Act of 1964 and related equal employment legislation. The Commission stresses the need for new equal employment guidelines

> . . . based on the principle explicitly stated that all seniority-based lay-off policies should be invalid as they apply to any work force that does not mirror the relevant labor market and the composition of which cannot be explained successfully by the employer.[30]

Various alternatives to seniority-based layoff are recommended by the Commission. They include work sharing, reduction of the labor force through attrition, payless holidays, and subsidization of employees who accept a reduced work week with increased unemployment insurance benefits. These policies, it was felt, would reduce the restrictive effects of seniority and nurture equal employment programs.

The reorganization of civil rights enforcement progress is one of the most relevant policy developments at this time. The need for reorganization has been documented by the Commission in a series of reports. The Commission has stated that the present civil rights enforcement efforts are still plagued by an overall lack of leadership, suffering from duplication, inadequate staff and resources, and inconsistent policies and standards.[31] The proposed reorganization is presently being discussed on Capitol Hill.

Women

In October 1972, the jurisdiction of the Commission was expanded by Congress to include sex discrimination. Four crucial, separate reports were published during the past four years in order to focus on the unique problems of women. They deal with reproductive choice, sex bias in the *U.S. Code,* women and minorities as contractors, and domestic violence.

The Commission viewed with alarm the abridgment of a woman's right to select abortion as stated in two earlier Supreme Court decisions.[32] In 1976 and 1977, Congress restricted the use of Medicaid funds for abortion by amending appropriations bills for the Department of Health, Education, and Welfare and Labor. The "Hyde Amendment," as it was labeled in the legislative parlance, stipulated that none of the monies appropriated were to be utilized for abortions except where the mother's life would be endangered if she carried the fetus to birth. Law suits precluded the implementation, and the measure was enjoined. In 1977, the House inserted a more restrictive measure in the appropriations bill. The Senate modified the language of the measure. In December 1977, the House-Senate conference agreed on the proposed changes. The new legislation provides for Medicaid-funded abortions where the life of the mother is endangered if the fetus is carried to term; where there was incest or rape reported promptly to the public health or law enforcement authorities; or where two medical doctors determine that a full pregnancy would result in severe damage to the mother. Three recent Court decisions upheld the legislation.[33] The Commission feels that the present ban on abortion funding will disproportionately affect poor women, minority women, and rural women.

Sex-based differentials pervade the *U.S. Code*. The Commission calls for sex-neutral terminology "except in the rare instance where no suitable sex neutral substitute term exists, or the reference is to a physical characteristic unique to some or all members of one sex, or the Constitutional right to privacy necessitates a sex specific reference."[34] The Social Security Act illustrates one aspect of the differential. The Commission states that a "married women who pays social security taxes all her working life may receive benefits no larger than if she never contributed to the fund."[35] Benefits, it was learned, accrue primarily from the earnings of the husband, the independent variable. Moreover, the Aid to Families with Dependent Children considers only the man as the breadwinner or head of the family. The payments provide a disincentive for families to stay together. The report is also critical of separate penal institutions but not separate sleeping and bathroom facilities.

The extent to which women share in the $120 billion worth of contracts from the respective layers of government was a topic of a 1975 report. The investigation revealed conclusively that female-owned firms

> . . . encounter problems of staggering proportion in obtaining information on federal, state and local government contracting opportunities in time to submit bids and in obtaining the working capital necessary for effective marketing and bidding. Minority and female entrepreneurs also encounter a great deal of skepticism regarding their ability to perform adequately on government contracts. Government contracting officers and program officials expressed reservations concerning the ability of minority-owned firms to perform, although no specific cases of inadequate performance by minority firms were brought to the attention of the Commission's staff by their contracting officials.[36]

The Commission also found that the three special federal programs established to assist women and minorities have not helped them to surmount their working capital problems or to secure timely information on government contract opportunities. Officials at only 3 out of 125 minority- and female-owned firms indicated that they were helped by the three programs.

Unmitigated marital or domestic violence is also a concern of many women and policymakers. Only a few states have instituted innovative programs to assist battered women, including halfway houses, shelters, legal assistance, and specifically trained law enforement units.[37] However, a majority of states do not provide any assistance or protection in this area. The Commission will have more to say on this crucial matter in 1978.

Conclusions

An effort has been made to outline some major aspects of a national agenda of civil rights policy concerns as identified by the Commission on Civil Rights. The Commission, as noted earlier, for twenty-one years has been in the business of documenting various kinds of denials of equal protection under the laws based on race, color, sex, religion, or national origin. During those twenty-one years, the Commission has produced a staggering amount of data documenting discrimination and citing failures of enforcement of laws barring discrimination and proposed new and creative means for lessening discrimination. No single volume, let alone a single article, could do justice to the splendid efforts of the Commission. Such was not the task of this chapter. Rather this chapter attempted to discuss what its authors consider to be some of the more critical items on the Commission's national civil rights agenda.

Little or no mention has been made of many of the other items on this agenda. These would include the following problem areas: administration of justice; the special case of Hispanics; civil rights enforcement; the special case of native Alaskans; the special case of American Indians; the special case of native Hawaiians; prisons; police-community relations; information and communications; migrants; health and safety; undocumented aliens; and civil rights reorganization. These represent the Commission's national agenda.

Notes

1. Foster R. Dulles, *The Civil Rights Commission: 1957-1965* (Lansing: Michigan State University Press, 1968), p. ix.

2. U.S. Commission on Civil Rights, *Twenty Years after Brown: Equal Opportunity in Housing* (Washington: Government Printing Office, 1975), p. iii.

3. Berl Bernhard, "Equality and 1964," *Vital Speeches,* July 15, 1963, quoted in U.S. Commission on Civil Rights, *Twenty Years after Brown,* p. iv.

4. Theodore M. Hesburgh, "Integer Vitae: Independence of the U.S. Commission on Civil Rights," *Notre Dame Lawyer* 46, no. 445 (1971): 446. Reprinted with permission. © by the *Notre Dame Lawyer,* University of Notre Dame.

5. U.S. Commission on Civil Rights, *The Unfinished Business: Twenty Years Later . . .* (Washington: Government Printing Office, 1977), p. 4.

6. U.S. Commission on Civil Rights, *The Voting Rights Act: Ten Years After* (Washington: Government Printing Office, 1975), p. 330.

7. U.S. Commission on Civil Rights, *The State of Civil Rights: 1977* (Washington: Government Printing Office, 1978), p. 33.

8. See U.S. Commission on Civil Rights, *Using the Voting Rights Act* (Washington: Government Printing Office, 1976).

9. U.S. Commission on Civil Rights, *The Voting Rights Act: Ten Years After* (Washington: Government Printing Office, 1975), p. 330.

10. U.S. Commission on Civil Rights, *Understanding Fair Housing* (Washington: Government Printing Office, 1973), p. 1.

11. U.S. Commission on Civil Rights, *Above Property Rights* (Washington: Government Printing Office, 1972), p. 28.

12. U.S. Commission on Civil Rights, *Understanding Fair Housing,* p. 1.

13. U.S. Commission on Civil Rights, *Twenty Years after Brown.*

14. U.S. Commission on Civil Rights, *The State of Civil Rights—1977,* p. 16.

15. U.S. Commission on Civil Rights, *The Federal Civil Rights Enforcement Effort—1974: To Provide For Fair Housing* (Washington: Government Printing Office, 1974), p. 328.

16. U.S. Commission on Civil Rights, *The State of Civil Rights—1977.* p. 17.

17. Ibid., p. 20.

18. U.S. Commission on Civil Rights, *Fulfilling the Letter and Spirit of the Law: Desegregation of the Nation's Public Schools* (Washington: Government Printing Office, 1976).

19. U.S. Commission on Civil Rights, *Twenty Years after Brown: Equality of Educational Opportunity* (Washington: Government Printing Office, 1975).

20. U.S. Commission on Civil Rights, *Statement of Metropolitan School Desegregation* (Washington: Government Printing Office, 1977).

21. Ibid., pp. 113–14.

22. U.S. Commission on Civil Rights, *A Better Chance to Learn: Bilingual-Bicultural Education* (Washington: Government Printing Office, 1974). Also see the following Commission publications: *The Unfinished Education: Outcomes for Minorities in the Five Southwestern States* (Washington: Government Office,

1971); *Mexican American Education in Texas: A Function of Wealth* (Washington: Government Printing Office, 1972); *Teachers and Students: Differences in Teacher Interaction with Mexican American and Anglo Students* (Washington: Government Printing Office, 1973); *Toward Quality Education for Mexican Americans* (Washington: Government Printing Office, 1974); and *Homeownership for Lower-Income Families: A Report on the Racial and Ethnic Impact of the Section 235 Program* (Washington: Government Printing Office, 1971).

23. U.S. Commission on Civil Rights, *Statement on Affirmative Action* (Washington: Government Printing Office, 1977), pp. 8-12. The case was decided on June 29, 1978. The splintered Supreme Court decision upheld the principle of affirmative action to overcome past discrimination but at the same time ordered the University of California to admit the plaintiff. The impact of the nebulous case will be analyzed for some time by the proponents and opponents.

24. U.S. Commission on Civil Rights, *The Federal Civil Rights Enforcement Effort* (Washington: Government Printing Office, 1970); *The Federal Civil Rights Enforcement Effort: One Year Later* (Washington: Government Printing Office, 1971); and *The Federal Civil Rights Enforcement Effort—A Reassessment* (Washington: Government Printing Office, 1973).

25 U.S. Commission on Civil Rights, *The Federal Civil Rights Enforcement Effort* (Washington: Government Printing Office, 1974); and *To Eliminate Employment Discrimination,* vol. 5 (Washington: Government Printing Office, 1975).

26. U.S. Commission on Civil Rights, *The Federal Civil Rights Enforcement Effort—1977, To Eliminate Employment Discrimination: A Sequel* (Washington: Government Printing Office, 1978).

27. Ibid., p. 329.

28. U.S. Commission on Civil Rights, *The Challenge Ahead: Equal Opportunity in Referral Unions* (Washington: Government Printing Office, 1976).

29. U.S. Commission on Civil Rights, *Window Dressing on the Set: Women and Minorities in TV* (Washington: Government Printing Office, 1977).

30. U.S. Commission on Civil Rights, *Last Hired, First Fired: Layoffs and Civil Rights* (Washington: Government Printing Office, 1977), p. 63.

31. U.S. Commission on Civil Rights, *The State of Civil Rights.*

32. See *Doe* v. *Wade,* 410 U.S. 113 (1973), and *Doe* v. *Bolton,* 410 U.S. 179 (1973).

33. U.S. Commission on Civil Rights, *The State of Civil Rights—1977,* as well as *Constitutional Aspects of the Right to Limit Childbearing* (Washington: Government Printing Office, 1975).

34. U.S. Commission on Civil Rights, *Sex Bias in the U.S. Code* (Washington: Government Printing Office, 1977).

35. Ibid., p. 211.

36. U.S. Commission on Civil Rights, *Minorities and Women as Contractors* (Washington: Government Printing Office, 1975), p. i.

37. U.S. Commission on Civil Rights, *Colorado Advisory Committee to the U.S. Commission on Civil Rights, The Silent Victims: Denver's Battered Women* (Washington: Government Printing Office, 1977).

Part III
The Impact of Judicial Decisions

8

Sex and the Burger Court: Recent Judicial Policy Making toward Women

Leslie Friedman Goldstein

Beginning, perhaps, with the seminal article by Robert Dahl in 1957,[1] the past twenty years have witnessed an increase in attention to the Supreme Court's role as a policy-making institution.[2]

Dahl's article made an effort to identify a pattern of interaction between the Supreme Court and the other two major national policymakers within the U.S. regime—Congress and the President. Dahl claimed to have proved that the Supreme Court basically acted in partnership with, rather than in opposition to, dominant national political coalitions. In his words, "Policy views dominant on the Court are never for long out of line with the policy views dominant among the lawmaking majorities of the United States [and therefore] . . . lawmaking majorities have generally had their way."[3] Dahl also claimed that on the rare occasions when the Court *has* opposed legislative majorities, opposition has *not* generally been in a policy direction that favored the basic rights of minorities unable to exert power through the electoral or legislative process.

In other words, if correct, Dahl's article undermined one of the classic justifications for permitting nine unelected, life-tenured individuals, via judicial review, to thwart the will of the majority of the elected representatives of the U.S. people. As Alexander Hamilton had stated it, the Supreme Court's political independence would enable that institution

> to guard the Constitution and the rights of individuals, from the effects of those ill-humors which . . . have a tendency . . . to occasion danger-ous innovations in the government, and serious oppressions of the minor party in the community,[4]

Dahl's conclusions, if valid, would relegate Hamilton's case for judicial review to the dustbin of factual error. For judicial review looks far less palatable when one notices the Supreme Court overturning congressional statutes in a direction that aids the *oppressor* of the "minor party," as the Court did in nineteenth-century cases involving slaveholders and segregationists.[5]

Dahl's conclusions, however, have not stood the test of time. In a recent critique of Dahl's thesis, Jonathan Casper points out that the pattern of judicial policy making in the 1957–1974 period belies Dahl's conclusion concerning the direction of Supreme Court policy: both the Warren Court and the early Burger Court demonstrated a relatively consistent concern for the rights of racial and religious minorities and of other politically powerless groups (for example, the poor or persons accused of crime).[6] More importantly, Casper points out that in a number of respects Dahl's methodology led him to underrate substantially the degree of the Court's influence both as a national policymaker and as a protector of minority rights.[7] Casper's critique points to the conclusion that the Supreme Court does make significant contributions to national policy making and that, at least during certain lengthy historical periods, those contributions promote the rights of groups who lack clout in the majoritarian electoral and legislative processes.

In criticizing Dahl's research methods, Casper describes certain aspects of the Supreme Court's role in national policy making which are quite helpful for understanding the dynamics of recent judicial policy making toward women. Casper argues that a characterization of Court-Congress or Court-President conflicts that simply tabulates each side's "won" and "lost" record is of necessity misleading. This is because

> many of the issues in which national political institutions become involved are not "settled" but continue to recur. Conflicts among political institutions produce not "winning" and "losing" policies, but rather tentative solutions that themselves become the basis for future policy making. . . . Though at various times one position or another may carry the day, ultimate resolutions are not discovered, and the Court, like other political institutions, has and will continue to make important contributions to the "solutions" that carry the day, become the subject for further debate and are modified or rejected.[8]

The late Alexander Bickel identified essentially the same process more succinctly when he wrote that "virtually all important decisions of the Supreme Court are the beginnings of conversations between the Court and the people and their representatives."[9] Although we would modify Bickel's comment to the effect that the colloquy has often begun long before some of "the people" decide to bring the Court into the conversation, the implications of his metaphor are well worth heeding. For the metaphor of a "conversation" points to those elements of persuasion, consultation, education, and reciprocity of response, which are important elements of judicial policy making in the United States.

The development of Supreme Court policies toward women during the tenure of Chief Justice Warren Burger provides an intriguing set of examples of just this process of institutional interaction. Women are no longer a minority in the U.S. population, although they were in the eighteenth and nineteenth centuries. Even though they comprise 51 percent of the population, however, they comprise only 5 percent of public officials.[10] Thus, within policy-making institutions in this country, women are a *very* small minority. As any policy-making minority—that is, loser in the legislative and executive arena—does sooner or later, women took their case(s) to court. For many decades women's rights advocates fared poorly with the judiciary as well as elsewhere (in conformity with Dahl's thesis).[11] But during the years of the Burger Court this pattern changed rather abruptly.

Content of the Burger Court Policy toward Women

Despite the setbacks encountered by women's group litigants during the 1976–1977 Supreme Court term, the fact remains that the Burger Court has contributed more to the development of U.S. women's legal equality and constitutional freedom than any previous judicial body. In fact, on the basis of the abortion decisions of 1973 (*Roe* v. *Wade,* 410 U.S. 113, and *Doe* v. *Bolton,* 410 U.S. 179) and 1976 (*Planned Parenthood* v. *Danforth,* 428 U.S. 52),[12] one can build a plausible case that the Burger Court has done more to enhance the freedom of American women than any single policy-making body in U.S. history. Since 1973, literally millions of women have taken advantage of the legal right to have an abortion in the forty-six states where the Supreme Court established that right,[13] and this single policy change has almost certainly saved the lives of hundreds of women who would otherwise have died at the hands of incompetent criminal abortionists.

In addition to the much publicized (and politically controversial) abortion decisions, the Burger Court by the end of the 1976–1977 term had produced the following rules of public policy concerning women. (1) States may not require that men be automatically preferred to women as estate administrators (*Reed* v. *Reed,* 404 U.S. 71 [1971]).[14] (2) Women employees of the government are entitled to spouse dependency benefits equal to those given comparable male employees (*Frontiero* v. *Richardson,* 411 U.S. 677 [1973]). (3) Women may not be forced to take leaves from government jobs on account of pregnancy (*Cleveland Bd.* v. *LaFleur,* 414 U.S. 632 [1974]) or be denied unemployment compensation on account of pregnancy (*Turner* v. *Department of Employment,* 423 U.S. 44 [1975]). (4) Women may not be systematically excluded from jury duty (*Taylor* v. *Louisiana,* 419 U.S. 522 [1975]). (5) When Congress provides social security benefits for the surviving spouse of males who pay social security taxes, it must provide comparable benefits for the surviving spouse of females who paid similar taxes (*Weinberger* v. *Wiesenfeld,* 420 U.S. 636 [1975] and *Califano* v. *Goldfarb,* 97 S. Ct. 1021 [1977]). and (6) States must set the same age of majority for females as for males in respect to eligibility for child support payments (*Stanton* v. *Stanton,* 421 U.S. 7 [1975]) and in respect to the legal age for purchasing liquor (*Craig* v. *Boren,* 429 U.S. 190 [1976]). All these policies were established by means of interpretations of the Constitution's equal protection and due process clauses. That fact, of course, gives these rules the particularly durable status of all policies produced by constitutional adjudication: They may not be overturned by legislative majorities.

Although its policy-making authority is more limited in its role as inter-preter of national statutes, the Burger Court has nonetheless used that role also to effect important changes in women's status. Under the chief justiceship of Warren Burger, in 1971 the Court for the first time (*Phillips* v. *Martin-Marietta Corp.*, 400 U.S. 542)[15] applied the 1964 Civil Rights Act's prohibition on sex discrimination in employment. On that occasion the Court announced that a blanket refusal to hire mothers (but not fathers) of preschool children did amount to sex discrimination (and therefore was illegal). The Equal Pay Act of 1963 was also applied by the Supreme Court for the first time during the tenure of Chief Justice Burger (although he dissented).[16] In that 1974 case (*Corning Glass* v. *Brennan*, 417 U.S. 188), involving an extremely complex fact situation, the Supreme Court reversed one federal Circuit Court of Appeals (agreeing with another) to hold that the company in question had not gone far enough in its pay equalization scheme to undo the residue of *past* sex discrimination in wages. And, in June of 1977 (*Dothard* v. *Rawlinson*, 97 S. Ct. 2720) the Burger Court once again applied the sex discrimination prohibition of the 1964 Civil Rights Act to rule that minimum height and weight requirements which disproportion-ately eliminated women from eligibility for the job of prison guard constituted sex discrimination.[17] The 1977–1978 session brought two more applications of the 1964 Civil Rights Act to women. The Court held that to deprive women on maternity leave of accrued seniority did constitute sex discrimination (*Nashville Gas* v. *Satty*, 98 S. Ct. 347) and also that it was sex discrimination to deduct larger contributions to the pension fund from female workers' wages than from wages of male workers (*Los Angeles* vs. *Manhart*, 98 S. Ct. 1370).

But, as anyone who reads the newspapers knows, this profeminist descrip-tion of Burger Court policies toward women is only a part (albeit a big part) of the picture. The rest of the picture does include some major rejections of the demands and legal arguments of women's rights groups. In 1974 (*Geduldig* v. *Aiello*, 417 U.S. 484) the Court ruled that states were not violating the Four-teenth Amendment requirement of equal protection of the laws when they refused to include coverage for pregnancy-related disabilities in government-mandated employee disability insurance plans. Late in 1976 the Court, utilizing this precedent, ruled that similar exclusions of pregnancy-related disabilities by private employers did not constitute the "sex discrimination" forbidden by the 1964 Civil Rights Act (*Gilbert* vs. *G.E.*, 97 S. Ct. 401). In a trio of cases handed down in June 1977, the Burger Court ruled (1) that the federal law providing Medicaid funds for "necessary" medical services does not require that states allocate funds for abortions categorized as "unnecessary" by states (*Beal* v. *Doe*, 97 S. Ct. 2366); (2) that the constitutional right to privacy, which keeps the government from prohibiting abortions altogether, does not prohibit the govern-ment from refusing to pay for abortions, even when the government is paying the costs of live births (*Maher* v. *Roe*, 97 S. Ct. 2376); and (3) that the constitu-tional right to privacy does not forbid the government from refusing to allow abortions in its own tax-supported hospitals (*Poelker* v. *Doe,* 97 S. Ct. 2391). And, finally, the Burger Court did uphold, in 1974, 1975, and 1977, three "reverse discrimination" statutes providing special economic benefits to women. In each of these cases the Court majority ruled that the sex discrimination favoring women—a special property tax exemption for widows (*Kahn* v. *Shevin,* 416 U.S. 351 [1974]), a military officer promotion scheme allowing women officers more years in which to try for a promotion than men had (*Schlesinger* v. *Ballard,* 419 U.S. 498 [1975]), and a social security provision allowing to women a more generous income-averaging calculus than was permitted to men (*Califano* v. *Webster,* 97 S. Ct. 1192 [1977])—could be justified by a governmental desire to compensate for the preexisting socioeconomic disadvantage facing women.[18]

In short, the Burger Court, since 1971, has demonstrated a willingness to void any legislative gender discrimination that (in the eyes of the Court) is not designed to compensate women for disadvantages that they have suffered as a result of societal discrimination,[19] *unless* that legislative discrimination (or, in the case of employers, private discrimination) happens to involve that unique physiological condition—pregnancy—to which only the female sex is liable. In the latter situation, the Court flatly refused until recently to define special treatment of pregnancy as sex discrimination. The December 1977 case of *Nashville Gas* v. *Satty* (98 S. Ct. 347) muddied these clear waters. Now the law is that employers may not place extra *burdens* on women who take pregnancy leaves, but they still may deny women the *benefit* of disability leave pay for maternity leaves. (Justice Stevens argued that the new distinction made no sense.[20])

In addition, the Burger Court has created (or "discovered") a constitutional right to abort any nonviable fetus. This constitutional right belongs to the prospective mother of the fetus, and it is a "right" in the sense that the government may not punish her for exercising it. Whether, however, the government may *regulate* the practice of abortion so as to prevent some women from obtaining abortions is, as of 1978, still a confused question of law. In 1976, for example, the Supreme Court declared unconstitutional a "regulation" of the state of Missouri that prohibited the most commonly available type of abortion, saline amniocentesis (*Planned Parenthood* v. *Danforth*). The Court reasoned that this purported regulation, in practice, made abortion virtually unobtainable for most women in the state and that it therefore violated the right to privacy (that is, the right against "unwarranted governmental intrusion into matters so fundamentally affecting the person as the decision whether to bear or beget a child").[21] Yet in 1977 the Court upheld a "regulation" banning abortion in all tax-supported hospitals of a particular municipality (*Poelker* v. *Doe*). The latter decision would seem to permit at least some policies making abortions unavailable to persons living in particular locales, and thereby to conflict with the Court's policy rationale, if not its specific policy outcome, of 1976.

Of course, in the case of the judiciary, the policy rationale *is* part of the policy outcome, because the Court's reasoning is what provides guidance for lower-level policymakers (such as state legislatures and lower federal courts) in future situations that are similar to, but not exactly identical to, the situation being judged by the Supreme Court. As we have indicated, the Burger Court's attempt to base its abortion policy on the distinction between the imposition of a penalty by government (*Roe, Doe* and *Planned Parenthood*) and the refusal by government to provide a benefit (*Beal, Maher,* and *Poelker*) has resulted in an ambiguous policy articulation. The Court then proceeded to compound this ambiguity by applying the benefit/burden rationale as the test for whether discrimination against pregnant employees amounts to illegal sex discrimination (compare the *Gilbert* and *Satty* cases). These policies represent, therefore, an unstable situation that will probably continue to be litigated over the next several years.[22]

Analysis of the Policy-Making Process

The foregoing overview of Burger Court policies toward women gives rise to a number of queries: Why did the Burger Court, four-ninths the product of the supposedly conservative Nixon administration, initiate all these policy reforms expanding the constitutional equality and liberty of women? Why did the Court, so willing to flout legislative majorities in some of its policy pronouncements on women, stop where it did on these issues? Stating the second question in more systemic terms, what defines the limits of the Court's potential as a policy innovator? Although our answer cannot be exhaustive, a focus on Burger Court policies toward women can provide some insights concerning the potential of and the limits upon the U.S. judiciary as a policymaker.

First, why the dramatic shift in judicial policy toward women, beginning in 1971? We can reject the simplest explanation, namely, that the Warren Court would have initiated these changes if only the questions had been presented to the Court. The questions *were* presented: in 1961 (*Hoyt* v. *Florida*, 368 U.S. 57) the Warren Court *upheld* the then common practice of systematically excluding women from juries; and as late as 1968 the Warren Court turned down a request to reconsider this ruling (*State* v. *Hall*, 385 U.S. 98). We can also reject the hypothesis that Nixon had unwittingly appointed to the Court a group of closet feminist ideologues. The limitations of the Court's rulings on pregnancy and abortion make obvious (had anyone doubted it) that the Burger Court is not simply following a feminist party line.

At first glance, Dahl's description of the judicial policy role seems to apply rather nicely to recent policy developments concerning women. The Burger Court, after all, is no more immune from the changing winds of national political sentiment than was the proslavery Court at the time of *Dred Scott,* the prosegregation Court at the time of *Plessy* v. *Ferguson,* the post-1937 pro-New Deal Court, or the nigh-McCarthyist Court of *Dennis* v. *U.S.*[23] The "political" branches of the government were indicating in the early 1970s a new willingness to consider the long-denied claims of women, and the Supreme Court moved with them. In 1967 President Johnson (in Executive Order 11375) prohibited sex discrimination by employers under federal contract; in August, 1970, the House of Representatives endorsed the ERA by the astonishing margin of 350 to 15; the calendar year of 1970 witnessed the legalization of abortion in four states; and in 1972 the Senate, too, endorsed the ERA, and Congress gave the Equal Employment Opportunity Commission real power to enforce (via the initiation of lawsuits) the federal prohibition on sex discrimination in employment. New arguments were being presented and endorsed in public forums all over the country, and one might suppose that the Supreme Court justices were simply responding to these arguments, as was the rest of the nation.

But the proposition that the Supreme Court was simply responding to, or moving along with, dominant national sentiment in questions of women's rights obscures at least as much as it reveals. First, it obscures the fact that the Supreme Court, in a sense, *initiated* some of the change in sentiment regarding policies toward women. The Supreme Court during the late 1960s inaugurated very significant changes of legal doctrine regarding the due-process and equal protection clauses. In 1965 the Court announced that the due-process clause protected something called a "right to privacy" which covered the right of a married couple to use birth control without interference from the state.[24] To lawyers, trained to think in terms of general legal principles (that is, general rules of law, as distinguished from specific results), the question of whether this new rule would cover the case of a right to obtain an abortion was bound to occur. Thus, when four states legalized abortion in 1970, they may have been acting at least partly in *response* to the Supreme Court's stimulus.

Also, in a number of cases in the middle and late 1960s the Supreme Court used the equal protection caluse to strike down laws discriminating against the poor, against illegitimate children, and against persons migrating from other states.[25] Before this time, declarations of unconstitutionality based on the equal protection clause had been limited almost exclusively to laws discriminating against racial or nationality groups. The broadening of the import of that clause by the Court naturally promoted discussions in law shools, in law reviews, and among lawyers concerning possible *future* applications of that clause. In this sense, the Court can be said to *invite* certain kinds of lawsuits to be brought before it. And in the early 1970s a number of women's rights litigants did take up the Court's invitation.

Developments in Court doctrine can be said to initiate change in a broader sense, too (although this is harder to document, especially by counting techniques). As the Court declared unconstitutional certain legal discriminations against the poor and against illegitimates, the justices were, in effect, heightening the national consciousness on the question of what really was a "fair" or a "reasonable" legislative categorization. Journalists, professors, legislators, and lawyers found themselves forced to address this question more often than in the past, and this development meant that their various audiences, too, were pondering this question in new ways. In this sense, the Supreme Court does act as a kind of national educator: it shapes (as much as reacts to) the national climate of opinion. It is difficult to believe that the success of the ERA in Congress in the early 1970s was not at all influenced by this new climate of opinion.

Finally, Dahl's thesis simply cannot account for the fact that the Supreme Court did move in opposition to dominant national legislative majorities on the abortion question (as it had earlier on questions of reapportionment, prayers in public schools, desegregation, and the rights of those accused of crime). Although four states had legalized abortion in 1970, the forty-six other states still treated abortion as a serious crime as of 1973. Perhaps it is most accurate to say that the action of the four innovating legislatures signaled a new fluidity in popular opinion on the question of abortion, and the Court moved within this new context to institutionalize a policy result that the justices (and the majority of the college-educated sector of the population by that time) favored. It must be acknowledged, however (as Dahl's methodology did not permit him to acknowledge), that this movement by the Court itself *caused* additional shifting of public opinion on the abortion question. Polls now show very solid majorities of the public favoring a legal right to obtain abortions,[26] and this was simply not the case in 1972.

This brings us to the second query: Why has the Court stopped where it has? Why the refusal in 1974 to say that the equal protection clause requires state disability insurance programs to cover pregnancy disability? Why the refusal in 1976 to say that such pregnancy exclusion constitutes illegal sex discrimination? Why the refusal to require abortion coverage in government health care programs or abortion services in government-supported hospitals? On these two issues, one involving enormous financial costs and the other involving what is, next to race, the most heated issue in U.S. domestic policy, the Supreme Court has apparently decided to hand these very hot potatoes back to the legislative branch.

At this point, it may be helpful to note that Dahl himself recognized that there were occasions on which the Supreme Court could act as a national policy-maker (though he underestimated their frequency). His description of those occasions provides useful insight into the Court's predicament on the abortion issue:

> There are times when the ruling coalition is unstable with respect to certain key policies; at very great risk to its legitimacy powers, the Court can intervene in such cases and may even succeed in establishing policy. Probably in such cases it can succeed only if its action conforms to and reinforces a widespread set of explicit or implicit norms held by the political leadership; norms which are not strong enough or are not

distributed in such a way as to insure the existence of an effective law-making majority but are, nonetheless, sufficiently powerful to prevent any successful attack on the legitimacy powers of the Court . . .[27]

The acknowledgment that it is peculiarly the job of the Supreme Court to identify and articulate the explicit *or implicit* norms of the nation says a great deal about the Court's institutional role within the U.S. regime. When the nation's explicit norms clash with its implicit ones, or when there are intensely felt divisions within the nation concerning certain norms (implicit or explicit), the Supreme Court can provide valuable leadership. On divisive questions like busing and abortion it is true that the Supreme Court *can* move with more free-dom from popular opinion than the elected branches. But it cannot move in total disregard of that opinion. As pressure has mounted within the legislature for constitutional amendments on these two subjects, the Supreme Court has visibly backed off on both of them. On the abortion question as in the busing question, we are witnessing a particularly vivid example of the uneasy tension between the Court's special institutional role, on the one hand, and the commit-ment of the U.S. regime to democratic, that is, majoritarian, government, on the other.

Notes

1. Robert Dahl, "Decision-Making in a Democracy: The Supreme Court as a National Policy-Maker," *Emory Law Journal* 6 (Fall 1957): 279-295 (formerly *Journal of Public Law*) reprinted with permission. Perhaps the trend should be dated as far back as Herman Pritchett's *The Roosevelt Court—A Study in Judi-cial Politics and Values 1937-1947* (New York: Macmillan, 1948).

2. Dozens of recent articles and books exemplify this concern. Some of the leading examples are Jonathan D. Casper, "The Supreme Court and National Policy Making," *American Political Science Review* 70 (March 1976): 50-68; Karen Orren, "Standing to Sue: Interest Group Conflict in the Federal Courts," *American Political Science Review* 70 (September 1976): 723-741; Richard Funston, "The Supreme Court and Critical Elections," *American Political Sci-ence Review* 69 (September 1975): 795-811 and "Communications" thereon in *American Political Science Review* 70 (December 1976): 1215-1221 and (Sep-tember 1976): 930-932; Alexander Bickel, *The Supreme Court and the Idea of Progress* (New York: Harper & Row, 1970); Samuel Krislov, *The Supreme Court in the Political Process* (New York: Macmillan, 1965); and Martin Shapiro, *Law and Politics in the Supreme Court* (Glencoe, Ill.: Free Press, 1964). For earlier works see citations in the notes to chap. 1 of Shapiro's book.

3. Dahl, "Decision-Making in a Democracy," pp. 285-6, 291.

4. *Federalist Papers*, No. 78.

5. See *Dred Scott* v. *Sanford*, 19 How. 393 (1857), and *Civil Rights Cases*, 109 U.S. 3 (1883).

6. Casper, "The Supreme Court and National Policy Making," especially pp. 53–54.

7. Ibid., especially pp. 55–63.

8. Ibid., pp. 62–3.

9. Bickel, *The Supreme Court and the Idea of Progress*, p. 91.

10. Milton Cummings, Jr., and David Wise, *Democracy under Pressure*, 3d ed. (New York: Harcourt, Brace, and Jovanovich, 1977), p. 146.

11. For example, *Bradwell* v. *Illinois*, 16 Wall. 130 (1873); *Minor* v. *Hapersett*, 21 Wall. 162 (1875); *Buck* v. *Bell*, 274 U.S. 200 (1927); *Goesaert* v. *Cleary*, 335 U.S. 464 (1948); *Hoyt* v. *Florida*, 368 U.S. 57 (1961).

12. This 1976 case held that state laws may not put a veto power over the abortion decision into the hands of the husband of a married woman or the parents of an unmarried woman.

13. In 1970 four state legislatures had legalized abortion, those of New York, Hawaii, Alaska, and Washington.

14. This is the only one the cases listed in the text that predated the accession to the Burger Court of Justices Powell and Rehnquist (and Stevens).

15. At this time, neither Powell nor Rehnquist (nor Stevens) had joined the Burger Court. The opinion was unanimous, although Justice Marshall concurred separately.

16. Nixon appointees Rehnquist and Blackman also dissented, but Justice Powell joined the majority.

17. The majority also held in this case that a regulation calling for same-sex guards in "contact positions" in maximum security prisons, a rule that operated to keep women from such jobs in male maximum security facilities, did not amount to sex discrimination, because it genuinely contributed to the smooth operation of the prison system.

18. In the case of military promotions, the Court reasoned that women were denied combat opportunities and therefore might need more time then men to accumulate impressive records as officers.

19. It is not the place of this chapter to explicate the constitutional doctrines by which the Court justifies or arrives at these policy results. For a discussion of the evolution of these doctrines see L.F. Goldstein, *The Constitutional Rights of Women* (New York: Longman, 1979), esp. chap. 5.

20. Justice Stevens argued, in a valiant effort to find some clear principle to reconcile the result of *Gilbert* with the result of *Satty*, that the rule should be that women, while *on* the job, may not receive discrimination on account of past or present pregnancy, but that while they were on leave from work they could be treated differently from other persons on leave. There are problems with Justice Stevens' proposal, however: it would seem to preclude requiring women

even in the last few weeks of pregnancy to leave even very dangerous jobs. Surely this result is not what Congress intended when it passed the Civil Rights Act.

21. *Eisenstadt* v. *Baird,* 405 U.S. 438 (1972).

22. Since the *Gilbert* and *Satty* cases are essentially matters of statutory interpretation, Congress can resolve this ambiguity by adopting a clarifying amendment. The Senate already did this in response to *Gilbert,* but the House has not yet acted.

23. On the responsiveness of the Supreme Court to political trends, see Casper, Funston, and "Communications" in note 2 and Dahl, note 1. Also see David Adamany, "Legitimacy, Realigning Elections, and the Supreme Court," *Wisconsin Law Review,* September 1973, pp. 790-846.

24. *Griswold* v. *Connecticut,* 381 U.S. 479 (1965).

25. For a discussion of these developments, see Gerald Gunther, *Cases and Materials on Constitutional Law,* 9th ed. (Mineola, N.Y.: Foundation Press, 1975), chap. 10, secs. 3 and 4.

26. There is not a clear majority in favor of government financing of abortions for the needy, however. *Time,* November 21, 1977, p. 115, reports that the Yankelovich survey (of a representative sample of registered voters) found 58 percent opposing such funding. (It reported 64 percent favoring legal freedom for a woman to have an abortion.)

27. Dahl, "Decision Making in a Democracy," p. 294.

9

Incidence and Correlates of Second-Generation Discrimination

Charles S. Bullock, III and
Joseph Stewart, Jr.

In less than a decade, the schools of the South changed from almost total segregation to become the most desegregated in the nation.[1] However, as a fairly common level of desegregation has come to exist throughout the nation, some observers have questioned whether equal educational opportunity is an automatic outcome of school desegregation. Civil rights and children's groups have issued a number of reports charging that *de jure* discrimination has often been succeeded by a "second generation" of discrimination. This chapter indicates the extent of second-generation discrimination in the South and explores the relationships of several independent variables to its incidence. Our research assesses the responsiveness of Southern schools to a policy goal of equal educational opportunity.

Dependent Variables: Manifestions of Second-Generation Discrimination

Second-generation discrimination will be measured in three contexts: (1) black overrepresentation among students assigned to special education classes, (2) black overrepresentation among students suspended or expelled, and (3) black underrepresentation on faculties. Each measure has been used by various observers in assessing the extent of equal educational opportunity policy. Before analyzing conditions in the South, we review the research findings of others on the three aspects of second-generation discrimination and indicate current legal requirements.

Special Education

Assignment of students to special classes, especially those for the educable mentally retarded (EMR), is a discrimination technique which can be couched in "educational" terms. However, ability grouping or tracking, of which EMR classes are one type, has been found to reinforce class distinctions which are correlated with racial distinctions.[2] Tracking negatively reinforces students with a history of failure and may lead to further failures by those aware that they have been branded as slow learners.[3]

Tests used to track black students are frequently criticized.[4] Kirp and Yudof delineated three major defects:

1. The tests reward white middle class values and skills, and penalize minority children because of their backgrounds;
2. The impersonal environment in which aptitude tests are given depresses the scores of minority children, who become anxious or apathetic in such situations; and
3. Tests standardized for white, middle class children fail to adequately measure the intelligence of minority children with vastly different backgrounds.[5]

The Office of Civil Rights requires that special education programs be educationally necessary and successful; that is, students must perform better than they would if they were left in regular classrooms. This is a crucial requirement. If special education programs are successful, overrepresentation of blacks may help compensate for generations of racially segregated schools. If, however, no such case can be made for the program, it becomes a technique for racial isolation freighted with many of the negative consequences of the dual school systems.

There is evidence that successful special education programs are infrequent.[6] For example, students misassigned to a special education class may require several months of intensive work to regain the level of performance of their peers in regular classes.

The serious consequences of tracking are noted in a 1970 report which claimed that 35 percent of the remaining Southern high school segregation and 60 percent of the elementary school segregation were the product of achievement tests, often instituted at the time of desegregation.[7] Despite federal prohibitions against practices, including testing, which promote racial isolation, the Children's Defense Fund conservatively estimates that 32,381 more black students were in EMR classes in 1974 than one would expect given the ratio of black to white enrollments.[8]

In reviewing applications for the Emergency School Assistant Act (ESAA) funds, the Office for Civil Rights investigates districts where black enrollment in special education exceeds the black enrollment in the system by 20 percentage points. The efforts of the OCR have received some support from the courts. A Louisiana federal district court held ability grouping based on testing invalid because the procedure initiated coincided with desegregation.[9] A California federal district court found an equal protection clause violation when blacks constituted 28.5 percent of a district's enrollment but 66.0 percent of all students in

EMR classes.[10] The Fifth Circuit has prohibited use of ability grouping which promotes racial separation in previously segregated schools until time has erased the effects of earlier discrimination.[11]

Punishment

Another type of discrimination is unequal application of extreme discipline. Suspensions and expulsions have been widespread in newly desegregated schools. Because the burden of adjustment to desegregated schools has fallen largely on blacks, it is not surprising that they are disproportionately the subjects of these extreme forms of punishment. A 1970 evaluation of desegregation[12] reports that suspensions and expulsions were widely used to "keep black students in their place." Two years later *It's Not Over in the South*[13] documented sharp increases in suspensions, especially among blacks, during the first year of desegregation. Most observers who had input in *The Student Pushout*[14] "linked the number of suspensions and expulsions to the various forms of resistance to desegregation. . . ." Miller[15] finds a discriminatory pattern in Boston discipline practices.

A national survey of selected districts done by the Children's Defense Fund finds a "pattern of disproportionate suspensions of minority children."[16] A report devoted exclusively to suspensions concludes that

1. Black children were suspended at twice the rate of any other ethnic group;
2. disproportionate suspension of blacks reflects a pervasive school intolerance for children who are *different;* and
3. black children bear the brunt of tensions arising from desegregation.[17]

The Office for Civil Rights which monitors suspensions and expulsions has concluded that "minority students are being kept out of school as a disciplinary measure more frequently and for longer periods of time than non-minority students."[18] Peter Holmes, then the OCR director, acknowledged that "just a cursory examination of our data suggests the probability of widespread discrimination in the application of disciplinary sanctions."[19] Despite all this evidence, determinations of noncompliance with federal equal education opportunity requirements based on findings of discriminatory punishment have been rare.[20] This conclusion is reached even though the OCR applies the same 20 percent black overrepresentation criteria to suspensions and expulsions when evaluating ESAA grant applications as it uses in evaluating EMR placements.

Court decisions in discriminatory punishment cases have varied. The Fifth Circuit held in 1964 that even if the offense was real, racially discriminatory discipline was unconstitutional.[21] However, other courts have found no racial discrimination in discipline.[22] In a major punishment case, Judge Hughes found racism to be the major cause of a pattern of disproportionate black suspension. The Dallas, Texas, school system was ordered to institute "an affirmative program aimed at materially lessening 'white institutional racism' in the district."[23]

Faculty Discrimination

When dual school systems are dismantled, black teachers are dismissed and demoted on a large scale. A survey of 467 districts found that "34 districts had dismissed black principals, 194 had demoted black principals, 127 had dismissed black teachers, and 103 had demoted black teachers."[24] The 127 districts dismissed 462 black teachers. Common excuses were a reduction in the demand for teachers with the elimination of the dual school system, failure to meet standards set for the National Teachers Examination, and "incompetency," "lack of qualifications," or "improper credentials." These latter reasons were often patently discriminatory since the same teachers had taught in black schools for years without these deficiencies being noted.

Not only have blacks being dismissed when their duties corresponded with whites, but also blacks are often not recruited for new positions.[25] This resulted in an estimated net decline in the wake of desegregation of 526 black teachers in Georgia and 519 in Louisiana.[26]

Discrimination against black faculty and staff is illegal.[27] The Department of Health, Education and Welfare has supported that ruling with its own regulation, and it reviews district personnel policies when checking ESAA grant eligibility. The courts have held that patterns of black faculty dismissal "cast the burden of proof on school boards to show that failure to rehire was for nondiscriminatory reasons, and require that such proof be clear and convincing, before the failure to re-employ may be upheld."[28]

Measurement of Possible Second-Generation Discrimination

The only systematic attempts to measure second-generation discrimination have been by Rodgers and Bullock[29] and Bullock.[30] There are, however, problems with their measure.[31] The measures used here rest on the same assumption as the Rodgers-Bullock index, but unlike theirs, the upper limit is not a product of the percentage of blacks in the system. The assumption is that blacks should be represented in special education classes, expulsions and suspensions, and faculty employment in proportion to their share of the system's student population. For special education the measure is the ratio of the percentage of blacks in a system in special education to the percentage of whites in the system who are in special education. A similar measure is used for punishment (that is, suspensions plus expulsions).

In the absence of discrimination, blacks and whites should be assigned to special education classes or punished at approximately equal rates. That is, if 4 percent of the blacks within the sytem are assigned to special education, 4 percent of the whites should be also. Such a situation would yield a score of 1.0 on this measure which indicates equality. Values greater than 1.0 indicate increasing evidence of racial discrimination.

This measure is, however, inappropriate for faculty discrimination. There is no category of faculty for which data are available which has the same discriminatory implications as categories for students do. Black faculty are employed, or they are not. The general assumption is that black faculty should be represented in the system in a proportion equal to the proportion of blacks in the student population.

Student-teacher ratios can be used to measure the likelihood of discrimination. If black teachers are employed in proportion to black enrollment, the ratio of black students to black teachers should equal the ratio of white students to white teachers. When the black student-teacher ratio is divided by the one for whites, a score greater than 1.0 indicates underrepresentation of black faculty and possible discrimination. By using this measure for tapping, the incidence of presumptive discrimination is reasonable since in the absence of racial bias the student-teacher ratio in all-black schools should have approximated the student-teacher ratio in white schools prior to desegregation.[32]

Data for the computation of the three measures are taken from forms filed with the OCR by each school system. Some gaps exist because of failure to file or unavailability of records at the time we were collecting data.

Levels of Second-Generation Discrimination

White it may be unreasonable to expect perfect equality, the higher a district scores above 1.0, the greater the likelihood of racial discrimination. But at what point is there a *prima facie* case of second-generation discrimination? As noted earlier, in reviewing applicants for Emergency School Aid funds, the OCR sets 1.2 as a threshold above which it holds a district's special education placement or punishment processes suspect. A more liberal standard of 2.0 would allow blacks to be overrepresented among those assigned to special education classes or punished by a factor of 2. Likewise, a score of 2.0 on the faculty index would indicate a student-teacher ratio twice as high among blacks as among whites.

Table 9-1 presents the proportion of districts scoring above 1.2 and 2.0 for each of nine Southern states in the 1973-1974 school year. By using the OCR standard of 1.2, the general conclusion is that in each state for each measure at

Table 9-1
Proportion of School Districts Exceeding Selected Levels of Probable Discrimination by State, 1973

State:	AL	ARK	FL	GA	LA	NC	SC	TX	VA
Type of Discrimination:				*Special Education*					
N	106	63	60	143	63	54	77	167	113
⩾ 1.2(%)	98.1	95.2	98.3	95.8	95.2	98.1	96.1	92.2	97.3
⩾ 2.0	84.0	82.5	93.3	85.3	84.1	92.6	76.6	76.0	87.6
Type of Discrimination:				*Punishment*					
N	96	92	59	142	62	53	77	147	116
⩾ 1.2	76.0	75.0	98.3	78.9	87.1	92.5	66.2	86.4	86.2
⩾ 2.0	54.2	48.9	84.7	52.1	51.6	56.6	35.1	60.6	47.4
Type of Discrimination:				*Faculty*					
N	99	95	57	146	37	50	73	124	119
⩾ 1.2	62.6	97.9	68.4	82.2	83.8	84.0	94.5	89.5	83.2
⩾ 2.0	25.3	78.9	21.1	39.7	24.3	22.0	46.6	50.8	45.4

least 60 percent of the districts could be declared in noncompliance on at least one count. Using the 1.2 standard, we find almost universal evidence of discrimination in special education, with Texas, where 92.2 percent of the school districts exceed this measure, appearing to be the least discriminatory state. For punishment, the proportion of districts exceeding 1.2 ranged from 66.2 percent in South Carolina to 98.3 percent in Florida. The faculty measures are lower, with the lowest being 62.6 percent in Alabama and the highest being 94.5 percent in South Carolina.

In using the 2.0 standard, there is still evidence of widespread possible discrimination. With a higher threshold, the presumptive evidence is more compelling, although fewer districts score this high. For special education, the proportion of districts exceeding 2.0 ranges from 76.0 percent in Teaxas to 93.3 percent in Florida.

There is substantially less evidence of discrimination in punishment than in special education when the 2.0 standard is used. The range is from 35.1 percent (South Carolina) to 84.7 percent (Florida) of a state's districts having a score of 2.0 or above on the punishment index.

In using the 2.0 standard, the least evidence of discrimination shows up for faculty. In four states 25.3 percent or fewer of the districts had black student-teacher ratios twice as large as white student-teacher ratios.

Whether one uses the 1.2 standard of the OCR or a standard of double overrepresentation among blacks, there is evidence that discrimination continues in enough districts that the reports cited earlier have not exaggerated the problem. Different states do, however, exhibit different patterns of presumptive discrimination.

The Independent Variables

School desegregation studies have used a number of independent variables. We examine the effects of several of these through multiple regression to determine the interstate differences in the amount of variance that can be explained and the pattern of the independent variables that contribute to that explanation across states. Since some of these variables are operationalized at the county level, only the four states (Virginia, Florida, Georgia, and Louisiana) in which school districts most closely correspond to county lines are used in this analysis. Independent variables and their operationalization are outlined here.

Local Response to Federal Desegregation Efforts

Districts varied in their resistance before finally coming into compliance with desegregation requirements. Bullock[33] uses an 8-point scale to measure the degree of pressure brought to bear on a district before it agreed to a terminal desegregation plan. We used this scale to measure local response. It ranges from voluntary compliance without the imposition of sanctions to the loss of federal funds coupled with threatened loss of state funds.

Wallace Vote, 1968

Fitzgerald and Morgan[34] report that support for Wallace's 1968 Presidential candidacy was negatively related to the amount of desegregation in Southern cities in 1972. The percentage of the popular vote won by Wallace by county is used here.

Percentage of Blacks

Percentage of blacks has been one of the most widely used correlates of difficulty in achieving school desegregation. Districts with a small percentage of black students were the first to desegregate. A number of studies have found the percentage of blacks in the population to be an important positive correlate of difficulties in school desegregation.[35] This study uses percentage of blacks in 1973 enrollment.

Urban-Rural Nature of the District

Southern rural school systems have been very effective in desegregating their schools.[36] Thus, the urban-rural nature of the district might affect the degree of second-generation discrimination present. This variable is measured as the percentage of the county designated as urban in the 1970 census.

Economic Discrimination

The premise for the use of this variable is that economic discrimination is indicative of underlying racial attitudes. Whites may want to keep blacks improverished in order to have a cheap source of labor and because they believe that the destitute are less likely to challenge white hegemony. The measure of economic discrimination here is the mean black family income divided by the mean family income by county for 1969 as reported in the 1970 census.

Federal Education Funds

The relative size of the federal contribution to a school district's budget may indicate the potential for the federal government to influence local education policies. The percentage of each district's 1973-1974 revenue which came from the federal government is included since the more a district gets from the federal government, the greater the potential for urging nondiscriminatory policies.

Index of Dissimilarity

The index of dissimilarity can measure the degree to which racial balance has been achieved among a district's schools.[37] It indicates what proportion of a district's black children would have to transfer from schools in which they are overrepresented to ones in which they are underrepresented so that all schools would have the same racial ratios. The range is from 0 (indicating that each school has the same proportion of blacks) to 100 (indicating complete segregation). The index of dissimilarity computed using data from the fall of 1972 is included as a variable since districts which have maintained schools with relatively high levels of racial isolation may find less need to engage in second-generation discrimination. If the schools are largely of one race, then there is less reason to use discriminatory punishment or tracking policies to exclude black pupils from regular classes. Moreover, districts with some largely black schools may staff these predominantly with black faculty, and therefore there would be less evidence of faculty discrimination.

Size

It is in school districts with small enrollments that racial balance among schools has come closest to being achieved.[38] Therefore, to the extent that second-generation discrimination is used to perpetuate racial isolation, it would be more attractive in less populous districts. Average daily attendance figures for the fall of 1973 are used to measure size.

Results of Regression Analysis

Table 9-2 reports the unstandardized regression coefficients for the eight independent variables for the three discrimination measures in the states analyzed. We also report the coefficient of multiple determination. Unstandardized regression coefficients are used because they, unlike other measures of relationships, can be compared across samples.[39]

Inspection of the unstandardized regression coefficients reveals that there are frequent differences among states in the magnitude of the coefficients and/or in the direction of the relationships for the three independent variables.

Despite a frequent lack of pattern in table 9-2, a few things become apparent. First, district size is insignificant as a predictor of second-generation discrimination. Second, local responsiveness to efforts to desegregate the schools is not a strong predictor of the incidence of later discrimination. Third, districts with large black enrollments tend to have lower scores on the special education and punishment indices but higher scores on the faculty discrimination index. Fourth, urban school systems are less likely than rural ones to have higher student-teacher ratios among blacks than whites. Fifth, systems in which more racial isolation persists among schools are less likely to discriminate against blacks in special education assignments or in faculty hiring. Sixth, districts which get relatively large shares of their school revenue from the federal government are less likely to give evidence of discriminatory punishment or personnel actions.

Looking at the coefficients of multiple determination, we see that with a few exceptions the independent variables do not succeed in accounting for much of the variance. Of the twelve values of R^2, seven are .16 or smaller and only two exceed .30. For all three types of postdesegregation discrimination, the independent variables explain more of the variance in Louisiana than in the

Table 9-2
Unstandardized Regression Coefficients and R^2 for Second-Generation Discrimination Measures Using Selected Independent Variables by State, 1973

State	Constant	Local Responce	Wallace Vote	Percentage Black	Percentage Urban	Economic Discrim- ination	Federal Aid	Index of Dissimilarity	Size	R^2
						Special Education				
VA	2.06	+.36	+ 2.88	-1.58	+ .95	-1.15	+20.90	-3.98	+.004	.12
FL	6.29	+.17	- 1.67	-4.65	+ .28	+ .14	- 1.32	- .85	-.0008	.13
GA	3.01	-.07	+11.58	+4.91	-3.18	-1.25	-23.97	-2.43	+.006	.12
LA	3.56	+.36	- 1.95	-2.70	-4.63	+9.68	+ 2.33	-7.46	+.004	.21
						Punishment				
VA	3.21	+.03	.76	- .64	+ .36	-1.28	- 1.31	+ .19	+.0007	.15
FL	3.06	+.02	+ .34	-2.60	+1.70	+ .06	+ 1.68	- .39	-.0006	.09
GA	1.85	+.05	+ 5.64	-3.48	- .53	+ .53	- 7.54	+1.06	-.003	.11
LA	8.19	-.14	- 4.21	-4.55	-1.18	a	.94	- .98	-.0004	.46
						Faculty				
VA	6.59	-.16	- 3.62	+1.24	-1.12	-3.47	- .89	- .97	-.0004	.22
FL	1.92	-.09	+ 1.17	+2.53	-1.14	+ .05	+ 2.49	- .96	-.0003	.16
GA	1.13	-.06	- .77	+1.09	- .34	+ .33	+ 5.05	+ .74	-.0006	.27
LA	.09	-.07	+ 1.04	+2.18	.48	a	a	.61	-.001	.49

[a]B too small to enter regression equation.

other states. This difference is especially pronounced on the punishment index. The R^2 tend to be smallest for the Florida schools. Overall, the independent variables are least successful in explaining variance in the special education index scores and most successful for the faculty measure. In summary, the independent variables do a reasonably good job of explaining variance in punishment and faculty discrimination in Louisiana. They display some, albeit lesser, utility in accounting for variance in faculty discrimination in Georgia and Virginia and special education in Louisiana.

Summary and Conclusions

This research provides a more comprehensive and more systematic look at the incidence of postdesegregation discrimination than had previously been available. The results confirm the impressions gathered by civil rights activists and scholars based on more limited data bases. We find that blacks are almost universally overrepresented in special education classes and among those suspended or expelled. While somewhat less extensive, there is also substantial evidence that blacks are underrepresented on school faculties. Despite some variations, there is strong evidence of extensive discrimination in every state on at least one dimension for each of the two thresholds used in table 9–1. With so many school districts having scores on the discrimination indices in excess of 2.0, it seems fair to conclude that federal policy is failing to achieve equal educational opportunities in the South on a massive scale.

Despite the frequently high levels of black overrepresentation in the student indices and underrepresentation in the faculty index, there is wide variation among states. This, coupled with the variations in the sizes and direction of unstandardized regression coefficients and the coefficients of multiple determination, suggests that the correlates of second-generation discrimination vary substantially from state to state. However, with a few exceptions, we have not succeeded in isolating the variables which are useful in accounting for variance in levels of discrimination. At best we had mixed success when using correlates of second-generation discrimination. Blacks are more seriously overrepresented in special education in districts having lower black enrollments, where desegregation is more complete and where more coercion was needed before the local school system responded positively and desegregated. This suggests that special education classes are being used to create largely one-race classes in relatively well-desegregated schools. Black exclusion through punishment is most common where there are relatively few blacks and where federal aid is a smaller component of the school budget. Black employment discrimination occurs in rural districts where black enrollments are high, black enrollments are fairly constant among schools, and the federal contribution to the school budget is low. From this we infer that districts underselect black teachers when a large black student population has been evenly distributed across a system's schools.

The policy implications of these findings are that considerations which were important to local school authorities when they were deciding how to respond to desegregation requirements may not have the same weights when the objective is equal treatment within the schools. The mix of factors underlying the practice of second-generation discrimination may be more complex than were that which motivated the persistence of segregation. Federal policymakers and those charged with policy implementation need to undertake critical reviews designed to identify the correlates of the discriminatory actions which persist today. Our findings should alert policy officials not to assume that a common set of factors underlies the behavior of all states or that the same considerations are related to different types of discrimination within a single state. Moreover, policymakers should be aware that different types of districts may indulge in different types of discrimination.

With all this in mind, federal officials need to systematically confront districts in which there is strong evidence of bias and see if there is a bias-free explanation. Where school districts cannot make such a case, corrective action should be taken. Federal officials should also undertake a search for combinations of inducements and penalties with which to persuade school policymakers to devise and implement programs free of overt or institutional bias. Our findings that discriminatory punishment and personnel practices occur in districts where federal aid is a small component of the budget suggests that something more than federal fund cutoffs will be necessary to achieve equal educational opportunities.

Notes

1. Charles S. Bullock, III, and Harrell R. Rodgers, Jr., *Racial Equality in America: In Search of an Unfulfilled Goal* (Pacific Palisades, Calif.: Goodyear Publishing Company, 1975).

2. Kenneth B. Clark, "Clash of Cultures in the Classroom," in Meyer Weinberg, ed., *Integrated Education—Learning Together* (Chicago: Integrated Education Associates, 1964), pp. 18-25; Ray C. Rist, "Student Social Class and Teacher Expectations: The Self-Fulfilling Prophesy in Ghetto Education," *Harvard Education Review* 40 (1970): 416-451.

3. Tom McCullough, "Urban Education: 'It's No Big Thing,'" *Urban Education* 9 (1974): 117-135; Anne Stein, "Strategies for Failure," *Harvard Education Review* 41 (1971): 158-204.

4. Dorothy C. Clement, Margaret Eisenhart, and John W. Wood, "School Desegregation and Educational Inequality: Trends in the Literature, 1960-

1975," *The Desegregation Literature: A Critical Appraisal* (Washington: National Institute of Education, 1976); Jane R. Mercer, "A Policy Statement on Assessment Procedures and the Rights of Children," *Harvard Educational Review* 44, no. 1 (1974): 125–141.

5. David L. Kirp and Mark G. Yudof, *Educational Policy and the Law: Cases and Materials* (Berkeley, Calif.: McCutchan Publishing Corporation, 1974), p. 668.

6. *It's Not Over in the South: School Desegregation in Forty-Three Southern Cities Eighteen Years after Brown,* Report by Alabama Council on Human Relations; American Friends Service Committee; Delta Ministry of the National Council of Churches; NAACP Legal Defense and Educational Fund, Inc.; Southern Regional Council; and Washington Research Project, 1974.

7. *The Status of School Desegregation in the South, 1970.* Report by American Friends Service Committee; Delta Ministry of the National Council of Churches; Lawyers Committee/or Civil Rights under Law; Lawyers Constitutional Defense Committee; NAACP Legal Defense and Educational Fund, Inc.; and Washington Research Project, 1971, p. 35.

8. *Children out of School in America,* Report by Children's Defense Fund of the Washington Research Project, Inc., 1974.

9. *Moses* v. *Washington Parish School Board,* 330 F. Supp. 1340 (1971).

10. *Larry P.* v. *Riles,* 343 F. Supp. 1306 (1972).

11. *McNeal* v. *Tate County Board of Education,* 508 F.2d 1400 (1975).

12. *Status of School Desegregation in the South,* pp. 62–63.

13. *It's Not Over in the South,* pp. 75–82.

14. *The Student Pushout: Victims of Continued Resistance to Desegregation,* Report by Southern Regional Council and Robert F. Kennedy Memorial, 1973, p. 22.

15. Joyce D. Miller, "Student Suspensions in Boston: Derailing Desegregation," *Inequality in Education,* no. 20 (July 1975): 16–24.

16. *Children Out of School in America,* pp. 5, 133.

17. *School Suspensions: Are They Helping Children?* Report by Children's Defense Fund of the Washington Research Project, Inc., 1975, pp. 12–14.

18. "Student Discipline," HEW Fact Sheet, Office for Civil Rights, May 1975, n.p.

19. Letter from Peter E. Holmes to Richard W. Boone, Director, Robert F. Kennedy Memorial, Washington, D.C., May 29, 1974, p. 3.

20. *School Suspensions,* pp. 72–73.

21. *Woods* v. *Wright,* 334 F.2d 369 (1964).

22. Cf. *Stevenson* v. *Board of Education of Wheeler County Georgia,* 462 F.2d 1154 (1970).

23. *Hawkins* v. *Coleman,* 376 F. Supp. 1330 (1974).

24. *Status of School Desegregation in the South,* p. 75.

25. *It's Not Over in the South*, pp. 84–95.

26. Junie Brown, "State School Hits Black Ousters," *Atlanta Journal*, March 18, 1971, pp. 1, 15.

27. *U.S.* v. *Jefferson County Board of Education*, 372 F.2d 836 (1966).

28. *Williams* v. *Kimbrough*, 295 F. Supp. 585 (1969).

29. Harrell R. Rodgers, Jr., and Charles S. Bullock, III, *Coercion to Compliance* (Lexington, Mass.: Lexington Books, D.C. Heath, 1976).

30. Charles S. Bullock, III, "Compliance with School Desegregation Laws: Financial Inducements and Policy Performance," Paper presented to annual meeting of the American Political Science Association, Chicago, September 2–5, 1976.

31. The major problem with the Rodgers-Bullock index is its variation and the cause thereof. The maximum of their index is determined by the percentage of black students in the system. The smaller the percentage of blacks in the system, the larger the maximum possible index. For example, a district with 2 percent black enrollment would have a maximum score of 50. This would be the score if the entire category were black. However, if the district were 40 percent black, the district's maximum could be only 2.5, even if the entire category were black.

32. The Supreme Court would reject our use of proportionality as a goal, at least in some types of districts. In *Hazlewood School District* v. *U.S.* (1977) the court held that the basis for evaluating whether a school district practiced racial discrimination in its personnel policies was the proportion of black teachers in surrounding districts and not the proportion of blacks among Hazlewood students. The decision did not, however, indicate whether the Hazlewood schools should be compared only with other suburban districts or if the St. Louis city schools where black faculty proportions were higher should be included. It may have been important that the Hazlewood schools have only a tiny black enrollment. Because of lingering questions it would be impossible to compute a faculty discrimination index along the general outlines of the *Hazlewood* decision.

The computation of our index is more in keeping with the standard used by the OCR in evaluating the faculty compositon of schools seeking Emergency School Aid funds. The OCR compares the present racial composition of the faculty with that of the year before desegregation began. At that time black student-teacher ratios tended to be only slightly higher than white student-teacher ratios.

33. Bullock, "Compliance with School Desegregation Laws."

34. Michael K. Fitzgerald and David R. Morgan, "Changing Patterns of Urban School Desegregation," *American Politics Quarterly* 5 (October 1977): 437–463.

35. Thomas R. Dye, "Urban School Segregation: A Comparative Analysis,"

Urban Affairs Quarterly 4 (December 1968): 141–165; Donald R. Matthews and James W. Prothro, "Stateways Versus Folkways: Critical Factors in Southern Reactions to *Brown* v. *Board of Education,*" in Gottfried Dietz, ed., *Essays on the American Constitution* (Englewood Cliffs, N.J.: Prentice-Hall, 1964), pp. 139–156; Thomas Pettigrew and M.R. Cramer, "The Demography of Desegregation," *Journal of Social Issues* 15 (Fall 1968): 440–443; and Beth Vanfossen, "Variables Related to Resistance to Desegregation in the South," *Social Forces* 47 (September 1968): 39–44.

36. Charles S. Bullock, III, "Desegregating Urban Areas: Is It Worth It? Can It Be Done?" *School Review* 84 (May 1976): 431.

37. Cf. Rodgers and Bullock, *Coercion to Compliance.*

38. Ibid.

39. Christopher H. Achen, "Measuring Representation: Perils of the Correlation Coefficient," *American Journal of Political Science* 21 (November 1977): 805–815.

10 Abortion Policy since 1973: Political Cleavage and Its Impact on Policy Outputs

Howard A. Palley

In 1973, the year of the Supreme Court's decisions of *Roe* v. *Wade* and *Doe* v. *Bolton* which limited the legal basis for forbidding abortions, 744,600 legal abortions were reported. By 1974 this rate had increased to 1,034,200.[1] In spite of the increased number of abortions obtained since 1973, political constraints within various states and within the health care service system have resulted in the denial of basic abortion services to hundreds of thousands of women in need of legal abortion services. This chapter examines the broad political processes surrounding abortion policies in the wake of the Supreme Court's 1973 abortion decisions and the impact of such processes on abortion policies culminating in the withholding of federal Medicaid funds in the case of nontherapeutic abortions in August 1977.

In a classic article on "incremental" decision making, Lindblom asserts that the "test of 'good' policy" utilizing the incremental method ". . . is [general] agreement on policy itself. . . ."[2] Elsewhere he notes: "Agreement on policy thus becomes the only practicable test of the policy's correctness."[3] The Supreme Court's abortion decisions of 1973, which affirmed (with some qualifications) a woman's right to choose abortion, represent a case of policy formulation which "preceded" overall societal agreement on policy. Although general public opinion increasingly supports a woman's right to choose abortion, intense opposition to this position is spearheaded by Catholic clerical and lay opposition. Also, such opposition is not limited to the Catholic Church, similar opposition stands having been taken by the Eastern Orthodox Church, the Lutheran Church-Missouri Synod, the Church of Jesus Christ of Latter-day Saints, and some fundamentalist denominations. Thus, the Supreme Court's decisions were rendered in an atmosphere of considerable political cleavage based on disagreement regarding basic social and human values.[4] Indeed, the value conflict discussed here involves conflicting ideological systems. *Ideology* may be defined as ". . . a set of beliefs revolving around one or a few pre-eminent values [which is] . . . generally comprehensive and tends to be reductionist, in other words complex issues are reduced to simple explanations."[5] Where disagreement on ideology is strong, such ideologies are incompatible and the relationships between adherents of rival positions result in conflict reflected by political cleavage.[6] The result of intense opposition to the Court's decisions has been a number of actions, pri-

marily at the level of state law and within the public and private hospital systems
—but also at the congressional level—to constrain and limit the impact of the
1973 Supreme Court abortion decisions.

This chapter reviews the Supreme Court's 1973 decisions. It discusses the
nature of both liberalization of abortion policy stemming from the 1973 decisions and constraints to a more liberal abortion policy reflected in state laws,
congressional action, restrictive hospital policies, and even in some subsequent
Supreme Court decisions.[7] The lens through which this discussion can best be
viewed is perhaps the recognition that political cleavage regarding ideological
differences with respect to basic social and human values will act as a significant
constraint on policy initiatives undertaken *in spite of* such basic disagreements
within the body politic.

Roe v. *Wade* and *Doe* v. *Bolton:* A Review of the Cases

On January 22, 1973, the Supreme Court passed judgment on two abortion
cases. These cases have had a profound impact on public policy concerning
abortion. The first case, *Roe* v. *Wade,*[8] concerned an 1857 Texas statute limiting
abortion to "the purpose of saving the life of the mother." The companion case,
Doe v. *Bolton,*[9] concerned a 1968 Georgia statute limiting abortion to cases in
which the health of a pregnant woman was endangered, the fetus was likely to
have a serious defect at birth, or the pregnancy was the result or rape. Furthermore, the Georgia statute required a number of other stipulations upon which
service was conditional. It required (1) Joint Commission on Accreditation of
Hospitals (JCAH) accreditation of the hospital where abortion services were to
be performed, (2) that the woman be a Georgia resident, and (3) that an abortion case have the concurrence of two additional physicians (besides the attending physician), approval by a three-member abortion committee within the
hospital, and certification in rape cases.

In introducing *Roe* v. *Wade,* the Supreme Court acknowledged that ". . .
one's philosophy, one's experiences, one's exposure to the raw edges of human
existence, one's religious training, one's attitude toward life and family and their
values, and the moral standards one establishes and seeks to observe are all likely
to influence and color one's thinking and conclusions about abortion."

The Court based its overall decision in *Roe* v. *Wade* on the Fourteenth
Amendment right of privacy. It held that "this right of privacy . . . [was to be
found] in the Fourteenth Amendment's concept of personal liberty and restrictions upon state action. . . ." It concluded: "[This right] is broad enough to
encompass a woman's decision whether or not to terminate her pregnancy. The
detriment that the State would impose upon the pregnant woman by denying

this choice altogether is apparent." This view was qualified by the observation that

> the privacy right . . . cannot be held to be absolute. . . . [T]he state may properly assert important interests in safeguarding health, in maintaining medical standards, and in protecting potential life. At some point in pregnancy, these respective interests become sufficiently compelling to sustain regulation of the factors that govern the abortion decision.

The Court went on to note that

> With respect to the State's important and legitimate interest in the health of the mother, the "compelling" point, in light of present medical knowledge, is at approximately the end of the first trimester. . . . [U]ntil the end of the first trimester mortality in abortion is less than mortality in childbirth.

Therefore, the state had no compelling right to intervene in abortion decisions during the first trimester. The Court also stated: "With respect to the State's important and legitimate interest in potential life, the 'compelling' point is its viability. This is so because the fetus then presumably has the capacity of meaningful life outside the mother's womb."

During the first trimester, the abortion decision is left to the pregnant women's attending physician. The Court states specifically that "for the stage prior to approximately the end of the first trimester, the abortion decision and its effectuation must be left to the medical judgement of the pregnant women's attending physician . . . in consultation with his patient."

Furthermore, in the second trimester, or more precisely,

> for the stage subsequent to approximately the end of the first trimester, the State, in promoting its interest in the health of the mother, may, if it chooses, regulate the abortion procedure in ways that are reasonably related to maternal health. . . . Examples of permissible state regulation in this area are requirements as to the qualifications of the person who is to perform the abortion; as to the licensure of that person; as to the facility in which the procedure is to be performed.

In the third trimester, or as the Court states, "for the stage subsequent to viability," the Court held that "the state, in promoting its interest in the potentiality of human life, may, if it chooses, regulate, and even proscribe, abortion except where it is necessary, in appropriate medical judgement, for the preservation of the life or health of the mother." Thus, the laws of the state may intervene to restrict the availability of abortion *except* in such cases where the "preservation" of a mother's life or health is involved.

In the companion Georgia decision, *Doe* v. *Bolton,* the Supreme Court dealt with four issues of state prerogative: residence requirement, JCAH accreditation requirement, abortion committee requirements, and the need for concurrence of two doctors, other than the attending physician, in abortion decisions.

With regard to the issue of residency, the Court succinctly noted: "We do not uphold the constitutionality of the residence requirement." It also held that as "in Georgia there is no restriction of the performance of non-abortion surgery in a hospital not yet accredited by the JCAH . . . the JCAH accrediation requirement [in order to perform an abortion] does not withstand constitutional scrutiny." The Court went on to reject the requirement under Georgia law of abortion committee approval of abortion and the Georgia requirement of concurrence by two additional doctors prior to permission for an abortion. In making such judgments, the Court clearly held that the state of Georgia could not place special barriers on hospitals and other health care facilities in the area of abortion services which did not apply in other areas of health services.

These two abortion decisions severely limited state action with regard to denial of abortion services by the states (at least in the first two trimesters of pregnancy) and limited the state's right to establish special barriers in terms of institutional requirements which limit abortion services where similar requirements are not provided for other health care services.

Other Federal Court Action

A number of state attempts to limit the applicability of the 1973 abortion decisions have been overruled or modified by the Supreme Court. On July 1, 1976, the Supreme Court made a number of abortion-related decisions. The Court ruled in a decision involving the state of Missouri that states may not give to a husband the right to veto a woman's decision to have an abortion.[10] In a companion case, the Court ruled that states may not give parents a blanket veto power over abortions which are sought by their unmarried daughters under 18 years of age and, in so doing, noted that "neither the Fourteenth Amendment nor the Bill of Rights is for adults alone."[11] The Supreme Court also reviewed a number of sections of the restrictive 1974 Missouri abortion law in *Planned Parenthood of Central Missouri* v. *Danforth.* In so doing, the Court upheld unanimously a requirement that pregnant women prior to submitting to an abortion during the first twelve weeks of pregnancy give written, uncoerced "informed consent" in advance of an abortion. The Court also unanimously upheld the requirement of detailed abortion record keeping by physicians as long as such requirements are "not absurd or overdone" by state officials. By a 5-to-4 vote, the Court overruled the Missouri prohibition against the saline method of abortion (saline amniocentesis) after the first 12 weeks of pregnancy on the grounds that the state ban was ". . . an unreasonable and arbitrary regulation designed to inhibit the vast majority of abortions after the first 12 weeks."

Thus, in these cases the Supreme Court sought to prevent states from developing laws intent on undermining or contravening its 1973 decisions. Specifically, it overturned a number of restrictive state laws passed in the wake of the 1973 decisions.

In 1977 in an attempt to avoid "the political thicket" the Court retreated somewhat from the 1973 decisions. It upheld state Medicaid laws and public hospital practices which forbade "nontherapeutic" abortions, that is, abortions in which the mother's life is not at issue. In its June 20, 1977 opinions, the Supreme Court held that states may refuse to spend public money for abortion services for poor mothers where the operations are not judged to be medically necessary. In *Maher* v. *Roe*[12] and *Beal* v. *Doe*[13] the Court noted that states are not required under Medicaid, the federal program in question, to provide nontherapeutic abortions. In a related case, *Poelker* v. *Doe,*[14] the Court held that a public hospital in St. Louis could not be required to perform elective abortions.

In *Beal* v. *Doc,* the Court also held that the language of Title XIX of the Social Security Act, which required states to establish "reasonable standards" for the first six months of pregnancy to only those certified as "medically necessary." In the Connecticut case of *Maher* v. *Roe* the issue was whether a state providing for Medicaid payments is denying equal protection of the laws by paying only for "medically necessary," first-trimester operations. The case of *Poelker* v. *Doe* involved curtailment of abortion services in a public hospital, Starkloff Hospital, in St. Louis. A policy directive by Mayor John H. Poelker forbidding elective abortions in the St. Louis public hospitals plus the long-time practice of staffing the Starkloff Hospital's obstetrics-gynecology clinic with faculty and students from a local Jesuit-operated medical school, St. Louis University School of Medicine, served to prevent women from receiving elective abortions. Mayor Poelker's directive which had been communicated to the City of St. Louis' Director of Health and Hospitals prohibited performance of abortions in city hospitals except in cases where there was a threat of grave physiological injury or death to the mother.

In the majority opinion in *Beal* v. *Doe,* Justice Lewis F. Powell, Jr., upheld the state's discretion to fund or not fund nontherapeutic abortions. Justice Powell declared, "The issues present policy decisions of the widest concern. They should be resolved by the representatives of the people, not by this Court."

In *Beal* v. *Doe,* the Court also held that the language of Title XIX of the Social Security Act, which required states to establish "reasonable standards" for determining the extent of medical assistance to be given in the state, allowed the states to decide not to fund elective abortions. In *Maher* v. *Roe,* the Court went on to observe that the constitutional guarantee of equal protection of the law was not violated where state Medicaid programs deny funding of elective surgery in the first trimester—even where such programs, as in the case of Connecticut, provide funding for women who choose to bear their children. The decision indicated that *Roe* v. *Wade* did not require state provision of abortion services. The opinion in *Poelker* v. *Doe* which went unsigned rested on the opinion in the Pennsylvania case.

The dissenters to the Court's opinion felt that the Court's rulings constituted significant retreat from the 1973 abortion decisions. Dissenting in the *Maher* case, Justice William J. Brennan, Jr., argued:

> None can take seriously the Court's assurance that its conclusion signals no retreat from *Roe* [v. *Wade*] or the cases applying it. Indeed, it cannot be gainsaid that today's decision seriously erodes the principles that *Roe* and *Doe* [v. *Bolton*] announced to guide the determination of what constitutes an unconstitutional infringement of the fundamental right of pregnant women to be free to decide whether to have an abortion.

Justice Blackmun, who delivered the Court's 1973 decisions, also was critical of this decision. He noted that the majority conceded that an indigent, financially helpless pregnant woman might, if denied help through public programs, not be able to implement her right to have an abortion. Blackmun observed that the Court:

> . . . denies the realization and enjoyment of that right [to decide the outcome of her pregnancy] on the ground that existence and realization are separate and distinct. . . . [T]he result is punitive and tragic. Implicit in the court's holdings is the condescension that she may go elsewhere for her abortion. I find that disingenuous and alarming, almost reminiscent of "let them eat cake."

The Court's decision buttressed the position of fifteen states with laws in 1975 that would deny Medicaid funds for elective abortion. It also buttressed the position of the 82 percent of the nation's public hospitals which did not perform a single abortion in 1975. During this period an estimated 83,000 women seeking abortions had to leave their home states to receive such health services.[15]

In the wake of the Court's decision, government officials in a number of states, such as Missouri, Connecticut, and New Jersey, sought to institute policies halting state financing of elective abortions—by reinstituting laws that had been previously nullified by the federal courts or by changing existing state policies.[16] As publicly supported elective abortion policies ended or were restricted in a number of states by state action and congressional action, such services then fell to a voluntary sector ill prepared to support delivery of such services. As of March 31, 1978, only sixteen state welfare programs and the District of Columbia's welfare program continued to pay for all or most abortions. These states were Maryland, West Virginia, New York, Massachusetts, Pennsylvania, North Carolina, Michigan, Wisconsin, Iowa, Colorado, Idaho, Washington, Oregon, California, Alaska, and Hawaii. In these jurisdictions, all or most abortions were financed entirely by the respective state's or the District's own welfare funds without federal reimbursement.

The series of decisions reached by the Court since 1973 have fallen on the issue of equal protection. The 1976 decisions essentially state that, where abortions are permitted, special procedural barriers cannot be created within the health system to obstruct the receipt of abortion services. The 1977 decisions, however, leave with the states and their subunits (that is, local public hospitals), the right to decide whether to provide abortion services. Judicial dissenters and other critics of this decision maintain that the de facto impact of the 1977 decisions is indeed to deny to poor women equal protection of the law with respect to their right to choose abortion.

The immediate impact of the Supreme Court's June 20, 1977, decisions seems to confirm the fears of critics of the decision, who have asserted that it would increase the difficulty of poor women of obtaining abortions in some areas. Of the fifteen states having laws barring women from receiving Medicaid help for most abortions as of June 1977, nine had been enjoined by court order which, in light of the Supreme Court's decision, appeared to be no longer binding.[17] In light of the decision, Mayor James F. Conway immediately suspended all abortions at two public hospitals in St. Louis, Missouri, while the St. Louis County Supervisor Gene McNary issued an order which suspended the county's program of referring indigent women to an abortion clinic in the city of St. Louis.[18] Thus, immediately after the Court's decision, it was clear that the right of indigent women to an abortion in nine states and in the city of St. Louis had been curtailed.

Political Conflict and Legislative Attempts to Restrict the 1973 Decisions

Since the decisions of *Roe* v. *Wade* and *Doe* v. *Bolton,* opposition to these opinions has generally taken two forms of action: a campaign for reversal of the Court's decisions and a campaign for minimization of the impact of these decisions. This section deals with the latter campaign.

This campaign has particularly involved the Catholic Church—formally through the National Conference of Catholic Bishops and through the lay group which is informally tied to the Church, the National Right to Life Committee.[19] In 1974 the Diocese of Pittsburgh alone contributed $60,101 to "prolife" programs.[20] Through appeals to public opinion, pressure for legislative action, and litigation in court seeking to limit the applicability of the 1973 decisions, the Right to Life Movement has had some successes and some failures. This effort in opposition continues to be sustained. In November 1975, the National Conference of Catholic Bishops indicated its intent to use "all Church-sponsored or identifiably Catholic national, regional or diocesan and parochial organizations and agencies to create an anti-abortion political action network throughout the country." In August 1977, Archbishop Joseph L. Bernardin, president of the National Conference of Catholic Bishops in a speech presented to a Knights of Columbus meeting in Indianapolis, indicated a continued Roman Catholic Church effort against abortion. The Archbishop noted that the ending of abortion in the United States ". . . is a crucial test case for our respect for the right to life." He urged strenuous efforts to defeat ". . . existing or proposed legislation which would require the expenditure or taxpayers' money for elective abortions."[21] That the Roman Catholic Church plays a very active role in financing the antiabortion movement is indicated by diocesan contributions of $906,404 from January 1976 to March 1977 for the antiabortion National Committee for a Human Life Amendment.

By June 1977, antiabortion forces claimed 11 million activists organized in 3,000 chapters which were federated under the umbrella of the National Right to Life Committee.[22] Antiabortion forces operating at the congressional level and in state capitals urged that Medicaid funds not be used for abortions but rather that they be used for counseling of women with so-called problem pregnancies, for developing sex education courses, and for research with respect to safer contraceptives. Activities by antiabortion forces have generated a great deal of grass-roots activism. The Right to Life Movement has utilized neighborhood bake sales, dinner dances, and nominal membership dues for financing.[23]

On the other hand, proponents of the right to choose an abortion—which include Planned Parenthood, Americans for Democratic Action, the National Women's Political Caucus, and the National Abortion Rights Action League—have tended to rely on traditional lobbying methods and have not generated the intensity of the antiabortion forces.

Increasingly, in the wake of political defeats of advocates of liberal abortion policies in 1977, such groups began to speak out more forcefully.[24] It is worth noting the ways in which a proabortion or Prochoice Movement is increasingly active in attempting to counter the Right to Life Movement.[25] Often the coordinative body for "prochoice" activities is the National Abortion Rights Action League (NARAL). Other groups involved in political activity supportive of "choice" are the Religious Coalition for Abortion Rights (which includes the Methodists, the Presbyterians, the YWCA, the Southern Baptist Convention, and the Lutheran Church) the National Women's Political Caucus, the National Organization of Women, Americans for Democratic Action, the American Civil

Liberties Union, the American Public Health Association, the National Association of Social Workers, and the American Association of University Women.

A recent example of an attempt at coalition to exert pressure at the national level for a more prochoice stand was the August 1977 recommendation to President Carter by a number of women's organizations that he reconsider his opposition to the use of Medicaid funds for abortions. The groups included the American Association of University Women, the Center for Women Policy Studies, Federally Employed Women, Leadership Conference on Civil Rights, Mexican American Women's National Association, the National Council of Negro Women, the National Women's Political Caucus, the Women's Equity Action League, the National Organization for Women's Legal Defense and Educational Fund, and the Women's Lobby.[26]

Among groups lobbying for more liberal abortion rights, a representative of NARAL often chairs national meetings concerned with political strategy. Many of the other groups listed seek to activate their local constituencies. NARAL works particularly closely with Planned Parenthood and the Religious Coalition for Abortion Rights. The Women's Political Caucus also conducts a special political action, prochoice project aimed at political leadership throughout the country at a state and national level. Prochoice groups have sought to influence Congress with telegrams opposing the so-called Hyde Amendment. They have avoided neighborhood grass-roots organization in part because they lack the necessary financial support. NARAL itself has also conducted a newspaper project which releases items to over 600 local papers which generally favor abortion rights. Increasingly the prochoice movement had become more intensely active by the latter part of 1977 as it had shaken off the complacency which occurred in the wake of the *Roe* v. *Wade* and *Doe* v. *Bolton* decisions.

An initial success by the opponents of liberal abortion policies had occurred in 1973. This event was Senator Frank Church's (D-Idaho) amendment to the Public Health Services Act. The amendment exempted institutions as well as individuals from being "forced" to provide or perform abortions which were against their moral or religious views. This law initially raised the issue as to whether tax-supported institutions could deny a basic health service—an issue which was subsequently raised in an unsuccessful federal court challenge.[27]

Opponents of liberal abortion policies also have sought to restrict the use of federal funds for obtaining abortion services. In September 1976, Congress passed a law which banned the use of federal funds to perform abortions for the poor unless the mother's life was endangered by pregnancy. This provision, the Conte Amendment [Rep. Silvio O. Conte (R-Mass.)] more popularly misnamed the Hyde Amendment, prohibited use of federal funds to pay for abortions "except where the life of the mother would be endangered if the fetus were carried to term." The Congressional Conference Committee, in accepting the Conte Amendment, issued in its report a statement indicating that the intent of the provision was to limit federal funding of abortions to cases where the life of the mother was "clearly endangered by disease" and to bar such funding for abortions for "family planning or the emotional or social convenience of the mother."[28] This law, which would have denied such elective health care services to Medicaid patients, was initially held to be unconstitutional by a New York Federal District Court judge. Judge John F. Dooling, Jr., held that "the state and Federal Governments are linked in a financial partnership to provide for medical assistance to the needy. . . . [Such] needy are citizens of the United States no less than of the states of their residence." Denial of such health care service, he noted, constituted unequal protection of the law for indigent women.[29]

On August 4, 1977, Judge Dooling, noting the June 1977 Supreme Court decisions, withdrew his order requiring the federal government to pay for elective abortions for the poor. This allowed the so-called Hyde Amendment to be enforced immediately. Secretary of Health, Education, and Welfare Joseph A. Califano quickly announced that the federal government would provide funds for abortions only in situations ". . . where the attending physician on the basis of his or her professional judgement, has certified that abortion is necessary because the life of the mother would be endangered were the fetus carried to term."[30] Shortly following these actions the Planned Parenthood Federation of American released a report indicating that publicly financed abortions for the poor had been abolished in over twenty states and that in only fourteen states were such abortions still easily obtainable.[31] In fiscal year 1976 Medicaid and Title XX funds were estimated to have paid for over 260,000 abortions at a total public cost of almost $61 million.[32]

Karen Mulhauser, executive director of the National Abortion Rights Action League, noted, "Ending federal funding of abortion will not stop abortions but will take away the choice of poor women to have a medically safe, legal abortion."[33] The opponents of abortion reform clearly have been politically effective. This is a reality in spite of the fact that general public opinion favors liberal abortion policies by a large majority. (The aftermath of the 1973 Supreme Court abortion decisions has been a period of greater general public acceptance of the right to abortion, as reflected in the results of a number of public opinion surveys conducted by the Roper Organization, the Harris Survey, the New York Times/CBS News Survey, and the National Opinion Research Center Survey.)

In spite of this support for the availability of abortion services, intense opposition by opponents of abortion reform has been effective in influencing Congress to pass restrictions on the use of federal funds for abortions. However, such restrictions, as we have noted, were blocked by federal court action until August 1977.

In December 1977, Congress again passed restrictive legislation preventing the use of federal funds for the performance of most abortions. This legislation forbade the use of such funds with respect to the performance of an abortion

. . . except where the life of the mother would be endangered if the fetus were carried to term; or except for such medical procedures necessary for the victims of rape or incest, when such rape or incest has been reported promptly to a law enforcement agency or public health service; or except in those instances where severe and long-lasting physical health damage to the mother would result if the pregnancy were carried to term when so determined by two physicians.

Conclusion

The 1973 Supreme Court decisions of *Roe* v. *Wade* and *Doe* v. *Bolton* have resulted in an increase in the provision of abortion services—in circumstances where a pregnant woman and her consulting physician viewed an abortion desirable. However, controversies have arisen as to the propriety and morality of abortions and the nature of circumstances which would "justify" abortion. Spearheaded by Catholic clerical and lay organizations, the opponents of liberal abortion policies have sought to curtail the availability of such abortion services. The strategies utilized have included effective grass-roots organization, letter writing, appeals to legislators on both state and congressional levels, appeals to public opinion, and court tests. Such activities have successfully limited the availability of abortion to many women desiring such services. As of August 1977, congressional and Supreme Court actions combined to limit sharply the availability of abortion to low-income mothers seeking such services under the federal-state Medicaid program. This action also serves to exacerbate regional inequities whereby major providers of abortion services are concentrated in the large cities of the East and West coasts.[34]

Those advocates of more liberal availability of abortion services are in the process of countermobilizing to fight battles which they had viewed as won in the wake of *Roe, Doe,* and subsequent lower-court rulings. In the short run, political conflict and debate about abortion will intensify. The political process surrounding policy outputs regarding availability of abortion services reflects intensely conflicting ideological systems. The political cleavages existing around this issue are unlikely to be resolved by a compromise satisfactory to all. However, recent public opinion studies indicating that sizable majorities of Protestants and Jews, as well as substantial numbers of Catholics, accept the performance of abortions in a number of circumstances may auger a *long-run* decline in the intensity of public debate and political conflict surrounding the availability of abortion services.

In spite of some setbacks regarding provision of abortion services in 1977, abortion services have increased greatly since the 1973 Supreme Court decisions. It is likely, however, that this trend of greater availability of abortion services will be reversed in the short run.

Notes

1. Ellen Sullivan, Christopher Tetze, and Joy G. Dryfoos, "Legal Abortion in the United States, 1975-1976," *Family Planning Perspectives* 9 (May/June, 1977): 116.

2. Charles E. Lindblom, "The Science of 'Muddling Through,'" *Public Administration Review* 19 (Spring 1959): 83.

3. Ibid., p. 84.

4. Arend Lijphart, "Cultural Diversity and Theories of Political Integration," *Canadian Journal of Political Science* 4 (March 1971): 1-6. Also see Yehezekel Dror, *Design for Policy Sciences* (New York: American Elsevier, 1971), pp. 57-58.

5. Derek Birrell and Alan Murie, "Ideology, Conflict and Social Policy," *Journal of Social Policy* 4 (July 1975): 244. Also see Giovanni Sartori, "Politics, Ideology and Belief Systems," *American Political Science Review* 63 (June 1969): 410-411.

6. Birrell and Murie, ibid., pp. 245-246.

7. For a discussion of the impact of political constraints on policy initiatives see Giandomenico Majone, "The Feasibility of Social Policies," *Policy Sciences* 6 (March 1975): 55-57.

8. 410 U.S. 113 (1973).

9. 410 U.S. 179 (1973).

10. *Planned Parenthood of Central Missouri* v. *Danforth*, 428 U.S. 52 (1976).

11. *Bellotti* v. *Baird*, 428 U.S. 132 (1976).

12. 45 L.W. 4787 (1977).

13. 45 L.W. 4781 (1977).

14. 45 L.W. 4794 (1977).

15. Morton Mintz, "Court Says State Needn't Fund Abortions," *Wilmington Morning News*, June 21, 1977, p. 2.

16. "Supreme Court Ruling Sparks Moves to Halt Medicaid Abortions," *New York Times*, June 27, 1977, p. 32.

17. Marc Charney, "Ruling Brings New Look at Free Abortion Policy," *Wilmington Morning News*, June 22, 1977, p. 13.

18. Ibid.

19. Marion K. Sanders, "Enemies of Abortion," *Harper's* 248 (March 1974): 26.

20. Beatrice Blair, "Men Vote, Women Die," *New York Times*, April 3, 1975, p. 37.

21. Kenneth A. Briggs, "Catholics Beginning an Expanded Drive against Abortions," *New York Times*, August 17, 1977, pp. 1, 44.

22. "The Showdown Seems Near," *New York Times*, June 26, 1977, sec. 4, p. 1.

23. Ibid.

24. "27 Groups Acclaim Women Who Oppose Carter on Abortion," *New York Times,* August 16, 1977, p. 13.

25. This section relies primarily on an analysis appearing in Joyce Gelb and Marian Lief Palley, "The Interest Group System and the Politics of Moderation," Northeast Political Science Association annual meeting, Mt. Pocono, Pennsylvania, November 10-12, 1977 (mimeographed).

26. "27 Groups Acclaim Women Who Oppose Carter on Abortions."

27. 513 F.2d 873 (1975); 423 U.S. 1000 (1975); 424 U.S. 948 (1976).

28. "Abortion Provision Compromise," *Congressional Quarterly Almanac,* vol. 32 (Washington: Congressional Quarterly, Inc., 1976), p. 803.

29. Max H. Seigel, "U.S. Court Voids Abortion Curbs under Medicaid," *New York Times,* October 23, 1976, p. 1.

30. E.J. Dionne, Jr., "Federal Judge Lifts Order Requiring U.S. to Pay for Abortions," *New York Times,* August 5, 1977, p. 1.

31. Briggs, "Catholics Beginning an Expanded Drive," p. 44.

32. Richard Lincoln, Brigitte Döring-Bradley, Barbara L. Lindheim, and Maureen A. Cotterill, "The Court, the Congress and the President: Turning Back the Clock on the Pregnant Poor," *Family Planning Perspectives* 9 (September/October 1977): 209.

33. Betty Ann Williams, "House Rejects Aid for Abortions," *Wilmington News-Journal,* June 18, 1977, p. 2.

34. Sullivan, Tetze, and Dryfoos, "Legal Abortion in the United States," p. 117.

Part IV
The Impact of Legislative
Enactments

11

Combating Dual Discrimination: The Impact of Civil Rights Policies on the Income Status of Black Women

Donald J. McCrone and
Richard J. Hardy

A great deal has been written under the rubric of public policy in the past decade and a half. Until recently, however, many political scientists were content with merely describing the origins and provisions of various public policies; little effort was expended on evaluating the consequences of policy decisions. Today's emphasis on relevancy has made members of the discipline keenly aware of the need to assess the impact of public policies. One policy area that offers a significant opportunity for political scientists to broaden their understanding of the impact process is that of civil rights.

The Civil Rights Act of 1964 and the policies it generated signify a dramatic change in the federal government's commitment toward ending discrimination in employment. Until the passage of Title VII of the Civil Rights Act of 1964, women—especially black women—had few legal weapons with which to combat discrimination in employment. Title VII is unprecedented in that it both prohibits job discrimination based on race and sex and provides the necessary machinery to enforce such a prohibition. We believe that if these policies have attenuated racial and sexual discrimination in employment, then this will be reflected in the aggregate income of black women. The purpose of this chapter, therefore, is to determine if the relative income of black women has improved systematically and significantly since the implementation of these civil rights policies in 1965.

Perhaps the best single indicator of the impact of these policies is change in the income ratio of black women to white men (BW/WM) over time. This ratio is obtained by dividing the annual median income of black women by the annual median income of white men from 1948 through 1976.[1] Our selection of white men as the criterion group for black women is based on the fundamental assumption that white men constitute the standard of economic success in U.S. society. Whereas black men suffer from racial discrimination and white women suffer from sexual discrimination, black women are afflicted by dual discrimination based on race *and* sex. A major concern of black women, then, is to close the gap between their income and that of white men. While an income ratio of less than unity is not a function solely of current discriminatory practices, the goal of civil rights policies is to move toward greater income equality. Hence, we focus not on the absolute magnitude of the income ratio, but on how the ratio does or does not change over time.

We address ourselves to three central questions in this chapter. Do changes in the BW/WM income ratio stem from cyclical economic conditions and/or government policies associated with the Civil Rights Act of 1964? Are changes in the BW/WM income ratio nationally and regionally a function of similar economic and/or political factors? And what income changes, if any, can we anticipate for black women based on the continued enforcement of current civil rights policies? We utilize an interrupted time-series analysis to determine the relative effects of economic and policy conditions on the BW/WM income ratio, both nationally and regionally, since 1948.

Civil Rights Policies since 1964

Before 1964 legal efforts to end discrimination in employment based on race and sex were practically nonexistent. Although eighteen states had laws banning both racial and sexual discrimination in employment prior to 1964, these laws were narrow in objective and limited to only piecemeal enforcement.[2] The first federal legislation prohibiting discrimination in employment was the Equal Pay Act (EPA) of 1963. This act prohibited differential pay rates to women and men who do equal work under similar conditions requiring equal skill, effort, and responsibility. Unfortunately, the EPA was devoid of provisions banning racial discrimination, and it allowed for three very large exceptions under which wage differentials could be justified—seniority systems, merit systems, and systems measuring earnings by quality or quantity of production. Furthermore, until it was amended in 1972, the EPA extended only to establishments covered by the Fair Labor Standards Act of 1938 which did business in excess of $250,000 per year. Thus, millions of women, such as those employed in small retail establishments, restaurants, and the home, were specifically excluded from EPA coverage.

There are five paramount reasons why we consider the Civil Rights Act of 1964 the watershed in federal policies aimed at improving the economic status of black women. First, the Civil Rights Act of 1964 embodies the most positive and pervasive effort ever made by the federal government to end racial and sexual discrimination. Initially Title VII forbade any union or firm employing more than twenty-five persons to discriminate, and it protected an estimated three-fourths of the national labor force.[3] To secure compliance under this act, the Equal Employment Opportunity Commission (EEOC) was established to investigate and negotiate complaints of discrimination, and the Attorney General was empowered to sue or intercede in civil litigation involving a "pattern or practice" of discrimination. Congress amended Title VII in 1972 to give the EEOC direct access to federal district courts and enlarged its jurisdiction to include state and local government workers as well as all unions and businesses employing fifteen or more persons. This amendment permits the EEOC to become directly involved with systemic problems affecting job equality throughout an entire employment operation, instead of relying entirely on individual complaints.[4] Although the EEOC has been criticized for being overworked and understaffed,[5] no one can deny that the EEOC has greatly involved the federal government in the area of civil rights.

Second, the courts have interpreted Title VII in ways likely to stimulate demand for blacks and women.[6] The importance of the courts in this matter cannot be overstated. According to Title VII, the EEOC is forbidden to require statistical balancing or preferential treatment in the hiring of blacks or women. With the aid of the courts, however, such practices have become common. In building a *prima facie* case of job discrimination, the courts have increasingly admitted statistical evidence regarding the number of blacks and women employed in various job categories[7] and have ruled it unnecessary for plaintiffs to prove job discrimination is intentional provided the effect of employers' actions are discriminatory.[8] In addition, courts have allowed individual blacks and women to wage class action lawsuits through liberal interpretations of Rule 23 of the Federal Rules of Civil Procedure.[9] Since 1965, such judicial decisions and out-of-court settlements have cost employers hundreds of millions of dollars in back pay and other benefits.[10] Thus, to prevent such litigation, major employing institutions have found it prudent to hire blacks and women in approximate proportions to their presence in the population.[11]

Third, the courts have invalidated many subjective selection and promotion criteria under Title VII that adversely affect employment opportunities for blacks and women. Concerning sex discrimination, for example, the courts have challenged state laws limiting the maximum number of hours that females can work and the maximum amount of weight to be lifted[12] and have ruled that the denial of employment to mothers of preschool children but not to fathers is unlawful in the absence of business justification.[13] Regarding racial discrimination, the courts have forbidden such practices as word-of-mouth job recruiting among white communities only,[14] seniority systems that lock minorities into low-paying jobs,[15] and educational and psychological tests that bar proportionally more blacks than whites.[16] Such decisions have undoubtedly alerted employers to the fact that unmitigated racial and sexual discrimination will no longer be condoned by the courts.

Fourth, Title VI of the Civil Rights Act of 1964 calls for the termination of federal funds from state or local programs administered in a discriminatory manner. In conjunction with this stipulation, twenty-one states passed legislation between 1965 and 1969 prohibiting discrimination, and many of these laws were passed in the South were discrimination was allegedly most egregious.

While the total number of federal subisides actually cut off from such programs has been relatively small, one could argue that without the threat of withholding federal funds national civil rights policies would be weakened.[17]

Finally, civil rights policies since 1964 have been buttressed by affirmative action programs. In 1965 President Lyndon Johnson issued Executive Order 11246 that requires all federal contractors to take affirmative action in the hiring and promotion of blacks. Two years later this order was amended to extend affirmative action to women. Contrary to previous executive orders that were of limited scope and duration, Executive Order 11246 carries affirmative action to all unions, private contractors, and subcontractors doing business with the federal government. Subsequent federal orders, regulations, and laws have forbidden job discrimination in special industries and occupations. When one considers that approximately one-third of the civilian labor force is employed either directly or indirectly by the federal government,[18] the importance of affirmative action programs becomes obvious. It is for these reasons that we believe that the Civil Rights Act of 1964 and the policies it engendered should have a salubrious impact on the relative income of black women. What quantitative evidence is there, if any, to support this belief?

Changes in Median Income Ratio for Black Women

Social scientists have long been concerned with changes in the economic status of minorities in the United States. Most quantitative analyses have concentrated on changes in the black-to-white median income ratio among men (BM/WM). Research has demonstrated amply that the BM/WM income ratio is highly sensitive to cyclical economic conditions. When the economy is healthy and jobs are plentiful, the BM/WM income ratio rises. This is because a healthy economy stimulates demand for all workers, including black men who, in the aggregate, possess less education and job skills than their white counterparts.[19] With the onset of recession the BM/WM income ratio again recedes because of the layoff of marginally skilled and poorly educated black male workers.

Most experts conclude that change in aggregate income for black men is generally a function of two components—cyclical economic conditions and racial discrimination. Hence, the task for anyone concerned with assessing the impact of civil rights policies on the income of black men is to separate the effects of these two components. Building on the seminal work of Rasmussen[20] and Masters,[21] McCrone and Hardy[22] specified an interrupted time-series regression model designed to separate the effects of policy change (Civil Rights Act of 1964 and subsequent federal actions aimed at ending job discrimination) on the BM/WM income ratio from cyclical conditions of economic growth and unemployment. This model, which uses 1965 as the breakpoint (the year the Civil

Rights Act of 1964 was implemented), was given by the following equation:

$$Y_t = a + b(\%\Delta GNP_t) + c(\%U_{t-1}) + d(T_1) + e(T_2) + f(D_t) + u_t \quad (11.1)$$

where Y_t = income ratio by year black male median income/white male median income $\times$ 100)

$\%\Delta GNP_t$ = yearly percentage change in the real gross national product (GNP) (1958 $)

$\%U_{t-1}$ = level of aggregate unemployment lagged one year

T_1 = time trend prior to 1965

T_2 = time trend from 1965

D_t = dummy variable to separate the two time trends

u_t = error term

Applying this model to annual data from 1948 through 1976, we obtained the following results:

$$Y_{BM/WM_t} = 59.29 + 0.84(\%\Delta GNP_t) - 2.66(\%U_{t-1}) + 0.29\ (T_1)$$
$$(0.16) \qquad\qquad (0.49) \qquad (0.11)$$
$$+\ 1.65\ (T_2) + 0.32\ (D_t)$$
$$(0.23) \qquad (1.43) \qquad\qquad\qquad\qquad (11.2)$$

$$R = .94 \qquad R^2 = .89 \qquad \bar{R}^2 = .86$$
$$F = 36.3 \qquad D.W.^* = 2.2$$

The parameter estimates indicate that while cyclical economic factors exert a powerful influence on racial income inequality among males, the marked departure in federal civil rights policies commencing with the Civil Rights Act of 1964 had a pronounced effect. The regression coefficients for our cyclical conditions show that for every 1 percent increase in the GNP the income ratio increased by 0.84 and for every 1 percent increase in the aggregate rate of unemployment the ratio declined by 2.68. Our primary concern, however, is with the statistically significant difference between the estimates of the two secular trends, T_1 and T_2. For the sixteen-year period prior to the implementation of the Civil Rights Act of 1964, the ratio of black to white incomes increased by only 4.6, or at the glacial rate of 0.29 per annum. The coefficient for the secular trend after the policy shift, T_2, was 1.65 per annum, or nearly six times that of the earlier period. This sharp departure in the two trends indicates that the implementation of civil rights policies decreased the degree of racial income inequality for black males.

This study raises the fundamental question of whether civil rights policies

---

*D.W. = Durbin-Watson.

have had a similar effect on the income inequality for black women. To answer this question, we modified our model so that the median income ratio of black women to white men (BW/WM) becomes the dependent variable. The new data[23] and revised model yield the following remarkably secure estimates:

$$Y_{\text{BW/WM}_t} = 19.19 + 0.01(\%\Delta\text{GNP}_t) - 0.30(\%U_{t\text{-}1}) + 0.19\,(T_1)$$
$$\phantom{Y_{\text{BW/WM}_t} =}\ (0.13)\qquad\quad (0.37)\qquad (0.08)$$
$$+\ 1.15\,(T_2) + 4.03\,(D_t)$$
$$\ \ (0.17)\quad\ (1.09)\qquad\qquad\qquad\qquad (11.3)$$

$$R = .98 \qquad R^2 = .95 \qquad \bar{R}^2 = .94$$
$$F = 94.5 \qquad \text{D.W.} = 1.83$$

Our results suggest that, unlike black men, changes in the gross national product and aggregate rates of unemployment for the period have little effect on the income ratio of black women. The cyclical variables possess the theoretically correct signs, but the standard errors are quite large. Our principal concern, again, is the estimates for the two secular trends. We find a slight but statistically significant trend (0.19 per annum) for the 1948–1964 period. Over this sixteen-year period, the BW/WM income ratio increased by only 3.0 percent. In sharp contrast, the income ratio for the period following the Civil Rights Act of 1964 increased by 10.0, or at a rate of 1.15 per annum. More important, the difference in slopes is significant at the .01 level and indicates a real change in trend. While the policy shift has definitely increased the income ratio for black women, the magnitude of the shift in trends for black women (1.15) is not as acute as for black men (1.65).

With these results we can estimate not only the current but also the continued impact of civil rights policies on the BW/WM income ratio nationally. First, we can estimate the upper-bound effect of the Civil Rights Act of 1964 and the policies it stimulated for the period 1965 through 1976. This estimate is obtained by adding the difference in the coefficients of the two time trends for a twelve-year period to the dummy variable. The estimated impact through 1976 is

$$\Delta Y_t = D_t + 12(T_2 - T_1)$$
$$= 4.03 + 12(1.15 - 0.19) \qquad\qquad (11.4)$$
$$= 15.55$$

If this estimate is correct, then the BW/WM median income ratio rose by more than 15 percent as a result of the policy shift.

Second, we can test the predictive power of our model by forecasting the BW/WM income ratio for 1977 and 1978.[24] We employ both actual and predicted data for GNP and unemployment:[25]

1977
$$Y_t = 19.19 + 0.01(4.8) - 0.30(7.7) + 0.19(0)$$
$$+ 1.15(13) + 4.03(1) \tag{11.5}$$
$$= 35.91$$

1978
$$Y_t = 19.19 + 0.01(3.6) - 0.30(7.1) + 0.19(0)$$
$$+ 1.15(14) + 4.03(1) \tag{11.6}$$
$$= 37.23$$

Since the BW/WM ratio stood at 34.2 in 1976, we foresee real economic advances for black women continuing in the immediate future. These estimates, of course, are based on our conclusion that the gap in income between black women and white men has declined and will continued to decline as a function of policy action. Is this conclusion supported by other research?

Evidence on occupational participation furnishes support for our general conclusion that black women have made real advances since 1965. One might suspect that any post-1965 occupational advances for black women would be confined mainly to lower-status jobs where gross turnover of the labor force is swift and cumulative experience and on-the-job training are less important.[26] Under such conditions, employment opportunities for older as well as younger black females would be much enhanced. To some extent, this has been the case; yet, since 1965, there has been a definite improvement in the share of black women in higher-skilled and better-paying jobs while the proportion of black women in less desirable jobs has generally diminished. For example, Garfinkle's[27] detailed analysis of occupational participation rates between 1962 and 1974 reveals that black women increased their relative occupational participation as professionals, social workers, clerks, teachers, accountants, and practical and registered nurses, while the proportion of black female farm laborers and domestic servants declined markedly. Although black women in technical, skilled, and professional positions are still statistically underrepresented, significant increases have been registered in these and other better-paying jobs since the Civil Rights Act of 1964 was implemented.

Before drawing too many conclusions about the ability of civil rights policies to effect change in the income of black women, we must elucidate two points. First, in 1976 the median income of black women was only 34.2 percent that of white men. At the present rate of change (1.15 percent per year), income equality between black women and white men would not be attained until well after the turn of the century. This is a significant improvement over the pre-1965 rate of change (0.19 percent per year), but a great deal remains to be done if income equality is to be realized. Second, until now, we have confined our analysis to national data. How valid is this analysis?

Regional Impact of Civil Rights Policies

It is essential to determine whether post-1965 civil rights policies have had a differential impact by region. If these policies have spurred across-the-board changes, as Masters,[28] for example, suggests, then black women should register significant changes in income in all regions of the country since 1965. Recently, McCrone and Hardy[29] found that increases in the income ratio for black males nationally were primarily a function of policy consequences in the South. Our estimated impact of the policy shift for black men (BM/WM) in the South was 15.6 percent. The same circumstances might apply in the case of black women. To test this, we apply our regression model to available annual regional data from 1953 through 1976:

South: $Y_t = 15.36 - 0.04(\%\Delta\text{GNP}_t) - 0.08(\%U_{t-1}) + 0.27\,(T_1)$
                      (0.11)   (0.35)   (0.12)
             $+ 0.87\,(T_2) + 3.73\,(D_t)$
             (0.15)   (1.02)   (11.7)

             $R = .98$ $R^2 = .96$ $\bar{R}^2 = .94$
             $F = 79.9$ D.W. = 2.26

Northeast: $Y_t = 37.10 + 0.23(\%\Delta\text{GNP}_t) - 1.17(\%U_{t-1}) + 0.51\,(T_1)$
                      (0.25)   (0.77)   (0.26)
             $+ 1.03\,(T_2) + 4.25\,(D_t)$
             (0.33)   (2.23)   (11.8)

             $R = .90$ $R^2 = .81$ $\bar{R}^2 = .76$
             $F = 15.4$ D.W. = 2.61

North $Y_t = 24.91 - 0.37(\%\Delta\text{GNP}_t) + 1.06(\%U_{t-1}) + 0.03\,(T_1)$
Central: (0.20)   (0.63)   (0.21)
             $+ 0.42\,(T_2) + 3.41\,(D_t)$
             (0.27)   (1.83)   (11.9)

             $R = .92$ $R^2 = .84$ $\bar{R}^2 = .80$
             $F = 19.0$ D.W. = 2.10

West: $Y_t = 26.84 + 0.03(\%\Delta\text{GNP}_t) - 0.00(\%U_{t-1}) + 0.58\,(T_1)$
                      (0.38)   (1.09)   (0.40)
             $+ 0.40\,(T_2) + 6.57\,(D_t)$
             (0.45)   (4.56)   (11.10)

             $R = .74$ $R^2 = .55$ $\bar{R}^2 = .40$
             $F = 3.6$ D.W. = 2.97

Equations 11.7 to 11.10 show distinctly that income for black women in all regions is unaffected by economic vagaries; none of the coefficients for the two cyclical variables $\%\Delta GNP_t$ and $\%U_{t-1}$ is statistically significant. Once again, our primary focus is on the coefficients for the two secular trends T_1 and T_2. As in the case of black men, only one regional equation shows any statistically significant *difference* in the slopes for T_2 and T_1—the South. The slope of 0.87 for the 1965-1976 period in the South is three times the 0.27 slope for the 1948-1964 period. Although the trend coefficient for T_2 in the Northeast is significant, it is not significantly different from that of T_1. Only the Southern equation (11.7) is truly robust (adjusted R^2 of .94) and relatively free of multicollinearity and autoregression. Hence, it appears that the dramatic improvement for black women indicated in our national analysis (equation 11.3) is a function of significant improvements in the South. Why should these improvements be confined mainly to the South?

Three plausible explanations may be advanced. First, the upsurge for black women, as well as black men, in the post-1965 period could be a function of migration of blacks from the South to higher-income and less discriminatory regions of the country. Gwartney,[30] for example, reports that virtually all the relative income gains for blacks from 1937 to 1967 could be eliminated by controlling for regional migration. This suggests that the two secular trends T_1 and T_2 could be a function of this process. A high rate of black migration after 1965 might account for the sharp trend in T_2. However, information on regional migration indicates that migration of blacks from the South was more common before the Civil Rights Act of 1964 than after. Migration of blacks from the South was most pronounced during the 1950s but subsided quickly afterward. Moreover, in the past few years, more blacks have moved into the South than have left.[31] Regional migration may account for the long-term secular trend before 1965 (3.0 percent increase), but it cannot be credited for the acute rise in the secular trend after 1965.

Another possible explanation for the increase in black income in the South concerns the processes of industrialization and urbanization. Wage rates have increased in the South at a pace faster than the national average as the South has become more industrialized and urbanized. While it is evident that the South did witness rapid industrialization and urbanization in the period following World War II, there is little evidence that these processes accelerated sharply circa 1965. Hence, we believe that the dramatic *change* in trend for black income cannot be attributed entirely to these phenomena.

We suspect that the more viable explanation for the significant increase in income for blacks in the South rests squarely on the implementation of the aforementioned civil rights policies. We expect greater increments for the South because the initial thrust of civil rights policies was on assuaging overt or purposeful discrimination based on race. Since income inequality for blacks is a dual function of purposeful discrimination and what might be labeled structural discrimination based on long-term factors such as occupational and educational inequalities, the region with the greatest purposeful discrimination should experience the greatest policy impact. In addition, the implementation of civil rights policies was more pressing and vigorous in the South. Consequently, what seems to be happening is a regression effect in which the most deviant case, the South, statistically regresses or moves toward the mean of the population as civil rights policies are enforced and purposeful discrimination is diminished.

We can now calculate the current and continued impact of civil rights policies on income for black women in the South. As before, we estimate the maximum effect of these policies by adding the coefficient of the dichotomous variable D_t to the difference between the two trend coefficients T_1 and T_2 for a twelve-year span.

$$\Delta Y_t = D_t + 12(T_2 - T_1)$$
$$= 3.73 + 12(0.87 - 0.27) \qquad (11.11)$$
$$= 10.93$$

Equation 11.11 reveals that the income ratio for black women in the South improved an estimated 10.9 percent as a result of policy action. This is still considerably less than the 15.6 percent increase registered by black men relative to white men (BM/WM) in the South for the same period. Dual discrimination based on race and sex is difficult to combat.

Finally, using equation 11.7, we can extrapolate the continued effect of current civil rights policies in the South for two years following available regional data:

1977
$$Y_t = 15.36 - 0.04(4.8) - 0.08(7.7) + 0.27(0)$$
$$+ 0.87 (13) + 3.73(1) \qquad (11.12)$$
$$= 28.59$$

1978
$$Y_t = 15.36 - 0.04(3.6) - 0.08(7.1) + 0.27(0)$$
$$+ 0.87(14) + 3.73(1) \qquad (11.13)$$
$$= 30.56$$

In 1976 the BW/WM income ratio for the South was only 28.8. If our estimates in equations 11.12 and 11.13 are correct, then income for black women in the South should remain stationary in 1977 but increase to 30.56 through 1978. These results are by no means trivial since it is the South where nearly half of the black population lives and where the gap between black and white income is greatest. Yet, it must be remembered that inequality for black women is a national concern. If black women are ever to gain an equal footing with white men, more needs to be done outside the South.

Conclusion

Black women have clearly benefited from the policy shift associated with the Civil Rights Act of 1964. While it would be inappropriate to assume that civil rights policies are solely responsible for recent economic advances recorded by black women, one cannot discount the fact that systematic progress has been made since 1965. This broad conclusion accords generally with the recent analyses of Freeman,[32] Garfinkle,[33] and the Congressional Budget Office.[34] They find that black women are advancing on a broad front including education, occupation, and income.

Unlike in these studies, however, we show that upturns in the median income of black women relative to white men after 1965, like that of black men, is largely a function of significant changes in the South where job discrimination was initially most egregious and where enforcement of civil rights policies has been most vigorous. Although the South witnessed rapid industrialization and urbanization as well as migration of blacks to less discriminatory regions in the period after World War II, there is scant evidence that these processes were accelerated sharply at or about 1965. Thus, we believe that the dramatic and significant *change* in trend for black men and black women should be credited to the policy shift associated with the Civil Rights Act of 1964.

Despite the basic similarity in the economic experience of black men and women in the post-1965 period, two specific differences between these groups exist. First, in contrast to black men, the median income of black women has not been sensitive to cyclical economic conditions. Though the median income of black women has not been adversely affected by periods of recession, likewise if has failed to improve significantly as a result of a growing economy. Second, the magnitude of the increase in median income of black women after 1965 has been less than that of black men, *relative to white men.* Black women, unlike black men, suffer from two forms of discrimination—one based on race and one based on sex.

In sum, while current civil rights policies appear to have a salutary impact on assuaging pruposeful discrimination, it must be remembered that in 1976 the median income for black females nationally was only 34 percent that of white male income. If the present rate of change (1.15 percent per year) were maintained, income parity would not be attained until well after the turn of the century. Thus, a great deal remains to be accomplished if racial and sexual income equality is to be realized.

Notes

1. The median income ratio is reported rather than the mean because it best reflects the economic status of the population and is the only statistic con-

sistently reported by the federal government from 1948. Median income is recorded annually for black women and white men 14 years and older. A 100 percent ratio indicates perfect income equality.

2. William M. Landes, "The Economics of Fair Employment Laws," *Journal of Political Economy* 76 (July 1968): 541–59; and Duane Lockard, *Toward Equal Opportunity* (New York: Macmillan Co., 1968).

3. U.S. Commission on Civil Rights, *Federal Civil Rights Enforcement Effort* (Washington: Government Printing Office, 1973).

4. Equal Employment Opportunity Commission, *EEOC 9th Annual Report* (Washington: Government Printing Office, 1975).

5. Charles S. Bullock, III, "Expanding Black Economic Rights," in ed. Harrell R. Rogers, Jr., *Racism and Inequality: The Policy Alternatives* (San Francisco: Freeman and Co., 1975), pp. 75–124; and Victor Perlo, *The Economics of Racism U.S.A.: Roots of Black Inequality* (New York: International Publishers, 1975).

6. Albert J. Rosenthal, "Employment Discrimination and the Law," *Annals of the American Academy of Political and Social Sciences* 407 (May 1973): 91–101.

7. For example, *Brown* v. *Gaston County Dyeing Machine Co.,* 457 F.2d 1377 (4th Cir. 1972); and *Parham* v. *Southwestern Bell Telephone Co.,* 433 F.2d 421 (8th Cir. 1970).

8. *Griggs* v. *Duke Power Co.,* 401 U.S. 424, 432 (1971).

9. For example, *Oatis* v. *Crown Zellerbach Corp.,* 398 F.2d 496 (5th Cir. 1968); and *Huff* v. *N.D. Carr Co.,* 485 F.2d 710 (1973).

10. Sandra Stencel, "Women in the Work Force," in *The Women's Movement: Achievements and Effects* (Washington: Congressional Quarterly Editorial Research Reports, 1977), p. 21–42.

11. Nathan Glazer, *Affirmative Discrimination: Ethnic Inequality and Public Policy* (New York: Basic Books, 1975); and Daniel Seligman, "How Equal Opportunity Turned into Employment Quotas," *Fortune* 87 (March 1973): 160–68.

12. *Rosenfeld* v. *Southern Pacific Railroad,* 293 F. Supp. 1219 (C.D. Cal., 1968).

13. *Phillips* v. *Martin-Marietta,* 400 U.S. 542 (1972).

14. *Parham* v. *Southwestern Bell Telephone Co.*

15. *United States* v. *Local 189, United Papermakers and Paperworkers,* 416 F.2d 980 (5th Cir. 1969).

16. *Griggs* v. *Duke Power Co.*

17. Thomas R. Dye, *The Politics of Equality* (New York: Bobbs-Merrill, 1971).

18. U.S. Commission on Civil Rights, *Federal Civil Rights Enforcement Effort.*

19. W.H. Locke Anderson, "Trickling Down: The Relationship between Economic Growth and the Extent of Poverty among American Families," *Quarterly Journal of Economics* 78 (November 1964): 411-524.

20. David R. Rasmussen, "A Note on the Relative Income of Nonwhite Men, 1948-1964," *Quarterly Journal of Economics* 84 (February 1970): 168-172.

21. Stanley H. Masters, *Black-White Income Differentials: Empirical Studies and Policy Implications* (New York: Academic Press, 1975), pp. 131-49.

22. Donald J. McCrone and Richard J. Hardy, "Civil Rights Policies and the Achievement of Racial Economic Equality, 1948-75," *American Journal of Political Science* 22 (February 1978): 1-17.

23. Note on sources: BW/WM income ratio: U.S. Department of Commerce, Bureau of the Census, *Current Population Reports* (Washington: Government Printing Office, 1948-76), series P-60, "Money Income of Families and Persons in the U.S."

Change in real GNP: U.S. Department of Commerce, Bureau of Economic Analysis, *Long Term Economic Growth, 1860-1970* (Washington: Government Printing Office, 1973), series A2, pp. 182-3. Also *U.S. Statistical Abstract: 1975*, "GNP in Current and Constant Dollars," no. 616, p. 381. The unit of analysis was real gross national product measured in billions of 1958 dollars.

$\%U_{t-1}$: *Long Term Economic Growth*, ibid., series B2, pp. 212-3. Also *U.S. Statistical Abstract: 1975*, ibid., "Employment Statistics of the Population by Sex and Race, 1950-75," no. 558, p. 343.

Regional data: U.S. Department of Commerce, Bureau of the Census, *Current Population Reports*, series P-60, ibid. The Census Bureau regions are: Northeast—Maine, N.H., Vt., Mass., R.I., Conn., N.Y., N.J., and Pa.,; North Central—Ohio, Ind., Mich., Ill., Wis., Minn., Iowa, Mo., Kans., Nebr., S.D., N.D.; South—Del., Md., D.C., W.Va., Va., N.C., S.C., Ga., Fla., Ala., Miss., Tenn., Ky., Ark., La., Tex., Okla.; West—all others. *Note:* 1953 was the first year that regional income data were reported by the government.

24. Robert S. Pindyck and Daniel L. Rubinfeld, *Economic Models and Economic Forecasts* (New York: McGraw-Hill, 1976), pp. 156-58; 177-81.

25. "Actual and Projected Economic Indicators," *Economic Outlook, U.S.A.* 4, no. 1 (Winter 1977): 4.

26. Richard B. Freeman, "Changes in the Labor Market for Black Americans," *Brookings Papers on Economic Activity* no. 1 (January 1973): 67-120.

27. Stuart H. Garfinkle, "Occupations of Women and Black Workers, 1962-74," *Monthly Labor Review*, November 1975, pp. 25-34.

28. Masters, *Black-White Income Differentials*.

29. McCrone and Hardy, "Civil Rights Policies."

30. James Gwartney, "Changes in the Nonwhite/White Income Ratio, 1939-67," *American Economic Review* 60 (December 1970): 872-883.

31. Current Policy Research, *Current Public Policy Research* 2, no. 6 (March 1978): 1.

32. Freeman, "Changes in the Labor Market for Black Americans."

33. Garfinkle, "Occupations of Women and Black Workers."

34. Congressional Budget Office, *Income Disparities between Black and White Americans* (Washington: Government Printing Office, 1977).

12 Women's Educational Equity: Favorable Student Response

Sarah Slavin Schramm

A learned woman is thought to be a comet that bodes mischief whenever it appears. To offer to the world the liberal education of women is to deface the image of God in man, it will make woman so high, and man so low, like fire in the housetops it will set the whole world in a flame. *

Introduction

The Women's Educational Equity Act (the Mink-Mondale bill, hereafter WEEA) became law on August 21, 1974, as section 408 of the Educational Amendments of 1974.[1] It provides educational equity for women by means of grants for research, training, guidance, curricula evaluation and development, and program expansion. The WEEA could have an impact on college students in the relatively near future as women in academia assume a more favored position than they have held in the past.

Tapp and Levine have shown that middle-class college-age youth are willing for daily behavior to be "guided predominantly by a law and order maintaining perspective for rule conformity."[2] In the case of the WEEA impact, however, such willingness would encounter still another socialization factor in the individual's makeup—the stereotype of women as essentially passive, inferior beings.[3] For the purposes of this study, it is assumed a tension will exist between, on the one hand, willingness for behavior to be guided by rule of law as exemplified in the WEEA and, on the other hand, the tendency to regard women as essentially inferior. Management of such tension is of special interest to those concerned with the administration of the WEEA on all levels and to those concerned with furtherance of equity for women in the field of education and beyond.

Revised version of paper presented to the American Political Science Association, Chicago, September 3, 1975.

*Bethsheba Makin, an Englishwoman, from a book she wrote three hundred years ago, quoted by Ann Scott, Vice President/Legislation National Organization for Women, in her testimony on behalf of the WEEA at the hearings before the Subcommittee on Education, Committee on Labor and Public Welfare, U.S. Senate, 93d Cong. (Washington: Government Printing Office, 1973), p. 69. Ann Scott died on February 17, 1975. This chapter respectfully is offered in her memory.

The purpose of this chapter is to determine if there are better or worse ways of handling the presentation of women's educational equity to college students, female and male. Specifically, will a more agreeable response to women's educational equity be forthcoming as a result of a particular mode of presentation? By presentation is meant a persuasive account. It is hypothesized that different modes of presentation will shape different responses to women's educational equity.

Research Design

For the purposes of this study, a fourfold typology was hypothesized as encompassing possible modes of presentation. The mental and external baselines are a function of both the mode and the subject. The mental baseline is dichotomized as rational/intuitional. A rational account is characterized by its appeal to a subject's power to comprehend and infer, that is, to intellect. An intuitional account is characterized by its appeal to a subject's power to know without recourse to inferences, that is, to instinct.

The external baseline is dichotomized as objective/subjective. An objective account is characterized by its appeal to something apart from the self. A subjective account is characterized by its appeal to one's self. The typology may be visualized thus:

| | | *Mental* | |
		Rational	Intuitional
External	Objective	Factual Mode	Dogmatic Mode
	Subjective	Consciousness Mode	Emotional Mode

A *factual mode* facilitates subject awareness of an actual state of affairs. The approach is rational and objective. There is no personal reference or connection. Reference is made to authoritative sources of information, that is, "studies." A *consciousness mode* facilitates subject awareness of self, relative to what is being discussed. The approach is rational and subjective. Reference is of or pertaining to the subject. A *dogmatic mode* facilitates subject awareness of matters of opinion. The approach is intuitional and objective. There is no personal reference or connection. Reference is made to authoritative proclamations as if they were matters of fact. An *emotional mode* facilitates subject awareness of his/her strong feelings relative to what is being discussed. The approach is intuitional and subjective. Reference is of or pertaining to the subject.

The relative agreeability of these modes is explored by randomly supplying each subject with a stimulus utilizing one of the modes. Then a comparison is made across the responses. The assumption is that by randomly distributing the stimuli among the subjects, any differences in response are facilitated by the stimuli. (See appendix 12A for the stimuli statements.)

Methodologically, the study utilizes survey and experimental techniques, drawing on both cognitive, or intellectual, and reactive, or behavioral, levels of response. This is reasonable because a subject's cognitive and reactive responses may or may not be congruent. In the case at hand, college students could favor educational equity for women in different degrees intellectually but react more or less agreeably to it according to the stimulus they encounter. This also could vary according to sex.

Subjects were students enrolled in PS004, Introduction to Political Science, at George Washington University for the fall semester 1974. There were approximately 220 students; 80.5 percent participated. Caucasians accounted for 83 percent of the sample population; 61 percent were 18 years old; 57 percent were male and 43 percent were female. College students' response is of interest, given the nature of the WEEA and of Tapp and Levine's findings. The selection of these particular students was a matter of access and convenience for the researcher. Additionally, the introductory course was required of a broad base of undergraduates.

Results

Statements used in designing stimuli were derived from testimony on behalf of the WEEA at the House and Senate hearings. A list of these excerpts was distributed among seven graduate teaching fellows in the political science department. The fellows were asked to categorize sixty statements according to the typology above. Five participated. They agreed 67 percent of the time or more on categorizations of dogmatic, emotional, and factual statements. They could not categorize consistently statements the researcher thought were of the consciousness mode, however. In other words, the fellows could not distinguish the two subjective modes from each other. The two subjective modes thus were combined into one mode named emotional.

The next stage involved administering a questionnaire randomly to students in six of twelve discussion sections. The sample size was 72. Each questionnaire consisted of twenty-five statements pertaining to one of the three modes. There were two sets of twenty-five statements for each mode. Students were asked to respond in close-ended fashion: Did they agree or not agree with each of twenty-five statements? Results were quantified as percentages. They were distributed along a two-dimensional continuum ranging from 0 to 100 percent. Statements producing the highest percentages of agreement or disagreement then were grouped within each of the four modes.

Judging from the level of agreement or disagreement to the different types of statements, the researcher's expectation was that (1) factual statements, especially those with which subjects generally agreed, would produce the most agreeable responses to educational equity for women and (2) dogmatic statements, especially those with which subjects generally disagreed, would produce the least agreeable responses to educational equity for women.[4]

Twenty-one questionnaires also were administered randomly with the scale questionnaires and later with the stimuli. These items were identical to five items on the questionnaire distributed with the stimuli. The assumption was that there would be no difference between the two average group responses. If there was a difference, it was facilitated by the stimuli.

The last stages involved designing six stimuli and randomly administering them to students in the remaining six discussion sections. The sample size was 63. Stimuli had identical introductory paragraphs and questionnaires. The stimuli themselves varied by high and low percentages of agreeability within each mode, as indicated by the aforementioned survey results. In other words, each stimulus varied with every other stimulus by valance, the degree of attractiveness each group of statements possessed as a behavioral goal.

Subjects were told the political science department was conducting a survey of students' attitudes toward women's educational equity. They were asked to read directions to the questionnaire carefully and to proceed as directed, without discussing the matter among themselves. Subjects were not informed of any differences in the questionnaires. While the subjects may have differed from one another in a number of ways, they may be assumed to have been distributed evenly throughout their discussion sections. Any differences apparent in their responses may be considered the effect of the stimuli to which they were exposed and not the effect of differences between sections.

There were no correct or incorrect responses to the items. This study was designed as a laboratory experiment looking at the effects of different modes of presentation of women's educational equity on subjects predisposed to a tension between their law-and-order-maintaining perspective and their stereotyped view of women. Subjects' responses to the items, which were intended to measure their agreeability to educational equity for women or toward women's liberation, are the study's central focus. About half the items originally were designed by Carol Tarvis to measure attitudes on male/female roles.[5] The University of Michigan's feeling thermometer for women's liberation also was used. Responses were scored as close-ended and dichotomous. Two-way analysis of

Table 12-1

Analysis of Variance of Percentage of Agreeable Responses: Educational Equity

Source	DF	SS	MS	F	Table F:05	Results
Stimulus	6	979,457.12	195,891.424	0.84689	2.53	NS
Sex	1	82,116.61	82,118.607	0.35502	4.17	NS
Interaction	4	451,768.19	112,942.047	0.48828	2.69	NS
Residual	31	7,170,518.52	231,307.049			
Total	42	8,683,862.42	211,801.523			

variance was used to determine if stimuli and sex were indeed a significant source of response variation.

In the first two-way analysis of variance, the question is, Can the variation in percentage of those who agree with educational equity for women be explained by the accompanying variation in stimulus and sex? According to table 12-1, the F test for interaction indicates additivity; thus it is assumed there is no interaction in the model. (Any additional amount explained by interaction is attributable to sample fluctuation.) Given no interaction, it is necessary to test stimulus and sex independently as possible sources of variance. The F test for stimulus indicates that the population column means are equal. There is no relationship between the stimulus and the percentage of agreeable responses. The test for sex indicates that the population row means are equal. There is no relationship between sex and percentage of agreeable responses.

In the second two-way analysis of variance, the question is, Can the variation in percentage of those who agree with women's liberation be explained by the accompanying variation in stimulus, including a control, and sex? According to table 12-2, the F test for interaction indicates there is no interaction in the model. (Any additional amount explained by interaction is attributable to sample fluctuation.) Given additivity, it is necessary to test stimulus and sex as possible independent sources of variance. The F test for stimulus indicates that

Table 12-2

Analysis of Variance of Percentage of Agreeable Responses: Women's Liberation

Source	DF	SS	MS	F	Table F:05	Results
Stimulus	6	3,592.514	598.7523	0.46869	2.09	NS
Sex	1	33,045.268	33,045.2684	25.86691	3.84	S
Interaction	6	2,131.888	355.3146	0.27813	2.09	NS
Residual	68	86,870.574	1,277.5084			
Total[a]	81	125,640.244	1,551.1141			

[a]The total in table 12-2 is higher than in table 12-1 because a control was added with the stimuli. Unfortunately, the control for table 12-1 vanished during tabulation.

Table 12-3
Mean Percentage of Agreeable Responses: Educational Equity

Stimulus Group			Female Percentage (N)		Male Percentage (N)	
Agree:	A	Dogmatic	100.0	(4)	73.3	(5)
	B	Emotional	100.0	(4)	44.4	(3)
	C	Factual	96.67	(5)	66.67	(3)
Not agree:	D	Dogmatic	6.67	(5)	22.2	(3)
	E	Emotional	88.89	(3)	66.67	(4)
	F	Factual	72.2	(3)		

the population column means are equal. There is no relationship between the stimulus and the percentage of favorable responses. The test for sex indicates that the population row means are not equal. There is a relationship between sex and the percentage of favorable responses.

Table 12-3 indicates that females generally agreed with women's educational equity somewhat less in responses to those stimuli made up of statements with which pretesting showed substantial numbers of respondents did not agree. The factual-agree stimulus was not associated with the highest percentage of agreement among females, with factual stimuli a near third.

Males agreed with women's educational equity less than females consistently throughout, except in response to the dogmatic, not-agree stimulus. Their highest percentage of agreement surprisingly was associated with the dogmatic-agree stimulus. Both factual stimuli were associated equally with a relatively high level of agreement as well; apparently there was no distinction between agree and disagree stimuli for males. The stimuli were generated into agreeable and not-agreeable responses to women's educational equity, but more so for women than for men.

Table 12-4 indicates that females generally agreed with women's liberation less in responses to those stimuli made up of statements with which pretesting showed substantial numbers of respondents did not agree, with the exception of the factual stimulus. The dogmatic- and emotional-agree stimuli again were associated with the highest percentage of agreeability among females. Males agreed with women's liberation less than females, and with only one exception, substantially less. Their highest percentage of agreeability was associated with the dogmatic, not-agree stimulus, but males agreed with women's liberation only one-third of the time there. Females who received the control questionnaire agreed with women's liberation 50 percent more than males receiving the questionnaire. For women at least, the control percentage of agreement was comparable to the higher percentages of agreeability associated with the dogmatic- and emotional-agree stimuli. Apparently some modes of presentation

Table 12–4
Mean Percentage of Agreeable Responses: Women's Liberation

Stimulus Group			Female Percentage (N)	Male Percentage (N)
Agree:	A	Dogmatic	75.0 (4)	22.2 (9)
	B	Emotional	75.0 (4)	20.0 (5)
	C	Factual	66.6 (6)	25.0 (4)
Neutral:	D	Control	71.4 (7)	26.9 (13)
Not agree:	E	Dogmatic	58.3 (6)	33.3 (6)
	F	Emotional	37.5 (4)	21.4 (7)
	G	Factual	66.6 (3)	12.5 (4)

do more harm than good so far as females' attitudes toward women's liberation are concerned, however. In only one instance did a stimulus-response percentage (factual, not-agree) differ noticeably from the control percentage for males. It appears that males have made up their minds independently not to agree with women's liberation, and the stimuli make little, if any, difference here. Here stimuli are not easily generated into agreeable or not-agreeable responses to women's liberation, although this is less true for females than males.

There was less variation in reactions among males than among females. For every group, the percentage of responses friendly to activity on behalf of women's equity, by means of education or women's liberation, was less among males than among females. Males see such activity as threatening their own advancement ultimately. Women's educational equity, however, was associated with a much higher friendly response, from either females or males, than was women's liberation.

It may be that education ultimately is seen as a more appropriate, perhaps even safer, means of advancement for an individual who is stereotyped as passive and inferior than women's liberation with its emphasis on full participation now. The presence of legislation such as the WEEA could be an important factor here as well. Many of the reforms sought by the feminist movement have not been translated into laws yet. Tapp and Levine's observation of a rule conformity perspective among middle-class, college-age youth may be the key to the tendency for subjects—male and female alike—to agree more with women's educational equity than to favor women's liberation.

Conclusion

It appears that arguments on behalf of women's educational equity have been of three types: dogmatic, emotional, and factual. These are associated with different levels of agreement in those to whom they are directed. Women seem especially susceptible to variance in this regard. Responses to stimuli based on these arguments, agreeing with women's educational equity, are not explained by interaction between stimulus and sex nor by stimulus or sex taken independently. Education may be viewed as an appropriate means by which to grant women equity, and legislation to that effect may contribute to the tendency to conform to such means. This may ease the tension between college students' law-and-order-maintaining perspectives and their stereotype of women as passive and inferior.

Responses to stimuli based on dogmatic, emotional, and factual arguments, agreeing with women's liberation, are not explained by interaction between stimulus and sex nor by stimulus taken independently. There is a relationship between percentage of agreement and sex, however. Both sexes nevertheless agree with women's liberation less than they agree with educational equity. The dogmatic-agree stimulus is more associated with high percentages of agreement with women's educational equity for both sexes. It should be remembered, however, that dogmatic statements taken out of context generally resulted in less agreement overall in the pretest and sometimes were associated with strong negative feelings in males. High female agreement generally was associated with the emotional-agree stimulus as well, but this was not true for males. Factual stimuli, agreement and disagreement, while not associated with extraordinarily high responses, nevertheless consistently were associated with relatively high responses. In addition, factual statements presented out of context generally were associated with strong positive feelings all around.

In conclusion, it may be said that women's educational equity seems destined for acceptance among college-age youth. Reinforcement of this accepting attitude would best be undertaken by the presentation of noncontroversial factual arguments.

Notes

1. 81 Stat. 554–5.

2. "Compliance from Kindergarten to College," Paper presented to the American Political Science Association, Chicago, September 9, 1971.

3. Samuel W. Fernberger, "Persistence of Stereotypes concerning Sex Differences," *Journal of Abnormal and Social Psychology* 43 (1948): 197–208; Caroline T. MacBrayer, "Differences in Perception of the Opposite Sex by Males and Females," *Journal of Social Psychology* 52 (1960): 309–14.

4. The following ad hoc comments were written on the dogmatic instruments:

"I have come to the conclusion that you, you, my dear, are a female chavenist [sic]. That's how it is, live it or live with it."

"This survey is biased toward women's rights. The tone is very prejudiced. I suggest any future surveys have more fairly-worded questions."

"This is foggy, poorly phrased, and highly biased. Most statements here are *lies. . . . This survey isn't a survey!* It is a slanted, biased, uninformational [sic] essay which only proves how ignorant the composer was and how, if anything, such corruption of truth should be weeded out of our already faulty educational system."

All these subjects were male. Only one factual instrument was returned with such a comment, and it was worded less forcefully.

5. "Woman and Man: A *Psychology Today* Questionnaire," *Psychology Today,* February 1971, pp. 82-88.

Appendix 12A
Stimuli Statements

Dogmatic-Agree Statements

The United States is in a values dilemma, regarding woman, her role, status, and equity. A first line of attack must be against sex discrimination rooted in and perpetuated by traditional sex stereotyping, the practice of viewing certain roles, activities, and qualities as proper only for boys and men—aggressive, decisive, wage earning—while regarding others as proper only for girls and women—submissive, supportive, homemaker. To merely end discrimination is not enough, however. New programs are vitally needed to deal with the issues arising as discrimination ends. Feminism must not be relegated to a two-week unit on women in history and then neglected for the rest of the year. Training and retraining as well as education for personal growth and pleasure should be available to all people regardless of age, sex, race, creed, or national origin. Much research and work needs to be accomplished and disseminated to assist the states (schools, family groups, legislatures, courts, and businesses) at all levels regarding issues inherent in problems of women in a pluralist society, and problems and procedures related to sex typing, especially motivation and economic aspects and possible viable solutions and ideas. It is not even accurate, to say nothing of honest, to expect little girls to become only housewives and mothers. Women deserve the right to fulfill themselves to their fullest potential and capabilities. The goal is to develop human beings who are free to act in ways that are appropriate to their interests and their values—not their sex.

Dogmatic, Not-Agree Statements

For too many women, education produces a sense of inferiority. There is a sexual track system in our schools that directs women from the outset to anticipate second-class status in the economic and sociopolitical mainstream of our country. For one thing, what universities are offering is a class education, designed to keep woman forever overcleaning her house and family and safely out of the career market, forever overproducing anything but babies, while forever overconsuming the gross national product—the last great leisure class of the world. Women are very much a class in need of remedial help. But many schools and departments, even tax-supported, have quotas for women and give them few scholarships, especially at graduate levels. Although the discouragement that women often receive from faculty may be benign in intent, it often has the effect of devastating career aspirations and feelings of self-worth in the embryonic stage. In addition, women are often discouraged from pursuing rigorous academic programs by counselors who urge them to train for traditionally female, dead-end, low-paying jobs, rather than for traditionally male, upwardly mobile, high-paying, high-status jobs. As long as the power structures in education are male-dominated, changes to provide equal opportunity for women will be gained at a snail's pace. Women have so far had little chance to participate in determining the character and features of the higher education system their taxes support. Even though education has traditionally been regarded as a "woman's field," it is mostly men who have had the opportunities and the power.

Emotional-Agree Statements

We are going to have to deal with male and female role playing. This is because we are continuing the locked-in mental attitudes of the chauvinist, even though we cannot afford (nor could we ever) the cost of ignoring the leadership potential of our women. We must not sacrifice more than 50 percent of the brain power of our nation to outmoded sex stereotypes. We must now educate the person, regardless of sex, to become more creative and productive. Our teacher training institutions must be encouraged to desex their courses and curriculum, bringing women into the mainstream and into equal partnership in education. Equally importantly, we must educate women so that they aspire to academic and career opportunities of all descriptions, rather than those traditionally left open for them. We still have "women's work" and "men's work" even though mechanization and automation have changed and virtually eliminated men's heavy and rough work. Somehow our society has tied women's role as child-bearer to every other aspect of her personhood. Our schools must begin to deal with the reality of people's lives, not with stereotyped or idealized concepts of life. We must particularly examine educational attitudes at all levels, hitherto unquestioned and taken on faith, affecting the role of women in society, and we must make sure that these attitudes keep up with the best and foremost of our thinking today. We will have taken a giant step toward educating the children of our country for survival when the product of education becomes more important than the container, when the educational atmosphere has become flexible enough so that females can make educational choices without fear of being stigmatized, and when educators can admit that there are many unexplored avenues to educational development.

Emotional, Not-Agree Statements

From nursery school through graduate education, our educational system is guilty of fostering and perpetuating rigid sex roles for men and women which result in stereotyped self-images and career choices for both sexes. We must listen to the cries of many women. So far a major theme has been one of regret for a potential identity which is now forever lost, of gentle mourning for a self who will never fully come to life. You find a young woman who has marked aptitude who wants to become an automotive mechanic being refused the opportunities to develop that vocation because this is not the acceptable thing to do. You might think of the needs of our society in urban planning, management of social institutions, crafts, services of all kinds, and ask, Why are we selecting from only a small segment of the society the ones to be trained, employed, or recruited for special responsibilities? Yet, our young women, even when allowed equal access, will still face a pervasive pattern of sex discrimination. Much of our present thinking results from attitudes that were valid decades ago, but which are invidious and unacceptable now. That is, we regard females, who make up more than half the population, as secondary in most instances. Half of our population, our girls and women, have their lives and talents and aspirations crippled by a society which sees them as second-class citizens. White men in power have been tracking us as women from the day we were born, and they will continue to do so. Still, we as women must share the brunt of perpetuating differences between the expectation and aspiration levels of boys and girls. Our educational system has given boys and men first place long enough.

Factual-Agree Statements

Raw data indicate just how few women are utilized as anything but support staff. When 700 fourth, fifth, and sixth graders were asked what they wanted to be when they grew up, girls' responses fell mainly into four categories: teacher, nurse, secretary, mother. The common findings of numerous studies of the image of women in textbooks reveal that women are underrepresented as main characters in stories and illustrations; are shown as passive, dependent persons; are characterized as unstable and weak; and are labeled in negative terms. One study of textbooks established that sex stereotyping exists at every level and in every subject in elementary schools. In Jamie Frisof's analysis of social studies textbooks, men are shown or described in over one hundred different jobs and women in less than thirty; and in these thirty jobs, women serve people or help men to do more important work. In a survey conducted in 1966 throughout the state of Washington, 66.7 percent of boys and 59 percent of girls stated that they wished to have a career in professional occupations. However, 57 percent of the boys and only 31.9 percent of the girls stated that they actually expected to be working in such an occupation. A study has indicated that fewer than 5 percent of all professional women fill those positions which to most people in the United States connote professions: physician, lawyer, judge, engineer, scientist, editor, reporter, college president, or professor. Studies show (from the data bank) that 85 percent of women with a B.A. in liberal arts are working in jobs that have nothing to do with their degree.

Factual, Not-Agree Statements

Research has shown that different attitudes are expressed toward female and male infants as early as two days of age. Available evidence suggests that sex role stereotyping has increased significantly in the past quarter-century and that the educational system is one of the social institutions which has reflected this trend in both curriculum and personnel practices. During the high school years, for example, girls' performance in ability tests begins to decline. A study by Hartley showed that girls' intention to work after marriage likewise declined with age. Yet a study by the Center for Continuing Education at Sarah Lawrence College documents that women who return to college to earn undergraduate degrees demonstrate notably higher achievement and motivation than young under-graduates who complete their degree in four years. In spite of this, Dr. Helen Astin, in a study of women doctorates, noted that women were less likely to receive aid from the government and from their institutions and were therefore more likely to rely on their own savings or support from their family and/or spouse. The decreasing status of women in the labor force, the ever-widening salary gap, the continuation of women in limited female occupations—these facts have been widely documented. For example, the average woman with a bachelor's degree who works full time earns about the same median income as a man who is a high school dropout.

**Part V
Policy Impacts in the States**

13 Policy Impacts on Hispanics and Women: A State Case Study

Cal Clark, Janet Clark
and *Jose Z. Garcia*

Disadvantaged minorities are likely to be the subject of a vicious cycle in their relationship to the political system. In the United States particularly, people with lower statuses as denoted by education, income, and other socioeconomic status (SES) indicators have significantly lower participation rates than their more fortunate brethren. As a result, their political wants or demands are not nearly so well communicated to the political decisionmakers, and the public policies which emerge are not well tailored to their political needs.[1] When the disadvantaged form a distinctive minority on some basis considered salient by the society, their opportunity for political aid or redress would appear particularly low, barring a normative "change of conscience" in the population at large, since their very lack of numbers inhibits effective political action.

Yet the relationship of these groups to the political processes might well be expected to differ in contexts where their minority status is not as pronounced as it is in U.S. society as a whole. New Mexico should provide an excellent place for studying policy impacts on minorities where their numerical disadvantage is greatly attenuated. The majority, Anglos, constitute just a fraction over 50 percent of the state's population while the largest minority group, Hispanics, are 40 percent. Women compose another group, generally considered a "minority," whose numbers are such that they should not be "locked-in losers" on the basis of simple arithmetic. Women differ from ethnic minorities such as Hispanics in one vital respect, however, since they are distributed approximately proportionately over the various social strata in the population. Hence, comparing women and Hispanics in New Mexico should provide an interesting case study of policy impacts on minorities. While they are two different types of minorities, both have the potential to numerically exert substantial political leverage at the polls.

This chapter describes and compares the position of Hispanics and women

The authors gratefully acknowledge the cooperation of Dr. Garrey Carruthers, State Chairman of the New Mexico Republican Party; Dr. Glen Gares, Personnel Director of the State of New Mexico; and the Honorable Gladys Hansen, State Senator from Dona Ana County, in obtaining data for this chapter. They are not responsible for the analysis and interpretations herein, however, which are solely our own.

177

in the New Mexico polity during the 1970s. Political events during even the limited time span of this decade should have significantly improved the status of women and Hispanics in the state. In terms of legal and constitutional status, the New Mexico legislature passed the Human Rights Act in 1969, creating a Human Rights Commission to receive and investigate complaints and to prevent discriminatory practices based on race, religion, color, national origin, or ancestry in regard to employment, public accommodations, housing, and financial assistance. Three years later the voters of the state added a constitutional amendment which prohibits discriminatory legislation based on sex. Subsequently, state laws have been brought into conformity with the amendment, and the Commission on the Status of Women was created. Finally, several events in the more intangible political realm also seemed to signal a more favorable environment for minorities. Court-ordered reapportionment in 1965–1966 led to significant shifts in the composition of the state legislature. In the early 1970s a liberal coalition of Hispanics and Anglos gained ascendency in the House, and at present the leadership of both the House and Senate is Spanish-surnamed. In 1974 a Hispanic, Jerry Apodaca, was elected Governor for the first time since 1918, an event widely perceived as having significance for the Spanish-speaking people of the state.

In particular, we examine three specific facets of Hispanics' and women's place in the political system of New Mexico. The position of women and Hispanics in New Mexican society is of central importance to assessing their status; so the first empirical section considers their degree of equality with Anglos and males in terms of education, employment, and income. The second facet is the composition of the political elites, and data are presented on the state legislature, Supreme Court, and political party leaders during this time frame. Policy outcomes form the third topic. In this area, we consider state laws of special relevance for women and Hispanics and state employment practices.

The Socioeconomic Status of Hispanics and Women in New Mexico

If women and Hispanics do constitute disadvantaged groups in New Mexican society, this should be reflected in their educational achievement, unemployment rates, and income levels. Tables 13–1 through 13–4 present 1970 census data on these variables. The percentage of the two ethnic and two sex groups in subcategories of these variables are reported first, and an index of representation in each category of Hispanics relative to Anglos and of women relative to men is computed by dividing the percentage of Hispanics (or women) in each category by the proportion of Anglos (or men) in the same category. Thus, equality in social status would be indicated by all the categories of a variable having representation ratios of approximately unity. The expected disadvantaged position of

Table 13-1
1970 Education Levels by Ethnicity and Sex

	Male (Percent)	Female (Percent)	Female Representation Ratio	Anglo (Percent)	Hispanic (Percent)	Hispanic Representation Ratio
Less than high school	27.1	25.2	.93	14.8	39.1	2.64
Some high school	22.2	24.5	1.10	20.7	26.7	1.29
High school	25.7	30.6	1.19	32.0	24.2	.76
Some college	13.1	12.0	.92	17.5	6.6	.38
College	5.8	5.1	.88	8.3	2.0	.24
Graduate school	6.0	2.8	.47	6.7	1.5	.22

Table 13-2
1970 Unemployment Rates

	Males	Females	Female Representation Ratio	Anglos	Hispanics	Hispanic Representation Ratio
Number in work force	234,249	123,988		213,518	122,054	
Number unemployed	11,323	8,322		8,565	8,865	
Percentage unemployed	4.8	6.7	1.40	4.0	7.3	1.83
Percentage not working in 1970	2.5	4.7	1.88	2.3	4.4	1.93

Table 13-3
1970 Income Distribution by Race and Sex

	Male (Percent)	Female (Percent)	Female Representation Ratio	Anglo (Percent)	Hispanic (Percent)	Hispanic Representation Ratio
Under $2,000	23.4	51.4	2.20	30.3	39.6	1.32
$2,000 –3,999	16.3	23.1	1.42	17.2	21.7	1.26
$4,000 –5,999	14.7	12.6	.86	12.7	15.6	1.23
$6,000 –7,999	14.6	7.6	.52	12.3	11.3	.92
$8,000 –9,999	11.1	3.1	.28	9.5	6.0	.63
$10,000–14,999	12.6	1.8	.14	11.3	4.3	.38
Over $15,000	7.4	0.6	.08	7.0	1.4	.20
Median income	$5,415	$1,929	.36	$4,252	$2,938	.69

Table 13–4
1970 Median Income by Education

	Males	Females	Female Representation Ratio	Hispanic Representation Ratio within Males	Hispanic Representation Ratio within Females
Less than 5th grade	$ 2,170	$ 911	.42	.66	.54
5th to 7th	3,586	1,219	.34	.98	1.04
Grade school	4,616	1,446	.31	.82	1.04
Some high school	5,132	1,635	.32	.71	.87
High school	6,353	2,636	.41	.77	.95
Some college	6,314	2,641	.42	.85	.99
College	10,017	4,524	.45	.76	1.43
Graduate school	11,533	7,024	.61	.80	1.05

women and Hispanics, on the other hand, would be shown by ratios substantially greater than 1 in the lower categories and less than 1 in the higher ones.

The data on education in table 13-1 show substantial differences between women and Hispanics. The latter are substantially overrepresented in the lowest two education categories, slightly underrepresented in the third category, and greatly underrepresented among college attenders who compose about 22 percent of the population. Thus, Hispanics definitely conform to the prediction of educational inequality. Women, on the other hand, differ little from men in educational achievements as they are significantly underrepresented only among those who have done graduate work beyond their initial college degree. This finding is consistent with the previous observation that women can share to some extent the social status of the other nonsexual reference groups to which they belong.

When we turn to actual participation in the economic sector, however, women join Hispanics in a position of clear inequality. Table 13-2 shows that both women and Hispanics have significantly higher unemployment rates than have males and Anglos, respectively. Hispanics are almost twice as likely as Anglos to be unemployed and to have suffered the long-term unemployment indicated by not having worked at all in 1970. Women's overall disadvantage in employment is slightly less; but, unlike Hispanics relative to Anglos, they are especially concentrated in the long-term unemployment category. Women's much lower participation in the labor force than men's, in addition, almost certainly results to some extent from perceptions of limited female access to the job market.

In terms of the individual income data reported in table 13-3, Hispanics and women are again clearly disadvantaged in New Mexico since both are concentrated in the lower income categories and almost totally absent from the group earning more than $10,000 a year. In contrast to the unemployment situation, women appear significantly worse off than Hispanics in terms of the relative "majority-minority" gap. Women's median income is only 36 percent of men's while the Hispanic median is 69 percent of the Anglo, and women are greatly underrepresented among those earning over $6,000 per year while the under-representation cutoff line for Hispanics is $8,000.

If income is assumed to be tied to qualifications as roughly indexed by education, this finding may seem to depart from the previous implications of the education data which showed minimal male-female differences in educational achievement in contrast to quite substantial Anglo-Hispanic ones. Therefore, table 13-4 introduces education as a control variable to further explain the relationship between minority status and income by presenting the median income of these sex and ethnic groups broken down by eight levels of education. (Since there is a somewhat different pattern, Hispanic-Anglo comparisons are made separately for men and women.) Women's disadvantaged position is starkly evident. For all levels of education, except those few going beyond a college B.A., women's median incomes are only about 40 percent of men's with a comparable education, and this ratio rises to only 60 percent for those having some graduate education.[2] The relative position of Hispanics is much better. Among women, there is little, if any, difference between Anglos and Hispanics, while Hispanic men have median incomes about 80 percent as high as Anglo males with comparable edcuation. Hence, at least in 1970, Hispanics do suffer some disadvantage in the New Mexican economy even after their lower level of education is taken into account, but the gap is not nearly as wide as for women.

The income figures suggest that the position of Hispanics compared to Anglos in New Mexico is somewhat disadvantaged when education is controlled. A bleaker picture of relative and absolute deprivation emerges, however, when we consider two further sets of data in tables 13-5 and 13-6, poverty status in New Mexico and comparisons between New Mexico and the rest of the United States. The position of Hispanics in New Mexico is woeful in regards to poverty conditions. Almost one-third are below the poverty line, and about 12 percent of them are in the extreme poverty category of having a family income that is less than half the official poverty level. In comparative terms, Hispanics are more than four times as likely as Anglos to be in these categories of economic distress—a disadvantage substantially more extreme than implied by the income data. Moreover, Hispanics relative deprivation is much greater in New Mexico than in the nation as a whole. Table 13-5 shows that the poverty rate for Hispanics is 40 percent higher in New Mexico than for all the United States and that the Anglo-Hispanic gap is much worse in New Mexico than in the country at

Table 13–5
1970 Poverty Status

	New Mexico			United States		
	Anglo	*Hispanic*	*Hispanic Representation Ratio*	*Anglo*	*Hispanic*	*Hispanic Representation Ratio*
Percentage below poverty	7.6	31.7	4.17	7.9	22.7	2.87
Percentage half of poverty	2.6	11.7	4.50	2.9	7.9	2.72

large. Table 13-6 compares the median income of Hispanic males in the four states bordering Mexico and the country as a whole; and New Mexico, along with Texas, displays comparatively great ethnic differentiation in income.

Despite extenuating circumstances such as part-time and noncareer employment status for women and lower educational achievement for Hispanics, both groups appear to be significant "losers" in New Mexico's socioeconomic system. There is a tremendous income gap between men and women at similar education levels, and Hispanics in New Mexico have a relative income level substantially worse than Hispanics in the nation as a whole. These conditions might well be expected to generate poltical demands for relief and redress. Women and Hispanics, to a lesser extent, should be vitally interested in nondiscrimination and affirmative action laws to ensure competition for jobs based on ability. Hispanics should be interested in measures equalizing educational opportunities in the state. An attack on poverty, furthermore, should directly benefit a substantial proportion of the Hispanic population. Political leaders obviously have a paramount role in determining what issues and needs are considered politically rele-

Table 13–6
Male Median Income

	Hispanics	*Anglos*	*Representation Ratio*
United States	$5,249	$6,918	.76
Arizona	5,150	6,748	.76
California	6,054	7,798	.78
Texas	3,917	6,643	.59
New Mexico	4,207	6,896	.61

vant and what public policies will emerge in response to them. Thus, we now examine the political elites in New Mexico to see how well Hispanics and women are represented among them.

Political Elites and Minority Representation

Hispanic and female membership (or lack of it) in the political elites of New Mexico is important for several reasons. Political life might theoretically provide a path to status and upward mobility that could serve as an alternative to economic advancement. Of more direct political relevance is the presumption that the composition of the state's leadership should affect the policy response, if any, to the inequalities outlined above. Therefore, the likelihood that the problems confronting women and Hispanics will be perceived as politically relevant and will elicit attempted government redress should be significantly influenced by whether or not they receive proportionate representation among New Mexico's policymakers.

Hispanics and especially women have certainly not fared very well in attaining the top positions in New Mexico's executive and judical structures. No women have been governor or served on the state supreme court. The present governor, Jerry Apodaca, is the first Hispanic chief executive since 1918. Until recently Hispanics have been underrepresented on the Supreme Court bench. No Spanish-surnamed individual served on the Court from statehood in 1912 until the 1950s when two gained this distinction, and up through 1970 only two of the thirty-five justices had possessed Spanish surnames. In the 1970s, Hispanics have fared much better. Three of the nine new members of the bench are Spanish-surnamed individuals; and since 1973 two of the five judges have been Hispanics, making their representation on the court 40 percent, which equal their proportion of the state's population. In addition, an unusually activist attorney general, Toney Anaya, has made this post clearly the second most important statewide elective office in New Mexico. Therefore, in the late 1970s, Hispanics have been well represented in the top executive and judicial positions; however, following the 1978 elections, both the governor and attorney general will again be Anglos.

Hispanic representation in the state legislature has been more consistent since Spanish-surnamed legislators have constituted about 25 percent of both houses since the late 1950s. Even the substantial legislative reapportionment of 1966 and 1972 had little impact on the data in table 13–7. Reapportionment was of vital political importance to the state, however, since it ultimately led to a realignment of the power structure in the legislature and to Hispanics' gaining the top leadership posts in the House. Also, unlike the census data in the previous section which classified all people of Spanish heritage as Hispanics, these elite ethnic classifications are limited to leaders with Spanish surnames so that

Table 13-7
Percentage of Hispanics and Women in New Mexican Legislature

	Hispanics		Women	
	House (%)	Senate (%)	House (%)	Senate (%)
1959	23	22	3	0
1961	21	22	2	0
1963	26	22	2	0
1965	26	22	1	3
1966	24	25	1	3
1969	27	26	3	0
1970	27	24	3	0
1972	22	29	3	0
1973	23	22	0	5
1974	20	24	0	5
1975	24	24	4	5
1977	24	24	6	2

the actual number of Hispanics is somewhat higher—8 percent higher in 1972, for example.[3] Thus, while Hispanics may be slightly underrepresented in numbers in the legislature, their current leadership positions indicate that they have attained their share of legislative clout.

Women, in contrast, have gained only token representation in the legislature. There has been at least one woman in the legislature continuously since the late 1950s, but until 1975 when three women were seated in the House, there were never more than two women in either chamber during this period. The number of women legislators increased slightly between 1975 and 1978 to a total of five, the first time since 1950 that there have been more than three at any one time. Still, women have never formed more than a miniscule portion of the legislature.

Leaders of the two major parties comprise a more informal set of political elites and influentials. Table 13-8 summarizes the ethnic and sexual composition of the Republican and Democratic state central committees for 1974 and 1978. In addition to the state party officials, the members are broken down into four groups according to their county's "political culture": (1) the Hispanic north, which is composed of counties with predominantly (65 percent plus) Spanish populations, (2) the southeastern "Little Texas" region which is the most conservative part of the state on political issues and ethnic relations, (3) three "urban" counties, and (4) a residual category which we call, for want of a better term, central agricultural.[4]

The pattern of Hispanic representation in the party elites displayed in table 13-8 conforms well with a priori expectations. Given the very strong association of Hispanics with the Democratic party,[5] the parties' extreme difference in over-

Table 13-8
Hispanics and Women on State Party Central Committees

| | Republicans | | | | | | Democrats | | | | | |
| | 1974 | | | 1978 | | | 1974 | | | 1977 | | |
	Total	Hispanic	Female	Total	Hispanic	Female	Total	Hispanic	Female	Total	Hispanic	Female
State level	7	14%	43%	7	14%	57%	6	67%	33%	6	50%	50%
Hispanic north	41	54	29	46	52	35	35	89	26	40	75	30
Urban	82	20	30	81	12	36	60	47	28	63	43	38
Central agricultural	80	13	39	90	14	33	39	36	31	41	39	34
Little Texas	70	3	24	71	1	30	27	4	33	28	14	46
Other[a]	6	0	67	6	0	50	—	—	—	—	—	—
Total	286	18%	32%	301	16%	34%	167	47%	29%	178	45%	37%
County chairs	29	24%	10%	31	23%	16%	32	41%[b]	19%[b]	32	41%	9%

[a]These are representatives from the Young Republican and Republican Women's organizations.
[b]There is an overlap of one here since one Hispanic woman was a county chairperson.

all proportion of Hispanic central committee members (almost 50 percent for the Democrats to less than 20 percent for the Republicans) should be expected. Regional differences also follow our initial assumptions since within both parties Hispanics have by far their greatest representation in the north and almost none in "little Texas." Women, in contrast, have little significant variation in their degree of representation in the party elites by either party or region, although on the basis of imputed "liberalism" it might have been hypothesized that they should have done better among Democrats and in urban areas. While their approximately 33 percent level is much less than their proportion of the population, it is certainly well above their miniscule representation in public office; and in numerical terms, it is large enough to suggest at least the potential for political influence in party councils. In addition, both groups have scored major successes in winning county chairs, positions which connote more than a modicum of political accomplishment and power in New Mexico.

Women and Hispanics, in sum, differ very substantially in their position within the New Mexican political elite. Hispanics in the late 1970s are represented in the government and party elites just lightly less than proportionally to their share of the population. As a result, they appear to have an excellent opportunity to influence state policies substantially. Women, in contrast, compose a hardly noticeable minority of state public officials. Their much higher representation among the party leadership almost certainly stems from two reasons that are contradictory in their implications for women's political power. On the one hand, the absence of partisan and regional variation in women's party representation suggests the *pro forma* inclusion of a certain proportion of women on the central committees which would not necessarily bring effective political power. On the other hand, women's holding a significant percentage of county chairs coupled with the national trend of increased women's participation implies that the expansion of women's participation in party affairs may be a first step toward broader entry into the government leadership.[6]

This disparity in elite representation may be traced to the different roles of these two groups in the New Mexican political system. For reasons of both numbers and cultural-organizational heritage, New Mexican Hispanics differ from most other Spanish communities in the United States in that their political participation is at least as high as that of Anglos, they generally control communities in which they are a majority, and they are perceived as a "legitimate" political group deserving explicit representation according to the New Mexican "rules of the game."[7] In short, they have achieved an institutionalized position in the state's political processes. Women, unfortunately, have not, despite their numerical majority of the population. In any event, the importance, if any, of elite composition turns on leadership impact on public policy. Hence, we now turn to the question of how Hispanics and women fare in two policy areas.

Minority-Targeted Legislation and
State Employment of Policy Outcomes

In view of the marked economic inequalities existing in 1970, the potential minority demand for "equal opportunity" legislation would appear quite high. During the ten legislative sessions from 1969 to 1978, laws regarding fourteen issues of specific relevance to minority groups in New Mexico were passed. Of these, twelve issue areas applied mainly to women; one, the 1969 Human Rights Act, applied to minority groups in general (but excluded women until it was amended in 1975); and one, the Consumer Protection Act, was not explicitly targeted at minorities but encompassed a subject considered of special interest to women and of general benefit to minorities and the poor. No laws pertaining only to Hispanics were enacted.

The legislature tended to be sympathetic to the needs expressed by women's groups, and the legislative record of policies for women has been outstanding in recent years. The state abortion law was modified in a more liberal direction in 1969; the divorce law was liberalized in 1971 and 1973; credit qualifications were changed in 1975; and the rape law was replaced to ease the prosecution of offenders. In 1978 additional legislation provided major funding for sex-crime prosecution. Also funds were made available to assist "displaced homemakers" in receiving welfare assistance and vocational training. Perhaps the most significant achievements were the passage of the state Equal Rights Amendment in 1972, the modification of state statutes to make them conform with it, and the ratification of the federal ERA. Rcent efforts to repeal this ratification and to reduce the impact of the state ERA on certain sexist institutions have been beaten down, and the governor vetoed a 1978 bill limiting state funding of abortions. However, the actual impact of these new laws so far has been substantially less than anticipated. Several female officials attribute this lack of progress to the problems of implementation and administration. Many of the state bureaucrats as well as the general public still think and act in terms of old stereotypes and social standards.[8]

The policy outputs of the legislature during this period seem to be at variance with the levels of representation of women and Hispanics. While Hispanics enjoyed far greater numbers and power in the legislature, almost all the specifically targeted bills were directed toward the condition of women. This may be explained by the previous hypothesis that the place of Hispanics within the New Mexican political system is fairly well institutionalized. Thus, demands for change in their legal status should be fairly limited in nature, and the comprehensive Human Rights Act of 1969 could well have been seen as providing an adequate legal framework for attacking the economic inequities and the discrimination that still exists in some parts of the state. Women's status, in contrast, is undergoing rapid change which creates pressures for legal changes and equality. Many of the women's issues such as abortion, divorce, displaced home-makers, and sex crimes may increase the equity of women's position in New Mexico but should have little effect on the overall distribution of economic or political power. Other laws—amending the Human Rights Act to include women, bringing state laws into compliance with the ERA, and creating a Commission on the Status of Women—really do no more than give women rights equal to those guaranteed to ethnic and racial minorities. The ability of women to score these legislative successes stems from a combination of general liberal sympathy and backing, an absence (at the time) of a strong and vocal opposition, and the quiet work of a few key women legislators and politicians.

The second policy area concerns an affirmative action program for state employment inaugurated by Governor Bruce King in 1972, following the first comprehensive study of minorities' roles in the state labor force. This program should affect minority status both directly by its contribution to the overall employment situation and indirectly by determining the people who will actu-ally administer state laws and policies. It, in conjunction with the other favor-able political changes taking place at that time, should have led to a significant improvement in state employment of women and Hispanics, especially since the state workforce expanded by 27 percent during 1971-1977, permitting consider-able flexibility for minority hiring and promotion. To test this hypothesis, we examined data from three studies of the State Personnel Board conducted in December 1971, March 1974, and December 1977.[9]

Table 13-9 shows that in relation to their respective shares of the New

Table 13-9
State Employment of Hispanics and Women

	1971	1974	1977
Hispanics			
Percentage of population (1970 census)	40.10	40.10	40.10
Percentage of state employment	55.20	56.00	57.30
Population representation ratio	1.38	1.40	1.43
Representation ratio by county			
population	1.02	1.03	a
Women			
Percentage of population (1970 census)	50.70	50.70	50.70
Percentage of state employment	39.10	40.70	43.60
Representation ratio	.77	.80	.86
Percentage of labor market, 1970	33.90		
Labor market representation ratio	1.15		

[a]Cannot be computed because approximately 1,000 state employees were not classified by county.

Mexican population, Hispanics are signficantly overrepresented and women significantly underrepresented at all three time points and that the proportion of each group grew very slightly over the entire period. However, this picture of relative representativeness alters dramatically if the geographic location of state jobs and the proportion of women in the labor market are taken into account. If each county is assigned an "expected" number of Hispanic employees by multiplying its number of state workers by its percentage of Hispanic population, these "expected" figures sum to almost exactly the number of Hispanics on the New Mexican payroll.[10] Similarly, comparing the proportion of women state employees to women's 1970 share of the New Mexican labor market shows a very slight overrepresentation for female employees. Thus, if the county locations of state jobs and sexual shares of the job market are controlled, Hispanics and women are hired on an approximately proportionate basis.

While women and Hispanics may be proportionately represented in the entire state employment, this says nothing about their distribution within the workforce. If they were concentrated in menial jobs, for example, inequality would still exist. To examine this distribution, we divided the state grade steps into eight categories on the basis of the percentage of employees who were in them in 1971 and 1977. Status categories 1 (lowest) through 7 (highest) are derived from the regular state workforce while the exempt category is composed of the governor's political appointees (four in each department) who are outside the normal civil service system. The proportion of people in every category is made as similar as possible between the two years to promote comparability.

Table 13-10 clearly demonstrates that equal representation for women and Hispanics does not hold when it is defined as equal access to all levels of employment. Both groups are clearly underrepresented in the higher grades of state government, but there are some interesting contrasts between groups and years.

Table 13-10
Representation of Women and Hispanics by Job Status

	Cumulative Proportion of Workforce		Hispanic Representation Ratio		Female Representation Ratio	
	1971	1977	1971	1977	1971	1977
Status level 1	17.3	19.7	2.54	2.25	1.88	1.99
Status level 2	40.5	44.2	1.94	1.74	1.66	1.28
Status level 3	62.9	62.9	1.30	1.24	.73	1.50
Status level 4	80.2	81.7	.52	.55	.99	.52
Status level 5	91.6	91.4	.34	.40	.42	.38
Status level 6	96.0	95.9	.35	.36	.20	.13
Status level 7	97.5	97.5	.10	.12	.09	.16
Exempt	100.0	100.0	.32	.53	.71	.58

In 1971 women were significantly better off than Hispanics. They were significantly underrepresented only in the top 20 percent of state jobs while Hispanics were underrepresented in the top 40 percent. For both groups but especially for women, their underrepresentation was substantially less in the exempt category of political appointees than at the top of the regular state hierarchy, suggesting at least some political sensitivity to the question of minority and female hiring. By 1977 the position of Hispanics had improved slightly but consistently in all seven regular status categories, indicating that they received a slight preference in promotions and/or that the newly hired Hispanics were somewhat more likely to be placed in higher posts than those employed before 1971. Hispanics experienced their largest gain, however, in the exempt positions, indicating that Governor Apodaca's administration has made a strong effort to redress the ethnic imbalance in the top positions of New Mexico's government by its political appointments; however, in the regular state workforce, progress has been only glacial. In contrast to the muted advance of Hispanics, women suffered a significant setback in their distribution over the state workforce between 1971 and 1977. At the first time point, they were significantly underrepresented in only the top 20 percent of state jobs, but at the final one their underrepresentation had expanded to the top 40 percent. Further, there was a significant drop in their representation in the exempt group, in direct contrast to the Hispanics' gain. Hence, women seem definitely underrepresented in the hiring for and promotion to the upper positions of state government.

Therefore, in spite of the passage of a state ERA in New Mexico, the state's affirmative action program, and a seemingly more favorable public atmosphere signaled by the election of an Hispanic governor, the inequalities in state employment which existed in 1971 persist to this day. This should not necessarily reflect adversely upon the commitment of those public officials involved in these policies or upon the ultimate success of the policies themselves. Still, the one policy for which systematic impact data are available showed only minute improvement at best in the status of New Mexico's Hispanics and women over the 1970s.

Implications

The basic findings of this study can be summarized succinctly. Hispanics and women are both decidedly disadvantaged in the state's socioeconomic system. Unlike Spanish people in most of the rest of the United States, New Mexican Hispanics are represented among political elites almost proportionally to their share of the population and are thus able to exercise substantial political power. Women, in contrast, have yet to make more than the most token of entries into elite circles. Several legislative and political changes in New Mexico were expected to improve the position of minorities; but, at least in the area of state employment, no appreciable change in the status of women or Hispanics occurred. Whether these policies have narrowed the 1970 economic differentials will be seen in the 1980 census findings, but it is hard to be very optimistic on this account. That political power (for Hispanics) or favorable legislation (for women) does not inevitably eradicate socioeconomic inequalities follows Marshall's observation that the civil, political, and social components of citizenship may be quite different and that equality on one dimension does not necessarily bring (and may even conflict with) equality on the others.[11] Marshall's question of how much economic inequality can be considered consistent with the democratic assumption of equal political rights and social worth, then, is certainly applicable to New Mexico.

Several reasons come to mind to explain why a more favorable policy environment did not have a greater impact on hiring at the state government level. First, as Hispanics and women obtain the educational status required for access to higher-level jobs in state government, the probabilities that they will look for state employment may diminish as more lucrative job opportunities in private and federal job markets in New Mexico and elsewhere materialize. Thus, the labor "pool" of minority applicants may not increase even though educational levels and affirmative action programs do rise and surface. This explanation is understandably the one most favored by state employment officials (Anglo and Hispanic) themselves.

Second, given the differences between Hispanics and women in their levels of representation in the elite political structures, such as the state legislature, it may well be that ethnic political representation is largely irrelevant to the enforcement of policies designed to help ethnic and sex groups. The greater representation of Hispanics versus women in the political elite circles seems to have had little effect on the enforcement of the policies themselves since the position of neither women nor Hispanics changed significantly during the period studied. This would suggest that in New Mexico ethnic political representation may not necessarily raise the saliency of the issue of ethnic inequality in the political arena. The increase of Hispanics in the "exempt" category, however, indicates that some ethnic environmental factors may have been at work after all, although these do not seem to operate at an institutional level. That the governor appointed more Hispanics to exempt offices may be due to cultural affinities rather than to any overt ethnic solidarity or conscious attempt to improve affirmative action programs in state government. Finally, the negligible gains made by women and Hispanics may simply be due to inevitable time lags, inefficient administration, "institutional racism," or the persistence of overt discrimination. This study raises more questions than it answers.

Notes

1. Norman Nie and Sidney Verba, "Political Participation," in eds. Fred I. Greenstein and Nelson W. Polsby, *Handbook of Political Science: Nongovernmental Politics,* vol. 4 (Reading, Mass.: Addison-Wesley, 1975), pp. 38–68.

2. This wage differential can be explained partly by women's greater tendency to hold part-time jobs. Yet the close correspondence of these New Mexican differences to the findings of Barbara Deckard, *The Women's Movement: Political, Socio-economic, and Psychological Issues* (New York: Harper & Row, 1975), pp. 80–81, for fully employed men and women in the United States as a whole indicates that this bias should not be very great.

3. These comparative data are taken from F. Chris Garcia, "Manitos and Chicanos in New Mexico Politics," in ed. F. Chris Garcia, *La Causa Politicia: A Chicano Politics Reader* (Notre Dame, Ind.: University of Notre Dame Press, 1974), p. 274.

4. Paul L. Hain, "Voters, Elections, and Political Parties," in eds. F. Chris Garcia and Paul L. Hain, *New Mexico Government* (Albuquerque: University of New Mexico Press, 1976).

5. Garcia, "Manitos and Chicanos," p. 273.

6. Janet Clark, "Social and Political Attitudes of New Mexico Party Leaders," Paper presented at the annual meeting of the Western Social Science Association, April 1977, Denver. Clark found nearly universal perceptions of significantly increased women's participation in party affairs among county and state leaders of both parties.

7. Garcia, "Manitos and Chicanos," pp. 273–278, discusses the strengths and weaknesses of Hispanics' positions in New Mexico.

8. Interviews with Tasia Young, Executive Director of the New Mexico Commission on the Status of Women, state Senator Gladys Hansen, and state Representative Sharlyn Linard.

9. The 1971 data are contained in *Minority Groups in State Government: A Report to the Governor by the New Mexico State Personnel Board* (Santa Fe: State of New Mexico, 1972). The 1974 data are taken from *Indian Employment in New Mexico State Government* (Santa Fe: New Mexico Advisory Committee to the United States Commission on Civil Rights, 1974). And the 1977 figures are derived from unpublished computer printouts from the state of New Mexico.

10. This method of controlling for geographic location was developed by the authors of *Minority Groups in State Government,* p. 6.

11. T.H. Marshall, *Class, Citizenship, and Social Development* (Garden City, N.Y.: Doubleday and Co., 1965), pp. 71–134.

14 Women and Public Policy: A Comparative Analysis

Susan Welch
with the assistance of
Diane Levitt Gottheil

The purpose of the study reported here is to examine the impact of the social, political, and economic environment on a set of public policies directed toward women. States have been moving with varying degrees of enthusiasm and speed to broaden the rights of women, removing restrictions on property, contractual, and other rights in marriage, alleviating discrimination in jobs, and removing other impediments to full equality under the law. Nevertheless, there remain important differences in the treatment of men and women in many aspects of law. While some of these differences favor women (such as lower age limits on use of alcohol and the right to marry), most differences penalize them.

We begin by surveying some of the areas of public policy where there are significant differences in treatments of males and females. Then we examine the states to see if there are significant and consistent differences among the states according to the way they treat women. Finally, the characteristics of states that have more and less favorable laws concerning women are analyzed.

Women and Public Policy: An Overview

Several types of public policy are especially relevant to the legal rights of women. We focus specifically on employment laws, laws regulating the rights of women in marriage, rape laws, and a most recent focus of concern, passage of the Equal Rights Amendment (ERA).[1]

Employment

According to federal law, one cannot pay women less than men doing the same work, if the job requires equal skill, effort, and responsibility [Equal Pay Act 29 U.S.C. 206(d)]. Sex discrimination is prohibited by the Civil Rights Act of 1964

The authors would like to thank Alan Booth, David R. Johnson, and John G. Peters, University of Nebraska-Lincoln, for their many useful suggestions.

(Title VII) for employment, the Executive Order 11246 of 1965 for employment under federal contracts, and a 1969 Executive Order (11478) for the federal government itself. However, state laws on these topics are also important, because many women (and men, too) are not covered by federal laws.[2] Thus, a sizable part of the workforce must look to the state for protection; and, in fact, many states have enacted their own equal pay and fair employment practices laws.

Some state laws set conditions of work that are different for women than for men. For example, some states have maximum-hours-of-work laws that set different standards for women; others have mandatory rest periods for women but not men; others forbid women night employment; and so on. Many states have laws that simply bar women from certain kinds of jobs.[3] While these laws had the ostensible purpose of protecting the health and safety of women, they also protect males from female employment competition.[4] Their effect is to deny a woman the right to decide for herself whether a job is too demanding for her own skills and physique, thus in some cases depriving her of changes for better-paying employment.

Rights of Wives

According to common law, husband and wife were one person; a woman who married gave up most of her legal identity.[5] The husband, not the wife, had the right to control property, press legal claims, and make contracts. These restrictions on married women have gradually been mitigated through various state laws referred to as the Married Women's Property Acts. Despite these changes, some legal impediments for married women exist in many states. Most prominent are restrictions on entering into contracts,[6] engaging in a business, retaining one's maiden name, and maintaining a separate domicile for the wife after marriage. Some states also continue to have restrictions on the right of a woman to obtain or sell property in her own right.

Rape

Rape is a crime thought to be least often reported by its victim. Reluctance to report the crime is due in large part to the treatment that a woman can expect from the police, medical personnel, and in the courtroom while the accused assailant is being tried. In a rape case, unlike most other kinds of felony charges, the victim is traditionally as much on trial as the accused. This anomaly is due to the ambivalence that many have about rape (that is, the belief that women may have invited the attack) which is reflected in the laws that govern what is required for a rape conviction. The prosecution has to show not only that the woman did not consent, but also that she actively resisted the attack. The differences among the states in laws concerning rape convictions, then, revolve on the definition and extent of resistance that the woman has to offer, on the one hand, and the corroborative evidence, if any, necessary to prove this resistance, on the other. For example, in several states evidence other than the woman's own word is necessary. In most states, the prior sex life of the woman is considered relevant to evaluating her credibility. And many states specify that the woman must have shown resistance up to points that would seem ridiculous if applied to other felonies such as robbery or assault; for example, in Minnesota a woman must resist until she is unconscious or fears great bodily injury.

ERA

Though equal rights amendment proposals have been introduced in every Congress since 1923, it was not until 1972 that the resolution passed. After an initial flurry of twenty-eight ratifications the first year, the ratification process has slowed as opposition forces have been mobilized.[7] With thirty-five states having ratified the amendment, three more are needed to bring the amendment into force. The amendment would outlaw discrimination on the basis of sex, thus nullifying some of the laws discussed above.

Hypotheses

We assumed that policies toward women would be related to a variety of socioeconomic and political characteristics of the state. This relationship would not be remarkable, since such characteristics have been found to affect other state policies examined.[8] Our hypotheses concern the specific socioeconomic and political characteristics that are related to equalitarian public policies. Figure 14-1 illustrates the causal model we are proposing. We conceptualize our variables as part of four constructs; general socioeconomic status factors (SES), the economic potential of women (EPW), the political climate of the state (PC), and the political potential of women (PPW).

SES

Equalitarian policies toward women are more likely to be found in states that are highly industrialized and urbanized, with a population that is well educated and affluent. Education and urban residence have been found to be associated with tolerance and liberal social welfare policies, both of which would lead one to predict more equal treatment of women as well. Further, economic develop-

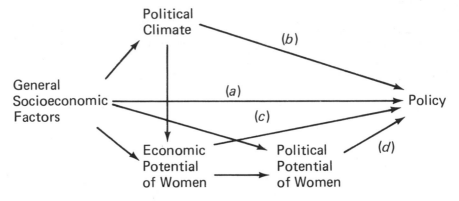

Figure 14-1. A Causal Model of Influences on Public Policy Toward Women.

ment tends to break down traditional sex roles, a factor again promoting equalitarian treatment. We hypothesize that SES factors influence policy both directly and through each of the other factors. In line with previous policy research that points to the dominance of socioeconomic factors rather than political factors in explaining policy,[9] we expect the direct impact of the SES (path *a*, figure 14-1) to be rather large in comparison to its indirect effect through the other constructs and in comparison to the direct paths of political climate (path *b*), economic (*c*), and political potential of women (*d*).

EPW

Equalitarian policies toward women are more likely to be found in states where women are a greater part of the workforce. Because political participation is greater among employed women than housewives, they may represent an independent force for improved public policies toward women.[10] We would expect that the direct path of EPW to be larger than that of PPW.

PC

Equalitarian policies toward women are more likely to be found in states with a supportive political environment. Where party competition is greater, parties are encouraged to offer benefits to the have-nots. Likewise, a competitive party system may lead parties to be more sensitive to demands of women in order not to lose support at the polls. Thus, we would expect competitive states to have the most equalitarian policies. One might expect states dominated by Democrats rather than Republicans to be the next most equalitarian since liberals are more sympathetic to women's rights than are conservatives;[11] however, given the predominantly Southern locale of strongly Democratic states, we do not expect them to be predisposed to pass equalitarian legislation. Thus, we expect no differences between states dominated by Republicans and those dominated by Democrats. We anticipate finding the most equalitarian policies in states with the most moralistic political cultures rather than the traditional or individualistic ones.[12] Overall, we predict PC variables to have a substantial direct path to policy, but not as substantial as that of SES.

PPW

Further, equalitarian policies toward women are more likely to be found in states where women have a greater role in political decision making. While certainly not all women in policy-making positions identify themselves with the women's movement, such women could be predicted to be more sensitive to inequalities written into law.

In sum, we expect that implementation of equalitarian policies toward woment is more likely to be successfully passed in states with populations that are well educated, affluent, urbanized, and industrialized and that possess a politically competitive and moralistic political culture. Additionally, we have postulated that the political and economic resources of the women themselves will increase the chances of equalitarian legislation.

Data and Methods

Policy Variables

Four variables were used to measure policy in the area of employment. State laws were considered equalitarian if they (1) require equal pay; (2) establish fair employment practices; (3) do not establish maximum hours of work for women; and (4) do not bar women from any specific occupations.[13]

In the area of rights of married women, three variables were used to measure state policy. Policy was considered equalitarian if laws (1) do not restrict a married woman's right to maintain a separate domicile for voting purposes; (2) do not restrict a married woman's use of her "maiden name," and (3) do not restrict, in a manner different from that of the husband, a married woman's right to enter into contracts.[14]

With respect to policy related to the crime of rape, two variables were used. Equalitarian laws would not require (1) corroborative evidence in rape trials and (2) unreasonable proof of resistance.[15]

Finally, states which have ratified the Equal Rights Amendment were considered more equalitarian in the area of policy toward women.

A composite scale was created by standardizing the scores on the employment, rape, marriage, and ERA variables and then summing them.

Independent Variables

To assess the socioeconomic status of the states' populations, we used an index of affluence and industrialization.[16] These indices are factor scores on two dimensions of state characteristics. The dimension labeled *affluence* is highly correlated with income, education, and urbanization, while *industrialization* correlates highly with the size of manufacturing establishments, value added by manufacturing, percentage of the population employed in manufacturing, and mean value per acre of farmland and buildings. These two indices provide a convenient and parsimonious way to summarize several characteristics of the states.

To measure political competitiveness, we used Ranney's compilation.[17] He examines party control of the gubernatorial and state legislative offices to measure competitiveness. These rankings were used to create two dummy variables: one, whether the state was rated as competive, and, two, whether the state was a modified, one-party Republican state. Sharkansky's operationalization of Elazar's state political cultures was also used to measure political coloration in the state.[18]

To assess the potential economic status of women, we used the percentage of the labor force that was female and the proportion of the female labor force comprised of women in the professional and managerial categories.[19]

We chose as our measures of the political potential of women the proportions of their membership in the upper and lower houses of the legislature.[20]

Findings

In table 14-1 we can see the relationships among the various aspects of public policy toward women. While there is some cohesion among these dimensions, it is modest at best. Five of the six relationships are positive, but one of them is less than .10. There are probably several explanations for these rather low correlations. One is simply the different time periods when the laws were enacted. Another is that these various laws are obviously not seen by many people as part of a common "treatment of women" dimension. While all these policies are of interest to women's rights groups, each has implications other than just for women, or at least may be seen to affect other groups in different ways.

We find an identifiable cluster of states at the bottom end of our scale and

Table 14-1
Correlations between Policy and the Independent Variables

Independent Variables	Employ-ment	Marriage	Rape	ERA	Composite Scale
General Socioeconomic					
Affluence	.47	.13	.07	.39	.45
Industrialization	-.27	.08	.25	-.08	-.01
Economic Status of Women					
Percentage of labor force					
women	.27	-.18	.01	-.28	-.20
Managerial proportion of					
female labor force	.26	-.05	-.12	.30	.16
Political Climate					
Party competition[a]	.27	.17	.07	.20	.30
Republican dominance[a]	.28	.06	-.01	.28	.26
Political culture[a]	-.50	-.18	.05	-.62	-.53
Political Potential of Women					
Percentage of lower					
house women	.19	.02	.09	.21	.22
Percentage of upper					
house women	.38	-.05	-.25	.31	.17
Employment	–	-.11	.07	.42	.58
Marriage		–	.13	.13	.48
Rape	–	–	–	.18	.58

[a]Party competition: 1 = competitive states; 0 = all others.
Republican dominance: 1 = modified, one-party Republican states; 0 = all others.
Elazar's political culture as operationalized by Sharkansky: 1 = moralistic; 5 = individualistic; 9 = traditional; various combinations are placed in between these points. All correlations are Pearson's r.

a mixed group at the top. The inequalitarian cluster is clearly defined by region. All states are either Deep South or Southwest.[21] The equalitarian states are a more mixed lot. Three are large Eastern industrial states, and three others are Western states of varying social and economic coloration.[22] However, they all are characterized by a mixed moralistic and individualistic political culture.

In table 14-1 the correlations between the independent variables and each of the six policy variables are also presented. In general, the employment laws, ERA passage, and the total scale are at least modestly related to all the independent variables, with the exception of industrialization. On the other hand marriage and rape laws are little related to any of the independent variables, except that rape laws are related to industrialization and proportion of women in the upper house. Most of the bivariate correlations are in the direction hypothesized, except that industrialization is negatively related to employment laws, rape negatively related to the percentage of women in the upper house, and in general Republican states have more pro-women's rights laws than do Demo-

Table 14–2
Policy and Independent Variables, Standardized Regression Coefficients

Independent Variables	Employ-ment	Marriage	Rape	ERA	Composite Scale
General Socioeconomic					
Affluence	.21	.12	.31	.09	.31
Industrialization	−.14	.13	.51[a]	.53[a]	.43[a]
Economic Status of Women					
Percentage of labor force women	.19	−.25	.01	−.18	−.10
Management Proportion of female labor force	.05	−.13	.31	.43[a]	.28
Political Climate					
Party competition[a]	.31	.16	.16	.28	.15
Republican dominance[a]	.33	.15	.30	−.11	.29
Political culture	−.11	.00	.37	−.70[a]	−.19
Political Potential of Women					
Percentage of lower house women	−.11	−.05	.26	−.01	.04
Percentage of upper house women	.21	.04	−.40	.15	−.04
R^2	.43	.12	.26	.57	.42

[a]Party competition: 1 = competitive states; 0 = all others.
Republican dominance: 1 = modified, one-party Republican states; 0 = all others.
Elazar's political culture as operationalized by Sharkansky: 1 = moralistic; 5 = individualistic; 9 = traditional; various combinations are placed in between these points. All correlations are Pearson's r.

cratic states. Percentage of women in the labor force is negatively related to equalitarian marrage laws, passage of the ERA, and the total scale.

In assessing which of the dependent variables are most strongly related to policy, we must look beyond the bivariate relationships. Thus, using multiple regression analysis, we have examined each policy variable and its relationship to the independent variables. This allows us to assess the relative impact of each variable while controlling for the others. (see table 14–2.)

Even though the nine predictor variables explained over 25 percent of the variance in four of the five dependent variables, and over 40 percent in three, our specific hypotheses were only partly confirmed: states with more equalitarian laws did tend to be the more affluent and industrial, had a larger female managerial class, and had a higher degree of party competition. These findings supported our hypotheses. On the other hand, Republican- rather than Democratic-dominated governments tended to have more equalitarian laws, in most cases more so than even competitive states. This did not confirm our hypothesis. Several variables showed little relationship to policy at all or were related but in inconsistent directions. These included the precentage of labor force that was female, the political culture, and the political-potential-of-women variables.

The pattern of relationships between the independent variables and the passage of the ERA is somewhat different from the relationships previously explored. Political culture has the strongest relationship to passage of the ERA; states with the moralistic political cultures are much more likely to have ratified the amendment than states at the opposite end of the spectrum. Passage of the ERA is also substantially related to industrialization and proportion of the female workforce that is professional and managerial. These relationships are in the predicted direction; a sizable middle-class female workforce does seem to be related to the passage of the amendment. In total, the nine independent variables explain 57 percent of the variance in the passage of the ERA.

In view of the topicality of the ERA question, a residual analysis was used to analyze individual states and their predicted position on the ERA. States with a predicted value near 1 would be most likely to ratify the amendment (using these variables as predictors); those states with a predicted value near 0 could be predicted not to ratify. Of the fifteen states that have not ratified, four have predicted values over .50; Utah, .74; Illinois, .65; Virginia, .62; and Louisiana, .51. At the other end of the scale the predicted values of South Carolina, Georgia, North Carolina, and Mississippi are .01, .02, .02, and .04, respectively.[23] Of course, these are predicted values based only on the nine variables used in this chapter; important contextual variables, such as personalities for and against the amendment, are not assessed.

A Causal Model

We had also posited a causal model specifying the various paths of impact on the policy, noting that we expected the socioeconomic factors to have a stronger impact than the political ones. We tested these assumptions for each of the five policy variables but present here only the findings for the composite scale. The results for the other policies are different in detail but generally similar.

Viewing our eleven variables as multiple indicators of four constructs (the SES, EPW, PC, and PPW noted above), we used the Sheaff coefficient method[24] to create a single coefficient representing the combined effects of the two variables measuring each construct (three variables in the case of PC).[25] This Sheaff coefficient can be thought of as a multiple partial beta.[26] Since we have multiple indicators at each point in our causal model, from these Sheaff coefficients we can calculate only the strength of various direct and indirect paths to the dependent variable, rather than calculating a path coefficient for each path of the path model.[27]

Table 14-3 summarizes the impact of the four constructs on the dependent

Table 14-3
Direct and Indirect Effects of Independent Variables

	Direct Effect	Total Indirect Effects	Indirect Effects
GSE	.54 (a)	−.09	Through EPW −.20
PC	.42 (b)	.08	Through EPW .11
EPW	.35 (c)	−.01	−
PPW	.03 (d)	−	−

variable—the scale comprising the sums of marriage, rape, employment, and ERA policies. As predicted, the socioeconomic factors have a very strong direct path to the policy scale—a coefficient of .54 (path *a*). The path from the political climate variables (path *b*) is also quite strong—.42—while the economic-potential-of-women variables also make a substantial independent contribution, with a coefficient of .35 (path *c*). Only the political-potential-of-women variables (path *d*) do not have an independent impact on policy (.03). In contrast with these robust direct paths, the indirect paths are by and large quite weak, as predicted. The socioeconomic factors do exert a modest negative effect acting through the women's-economic-status variables. This effect is due largely to the substantial negative relationship between proportion of female labor force that is professional and industrialization. Thus the SES tends to depress one aspect of PPW, which in turn increases the composite policy variable. The only other indirect path that is greater than .10 is that of the political coloration variables through EPW. In general, this path both confirms and rebuts our initial assumptions. On one hand, economic factors clearly are very important in explaining policy toward women; on the other hand, the general political climate, as measured by party competition and political culture, also exerts an important independent impact. As predicted, the political-potential-of-women factors were the least important, partly for reasons we will discuss now.

Conclusions

Clearly these findings indicate that correlates of state policies toward women tend to be similar to those of economic redistribution policies, such as welfare. Both socioeconomic and political variables such a party competition and political culture are highly related to this policy output. Their impact, however, was sometimes the contrary direction to that predicted. While some rather post hoc explanations were offered for certain of these findings, a more general view needs to be taken. What was the source of the error—the hypotheses themselves, the measurement of the constructs, or poor choice of policies?

The hypotheses were based on extrapolation from policy research in other areas combined with some knowledge of sources of various attitudes toward women. They suffer from the same defects as many hypotheses relating policy outputs to ecological variables. There is obviously something important that goes into policy formation which simply is not captured by these gross variables. That "something" could be the nature of legislative leadership, gubernatorial legislative relations, strength of party cohesion in the legislature, activity of lobbying groups, and so on. An attempt to operationalize these factors would result in about as many predictors as states, making the regression approach meaningless.

Measurement problems are certainly apparent. Social scientists have a reasonably good grasp of variables reflecting socioeconomic characteristics of societies. The political variables used here are probably less comprehensive but still adequate. The real gap between theory and measurement is found in the indicators of female economic and political potential. While the existence of a large female independent middle class seems a good indicator, the census categories of professions, technicians, and kindred workers and managers and administrators are heterogeneous. Along with bank vice presidents are managers of school cafeterias, for example. Percentage of women in the labor force represents an even more heterogeneous group: many of these women are in unskilled positions, unorganized by unions or other groups and hence not likely to be active participants in politics.

Ideally the choice of policies would be those under current consideration. That is practically impossible since different states attack different policies at different times. This means, however, that current characteristics of states are being related to policies that in some cases may be decades old. Of course, in some sense this is still valid, since the option to change the policy is always present.

Regarding policy, this chapter has committed the opposite sin from many other policy reports. Instead of using all expenditure-related policy variables, we have used none. Certainly it would be of some interest to examine the amount of money states are willing to allocate to activities benefiting women (such as rape prevention programs, abortion clinics, enforcement of fair employment laws, affirmative action programs).

After all these caveats, it still can be argued that something has been learned about public policies relating to women. Policies toward women, like many other policies, seem more related to socioeconomic aspects of the environment than political ones. Yet the fact that we can explain only one-fourth to one-half the variation in the policies leaves a large margin for political factors unmeasured here, and should in no way suggest a fatalistic attitude about the possibilities for change.

Notes

1. Because of the fairly rapidly changing status of state abortion laws, up-to date data were unavailable for twenty states. Thus this area was not investigated. An excellent source book on women and public policy published since this chapter was written is Barbara A. Brown, Ann E. Freedman, Harriet N. Katz, and Alice M. Price, *Women's Rights and the Law* (New York: Praeger, 1977).

2. For example, the equal pay law does not cover employers with less than twenty-five employees, nor does it cover professional executives, administrators, or people employed by state and local governments. See Thomas E. Murphy, "Sex Discrimination in Employment: Can We Legislate a Solution?" *New York Law Forum* 17, no. 2 (1971): 437–474; Brown et al., *Women's Rights and the Law.*

3. Some of these are occupations that might be considered hazardous; others do not seem to be particularly dangerous, such as bell hopping, reading electric or gas meters, working in shoe shine parlors, setting pins in bowling alleys, or tending bar.

4. For example, Ohio, like other states, had statutes forbidding night work by women. Yet exceptions were made for women working in typically female occupations, such as nurses, telephone operators, scrub women, and so on, but not for those working in "male" occupations. See Murphy, "Sex Discrimination in Employment."

5. Leo Kanowitz, *Women and the Law* (Albuquerque: University of New Mexico Press, 1969); Brown et al., *Women's Rights and the Law;* Caroline Bird, *Born Female* (New York: Pocket Books, 1971); Shana Alexander, *Women's Legal Rights* (Los Angeles: Wollstonecraft, 1975).

6. For example, in some states women need their husband's consent to make certain kinds of contracts.

7. Mary Eastwood, "Feminism and the Law," in ed. Jo Freeman, *Women: A Feminist Perspective* (Palo Alto, Calif.: Mayfield Publishers, 1975).

8. Thomas Dye, *Politics, Economics and the Public* (Chicago: Rand McNally, 1966); Andrew Cowart, "Anti-Poverty Expenditures in the American States," *Midwest Journal of Political Science* 13 (May 1969): 219–236; Ira Sharkansky, "Economic and Political Correlates of State Government Expenditures," *Midwest Journal of Political Science* 11 (May 1967); Richard E. Dawson and James A. Robinson, "Inter-Party Competition, Economic Variables and Welfare Policies in the American States," *Journal of Politics* 25 (May 1963): 265–289; Brian Fry and Richard Winters, "The Politics of Redistribution," *American Political Science Review* 64 (June 1970): 508–522.

9. See Dye, Dawson and Robinson, and Fry and Winters, ibid. But see also John Sullivan, "A Note on Redistributive Politics," *American Political Science Review* 66 (Dember 1972): 1301–1305.

10. Kristi Andersen, "Working Women and Political Participation, 1952–1972," *American Journal of Political Science* 19 (August 1975): 439–454; Susan

Welch, "Women as Political Animals?" *American Journal of Political Science* 21 (November 1977): 711–730.

11. Susan Welch, "Support by Women for the Issues of the Women's Movement," *Sociological Quarterly* 16 (Spring 1975): 216–227.

12. In a moralistic political culture, government is seen as a force to promote public good; political participation is encouraged. In individualistic political cultures, government takes little initiative except to protect property rights, while in traditional cultures politics is the prerogative of a small elite acting to protect the status quo. One would expect, therefore, legislation improving the status of women to be more popular in the moralistic rather than the more status quo–oriented traditionalistic and individualistic ones. See Daniel Elazar, *American Federalism: A View from the States* (New York: Thomas Y. Crowell, 1972).

13. See Alexander, *Women's Legal Rights.*

14. Ibid.

15. Some indication of resistance was considered reasonable, but not "until unconscious" or "to the utmost of her ability for as long as possible." See Alexander, ibid.

16. Richard Hofferbert, "Socioeconomic Dimensions of the American States, 1890–1960," *Midwest Journal of Political Science* 12 (August 1968): 401–418; David R. Morgan and William Lyons, "Industrialization and Affluence Revisited: A Note on the Socioeconomic Dimensions of the American States," *American Journal of Political Science* 19 (May 1975): 263–276.

17. Austin Ranney, "Parties in State Politics," in Herbert Jacob and Kenneth N. Vines, *Politics in the American States* (Boston: Little, Brown, 1976).

18. See Ira Sharkansky, "The Utility of Elazar's Political Culture: A Research Note," *Polity* 2 (Fall 1969): 66–83. Sharkansky's operationalization assumes that the individualistic political culture, where government takes little initiative except to protect economic rights, is a halfway point between the moralistic political culture, where government is seen as a force to promote public good and thereby where politics are issue-oriented, and the traditionalistic political culture, where politics is the prerogative of a small elite acting to maintain the existing social order. See Elazar, *American Federalism,* pp. 87–93. Moralistic political states are coded as 1, traditionalist as 9, with individualistic states given a score of 5. States that Elazar categorizes as being combinations of two cultures are scored in between these pure types.

19. U.S. Bureau of the Census, *1970 Census of the Population: Characteristics of the Population* (Washington: Government Printing Office, 1973), vol. 1, parts 2–51, table 46.

20. Wilma Rule Kraus, "U.S. State Environments and Women's Recruitment to Legislatures and Congress," Paper presented at the 1975 meeting of the American Political Science Association, San Francisco, September 1975.

21. The inequalitarian cluster includes Florida, Alabama, North Carolina, Virginia, Louisiana, Mississippi, Nevada, New Mexico, and Oklahoma.

22. The equalitarian states include Alaska, New Jersey, Wisconsin, Washington, California, Connecticut and Massachusetts.

23. Some question the use of regression analysis when one has a dichotomous dependent variable, as the ERA variable is. By using discriminant analysis, which computes the probabilities that a given case will fall into each possible group (ratified or not ratified, in this instance), the rank orderings of the states according to probabilities of passage were almost identical to the regression residuals.

24. David Heise, "A Model for Employing Nominal Variables, Induced Variables, and Block Variables in Path Analyses," unpublished manuscript, 1970; Heise, "Employing Nominal Variables, Induced Variables and Block Variables in Path Analysis," *Sociological Methods and Research* 1 (November 1972): 147-173.

25. Assuming that we are creating a Sheaff coefficient to measure path from PPW to policy while controlling for the other seven variables, we simply use the standardized regression coefficients (beta) for each of the two PPW variables in the following fashion:

B_u = standardized regression coefficient, percentage of women in upper house

B_L = standardized regression coefficient, percentage of women in lower house

r_{uL} = Pearson's r between percentage of women in upper house and percentage of women in lower house

Sheaff coefficient = $B_u^2 + B_L^2 + 2(B_u B_L B_{uL})$

If three variables are involved, the equation is expanded (let B_w be a third measure of PPW):

Sheaff coefficient = $B_u^2 + B_L^2 + B_w^2 + 2(B_u B_L r_{uL} + B_u B_w r_{uw} + B_L B_w r_{Lw})$

26. Heise, "Employing Nominal Variables," p. 164.

27. This is done by recalculating the regression equation with various combinations of the independent variables, that is, SES alone, SES with PPW, EPW, PF individually and in combination of two, then all variables together. By Calculating the effect of the SES variables under each of these conditions, the various indirect effects of SES through the other factors can be determined. See Duane Alwin and Robert M. Hauser, "The Decomposition of Effects in Path Analysis," *American Sociological Review* 40 (February 1975): 37-47.

15 Political Power and Policy Benefits: Voting Rights and Welfare Policy in Mississippi

Glen T. Broach

Studies of the political power of economically and socially deprived groups indicate that the poor are frequently unable to play even marginal, much less decisive, roles in the making of policy decisions which directly affect them.[1] This observation raises serious doubts about the validity of the pluralist thesis that the making of public policy in U.S. society is a process of inclusive group competition in which all segments of society are able to bring effective power resources to bear on those policies most relevant to their interests.[2] Unfortunately, little systematic comparative research has been conducted to determine if there are conditions under which deprived policy constituencies play more effective roles in influencing policies which directly affect their lives.[3] This chapter is based on an exploratory investigation to determine if differences in the effectiveness of welfare policy constituencies exist within the framework of the present federal-state welfare system and to identify some of the conditions conducive to the securing of greater benefits from that system by the poor. The ineffectiveness of deprived policy constituencies has been attributed both to the inherent bias of a system which legitimates certain kinds of policy demands and not others and to the difficulties of sustaining sufficient levels of organization and mobilization among the poor. This analysis therefore attempts to assess the relative impact on the distribution of benefits to the poor of both levels of mobilization among welfare constituents and relative systemic bias in the behavior of policy administrators.

The investigation centered on intercounty variation in total Aid to Families with Dependent Children (AFDC) payments as a proportion of total county welfare need in the state of Mississippi. Data on welfare payments and need among the counties of the state were available in connection with a larger study of within-state welfare policy in the South. It was decided to limit the present analysis to AFDC payments since this program more closely approximates a general relief program for the poor than do other categorical aid programs which require relatively obvious physical "excuses" for poverty such as old age, disability, or blindness.

The AFDC program is administered in Mississippi, as in all states within the framework of federal subsidies and guidelines, in conjunction with statewide provisions for eligibility standards and amounts of individual payments. Since both federal and state AFDC regulations are intended to be applied uniformly within states, variation among counties in benefits as a proportion of need can be attributed either to the proportion of the county's needy actually receiving benefits or to variation in the liberality of rule interpretation by local officials administering the program. These components of variation in county welfare policy are regarded in this study as indicators, respectively, of the level of mobilization of the poor and the favorableness of official attitudes toward the poor within the local welfare system. By examining these characteristics of the interaction between local welfare systems and the constituents they are intended to serve, this analysis seeks to identify the relative importance of local attitudes and the mobilization of the poor to the level of relief provided the poverty community by the welfare system. By further attempting to identify the characteristics associated with both systematic attitudes and poverty constituency mobilization, the study seeks also to identify the conditions which tend to encourage relationships between welfare officials and welfare constituents that are more beneficial to the aggregate poor.

With these objectives in mind, the study attempts to develop through exploration a model of the components of within-state welfare policy and the factors associated with variance in those components. Since it offers a distinct advantage in the decomposition of the elements of variation in a dependent variable, the technique of path analysis will be employed. Duncan has illustrated the utility of path analysis in assessing the contribution of persons per dwelling unit, dwelling units per structure, and strucutres per area to variance in population density.[4] The technique is used here in similar fashion to assess the relative contributions of official liberality and welfare constituency mobilization to intercounty variation in welfare benefits relative to need. The path technique will also be extended to explain variance in the components of the policy dimension under examination—constituency mobilization and liberality of official rule interpretation.

A further purpose of the analysis derives from a substantive interest in the development of black access to policy benefits within the Deep South following the political changes wrought by the civil rights struggles and federal intervention of the 1960s. Blacks in the Black Belt counties of the South have long been deprived of the economic advantages possessed by Southern whites. While the civil rights movement has produced manifest political changes in the South,[5] it is not yet clear that the movement has made any substantial change in the distribution of policy resources to Southern, Black Belt counties. Thus while demonstrating the utility of a distributional focus in state policy research, the analysis presented here also seeks to determine the extent to which change has occurred in the ability of Black Belt counties to secure policy benefits of concern to blacks in the South.

The Dependent Variable and Its Components

The measure of the dependent variable discriminates the effectiveness of the poor within individual Mississippi counties in securing the share of total benefits distributed within the state due them on the basis of presumed need. While the measure as used here is applied to the distribution of AFDC benefits within the state of Mississippi, in principle it can be generalized for application to the distribution of benefits across a wide range of state policies.

The distribution of AFDC payments within Mississippi was obtained by computing county proportions (P_b) of total state benefit expenditures for each of the state's eighty-two counties. This first step, of course, simply indicates how much of the total state AFDC "pie" was received by each county and is largely, but not exclusively, a function of the size of the county population. If benefit shares were distributed equitably according to need among the state's counties, P_b would be equal to each county's portion of the total need for AFDC relief within the state (P_n). Since AFDC benefits are paid to families, and since basic eligibility for benefits is determined by a maximum income ceiling defining those below the ceiling as "poor," P_n can best be estimated by taking the proportion residing within each county of all state families with incomes below the poverty level.

The measure of P_b was taken in 1972, the most recent year for which data were available.[6] Each county's proportion of total state AFDC benefit payments in 1972 was calculated by dividing total payments made within the state into payments made within the county. The measure of P_n was taken from the 1970 census using a similar procedure whereby each county's proportion of all state families below the poverty level was obtained. With measures of both P_b and P_n, the distributive equity (E) of each county's share of the state's AFDC payments is defined as follows:

$$E = \frac{P_b}{P_n}$$

Thus E is the ratio of the actual proportion of benefits received under the program to an estimate of the proportion the county could expect to receive on the basis of need. Values of E are theoretically distributed along a ratio scale, with increasing values indicating greater need-adjusted shares of the state's AFDC expenditures. If E equals 1, then the county receives precisely its equitable share of the AFDC payments made within the state. If E is greater than 1, the county is receiving more than it would expect to receive relative to its need, given total payments within the state. An E of less than 1 indicates that the county's poor receive less than their share of AFDC relief.

Now, E is presumed to be a multiplicative function of two components—the relative liberality of local welfare officials in fixing payments to families and the level of mobilization of poverty-income families within the county. Measures of each of these components were obtained for the purpose of determining their relative contribution to intercounty variance in E. The level of mobilization of the county poverty constituency was presumed to be indicated by the percentage of all county families with incomes below poverty level who received AFDC assistance in 1972.[7] This measure indicates only those poverty families who *successfully* became AFDC clients and fails to take into account differences in the flexibility with which local officials apply statewide eligibility requirements. But the latter is virtually immeasurable with aggregate data; and even if they were available, they would be unlikely to alter significantly relative county mobilization scores since official flexibility is likely to be in part a function of the intensity of client demands and the relative quiescence of a poverty population—factors which are themselves manifested in mobilization levels.

Variation in the liberality of local officials' attitudes toward the poverty population is measured by the average payment per case made to AFDC clients within the county. In a study of average welfare payments in thrity-six states, Sharkansky has shown that there is substantial variance among counties within states in average per case payments made under several public assistance programs.[8] He suggests that while county officials presumably apply uniform, statewide standards within their jurisdictions, payment levels can vary because of local propensities to apply regulations with greater or lesser flexibility. Thus patterns of administrative application, as reflected in the relative size of average payments, can result in counties receiving differential amounts of AFDC relief relative to their need for such relief.

Although we would expect official rule interpretation to have some effect on the relative success of county welfare constituencies in receiving AFDC relief, it is likely that the effect of the mobilization of the constituency itself is much greater. Increases in total AFDC expenditures occasioned by the addition of more clients to the welfare rolls will presumably be much greater than increases due to marginal fluctuations in payment liberality. As a result, mobilization is likely to have a more substantial effect on differences in payments made to welfare constituencies in proportion to need. In any case, E is expected to be a multiplicative function of the two components, mobilization and liberality. Thus the respective contributions of these factors will be determined by relating the logarithmic transformation of mobilization and generosity to the log of county scores on E.

Conditions of Welfare Constituency Mobilization and Official Liberality

Because of the scarcity of preexisting theoretical speculation bearing on the components of welfare distributions, the analysis of the environmental antecedents of mobilization and official liberality will be primarily exploratory in nature. All but one of the variables selected for inclusion in the analysis were chosen because they were representative of factors found important in studies of interstate variation in welfare policy. But while familiar influences from state policy research can be expected to be important to the distribution of welfare benefits in the states generally, the distinctive character of Mississippi's Deep South politics requires that county racial composition also be treated in this case as a potentially significant environmental variable. The inclusion of this variable in the system should also yield inferences about the relationship between the state's economically deprived black citizenry and the welfare system in the aftermath of the civil rights revolution of the 1960s.

In any study of the politics and policy of the Deep South, the analyst almost inevitably begins by taking account of the dominant concern of much of Southern political life—the politics of race. A long line of research, beginning with Key's seminal work, has impressively documented the dominance and pervasiveness of racial politics in the Deep South.[9] Thus in part as a matter of necessity dictated by previous research, county racial composition is expected to be related to the components of Mississippi's AFDC distribution. But given the temporal context of the study, there is reason to specifically expect the racial composition of the county electorate to be closely related to the level of mobilization of the poor. Numerous indicators such as increased voter registration and turnout and the election of blacks to public office provide evidence of an increasingly active orientation of Southern blacks toward the political system in the aftermath of the Voting Rights Act of 1965.[10] The development of general political awareness among blacks can be expected to be coincident with higher levels of policy mobilization among the black welfare constituency in the South—a constituency which comprises a substantial proportion of both the black population and the total poverty population in the region.[11] It is unlikely, however, that increases in the mobilization of the black poor have been accompanied by mobilization of equivalent dimensions among the nonblack poor in the South. Indeed, one suspects that, given the racial attitudes of whites generally in the South, increases in the mobilization of the black poor may have tended to harden individualistic white resitance to poverty relief. In the South's racially polarized environment, this resistance to welfare is likely to be common even among whites who themselves are potential welfare clients. Consequently, the mobilization levels of poverty constituencies in Mississippi counties can be expected to vary with the racial distribution of the county's registered voters, producing a positive relationship between mobilization and percentage of blacks.

For somewhat similar reaons we expect official liberality, as measured by the size of average payments to be greater in Mississippi counties where blacks constitute a greater proportion of the population and, inevitably, a more sizable segment of the poor. If increased levels of mobilization and awareness can be viewed as likely to create pressures on officials for more generous policies, then one would expect (via the reasoning of the preceding paragraph) that the more mobilized black poverty population would receive more liberal AFDC payments. Moreover, given recently adopted federal safeguards against discrimination in the use of federal funds, welfare officials in Black Belt counties are likely to feel constrained to be more responsive to their clients, and thus more liberal in rule interpretation, than officials in the remainder of the state.

Previous research on differences in welfare liberalism among the states suggests several additional factors which may be expected to influence the components of the distribution of welfare benefits among counties within states. Studies by Dye, Hofferbert, and Dawson and Robinson have found that those states with more liberal welfare policies tend to be more urbanized and prosperous with relatively high levels of interparty competition and electoral participation.[12] Assuming that these relationships will also hold for the components of welfare policy under consideration here, county measures of urbanization, affluence, electoral competition, and political participation will be related to levels of mobilization and liberality among Mississippi counties.

The measure of urbanization was simply the percentage of urban as defined by the 1970 census. Instead of more frequently used measures of aggregate affluence such as per capita and median income, the present analysis employed the proportion of the county income below poverty level as a means of differentiating county prosperity. This characteristic would seem to be more appropriate for the purpose here since it directly discriminates those counties with relatively large welfare burdens—a condition which can be expected to depress both mobilization and generosity.[13]

Two political variables found to be important in previous welfare policy research—electoral competition and political participation—were also included in the analysis. Some of the most well-known studies of state policies relate these factors to the conditions which generate active and effective political participation by the less prosperous members of society. In separate comparative studies of state government, Key and Lockard obtained results which suggested that the existence of competitive party politics tends to result in increased and more effective political participation by the have-nots of society.[14] These findings lead one to expect a strong positive relationship between interparty competition and the levels of mobilization and liberality within local welfare systems. While the effects of competition and participation on welfare policy have generally been found to be minimal once socioeconomic effects are controlled, their impact should be much greater *within* states where the variance in both socioeconomic conditions and welfare regulations is less dramatic.

Unfortunately for this analysis, the state of Mississippi is not internally competitive between parties. The slight intercounty variations in one-party Democratic dominance which do occur are not sufficiently large to produce the kinds of conditions that one would expect to lead to increased electoral awareness and effectiveness among the poor. But the noncompetitive situation in Mississippi does present an opportunity for an examination of Key's contention that the transient factional competition characteristic of one-party politics fails to stimulate active political participation by the less prosperous.[15] Key based his contention largely on his observation of elite dominance and low levels of participation in the one-party electoral politics of the South. If Key's conclusion about factional conflict is valid, then the degree of intercounty variation in levels of primary competition will be unrelated to county levels of welfare constituency mobilization. In order to examine this relationship, the mean of the vote percentage margins for the leading candidate in each county was computed for the three gubernatorial Democratic primary runoffs prior to 1972.[16] Each primary involved entirely different sets of candidates, which is typical of the transient factionalism Key observed in his study of Southern electoral politics. We would thus expect that the measure of intraparty competition computed from these primaries will be unrelated to intercounty differences in welfare constituency mobilization and official liberality.

Voting studies have found that increased aggregate participation levels usually mean the involvement of more representative proportions of the less prosperous in the electorate. If it can be assumed that greater electoral participation by the poor involves an accompanying mobilization relative to their policy concerns, then higher levels of county electoral participation can be expected to be positively related to welfare constituency mobilization. As a measure of differences between counties in participatory traditions, the mean of the proportions of the county adult population voting in the 1963, 1967, and 1971 gubernatorial runoff primaries was computed. As this measure increased across counties, levels of welfare constituency mobilization were expected to increase also. Assuming further that increased mobilization creates pressures on officials for greater liberality, participation should also be positively related to official liberality.

Analysis of Benefit Distribution

One of the chief advantages of path analysis is that it encourages, through the elimination of weak relationships, a parsimonious statement of the relationships among a set of variables. Since this attempt to identify the conditions of both mobilization and generosity is exploratory in nature, the path technique is used here as search device for discovering the most parsimonious explanation of the Mississippi AFDC distribution using the variables described above.

Thus table 15-1 displays only those relationships which the path exploration found to be statistically significant at the .05 level. Strictly speaking, tests of statistical significance are inappropriate in the present case since we have data on the entire universe of eighty-two Mississippi counties. The significance criterion was not used here, however, for the purpose of generalization to a universe from a sample: instead it was employed as a somwhat arbitrary, but nevertheless functional, criterion for uncluttering the model of weak relationships without at the same time greatly increasing the size of the residuals.[17]

Table 15-1
Path Exploration of Mississippi AFDC Distribution, Significant Relationships

		Dependent Variable			
Independent Variable	E	Constituency Mobilization	Official Liberality	Primary Competition	Primary Participation
Constituency mobilization	.941				
Official liberality	.123				
Primary competition		−.165			.174
Primary participation			−.425		
Black voter registration		.672	.594		
Percentage urban		.219		.394	.516
Percentage below poverty			−.449		−.589
Residual (unexplained variance)	.031	.621	.761	.919	.501

As expected, virtually all the variance in E is explained by official generosity and welfare constituency mobilization, with by far the greatest determinant of intercounty benefit differences being the rate at which the poverty constituency takes advantage of the benefits offered by the AFDC program. This finding emphasizes the crucial requirement of poverty constituency mobilization for the attainment of greater relief by the poverty community under the present welfare system. While most previous studies of intersystem differences in welfare policy have emphasized differences in payment levels as indicators of differential policies, this analysis of intercounty policy differences in Mississippi reveals that in terms of differences in the effect of policy on the aggregate policy constituency, the rate at which policy constituents take advantage of benefits is much more crucial than marginal fluctuations in official liberality.

Given the importance of welfare constituency mobilization to the aggregate effect of welfare policy on its constituents, the prediction of mobilization is especially critical to an understanding of the within-state distribution of welfare expenditures. Unfortunately the independent variables selected for inclusion in the model underlying table 15-1 explain only a moderate amount of variance in mobilization, leaving a rather large residual path of .621. Two of the variables expected to be related to mobilization fail to appear as significant influences.

Both the proportionate size of the poverty constituency and political participation produced paths of insignificant and low magnitude to mobilization.

The factor of greatest influence on mobilization is black voter registration, indicating that the relatively high awareness levels of the state's black poor substantially affect the distribution of welfare benefits among the counties within the state. Both urbanization and, unexpectedly, primary competition are significantly and positively related to mobilization, but the paths are considerably weaker than that for voter registration. The path schema enables us to observe that urbanization affects mobilization both directly and indirectly through primary competition. The strength of the indirect influence is given by $P_{64}P_{62} = .0650$, which is much weaker than the direct path from urbanization to mobilization. In general, while it is possible to state that urbanization, a larger percentage of blacks in the electorate, and primary competition tend to increase poverty constituency mobilization within the context of Mississippi politics, there is substantial variance in mobilization left unaccounted for by the environmental and political variables included in table 15-1.

Just as the system does not adequately explain mobilization, so there is also a large error term associated with intercounty variance in official liberality. With this component the dominant and pervasive influence of race on the state's politics and policy is again illustrated. The strongest path influencing official generosity is, as was the case with mobilization, that from percentage of blacks in the electorate. Yet unlike the model's explanation of mobilization, two other paths rival the strength of the racial variable in their ability to explain variation in generosity, although the interpretation of each of these paths presents some difficulty.

The negative path from participation to liberality presents the most perplexing anomaly of the findings displayed by table 15-1. It was expected that higher participation levels would mean greater political participation by the poor and greater pressure from the welfare constituency for official liberality. We have already noted that general political participation is not significantly related to mobilization, and the fact that liberality is negatively influenced by participation presents what at this juncture is an uninterpretable finding. We can only point out that the relationship is probably accounted for by other variables not included in the system, and would probably disappear if these other unknown variables were discovered and the error term for liberality were substantially reduced.

The path results of table 15-1 also contain some interesting revelations about the demographic characteristics associated with variance in competition and turnout among Mississippi's county primary electorates. As is generally the case outside the South, the poorer counties tend to have significantly lower participation levels. Somewhat surprisingly, racial composition of the electorate significantly affects neither competition nor participation in primaries. In light of the frequent findings in studies of earlier time periods that race was significantly associated with the nature of the electorate in the South, this suggests that the emergence of black voting rights may have altered the long-standing nexus between racial composition and the characteristics of the electorate in Southern states. Yet the Mississippi electorate continues to retain some of the traditional distinctiveness of Southern electorates. Consistent with previous studies of Southern political participation, and at variance with the relationship normally found outside the South, rates of aggregate participation are higher in the rural areas of the state.[18] Despite sizable increases in total turnout in Mississippi, rural citizens continue to outvote their urban brethren.

The significant paths also reveal that urban areas tend to be more factionally competitive than rural areas, although demography is able to explain but little of the variance in primary factional competition. Yet the behavior of the competition variable suggests that the conventional wisdom on the effects of factional competition may warrant reassessment as applied to variation in competition *within* one-party settings. Key concluded that factional competition within the one-party environment does not produce the kind of issue-based popular interest which is necessary for high rates of participation. And as one would expect from this assertion, the path from competition to participation is relatively weak and indicates that more competitive counties tend to have lower levels of participation. (As defined above, higher scores on the measure of primary competition indicate lower levels of competitiveness.) But while factional competition does not increase general electoral participation, it is positively associated, albeit weakly, with the level of mobilization of the poverty constituency. The significant path from competition to poverty constituency mobilization suggests that the effect of the salience of factional rivalries on the political awareness of the poor within the one-party setting should be examined in greater detail. Competitive factionalism may turn out to be functionally conducive, if not to electoral participation generally, then to greater awareness and more effective participation by society's have-nots. The greater attention normally given to more competitive areas by political candidates may induce the kind of political interest and organizational awareness among the poor which is necessary if they are to participate more.

Change in the Benefit Distribution, 1964–1972

The results of the foregoing analysis sharply emphasize the importance of mobilization of the poor as a factor contributing to the effective implementation of redistributional public policies. This point can be further illustrated by a comparison of the distribution of E among counties arranged by categories of racial composition for 1964, when suppression of black mobilization in Mississippi was

Table 15-2
Mean County *E* Scores within Categories of Racial Composition

	Mean E Score	
Percentage Black	1964	1972
Less than 30 percent	.852	.590
30 to 49.9 percent	1.155	.945
50 percent or greater	.933	1.179

relatively unfettered by the national political system, and 1972, after the events of the 1960s had their impact on black awareness and political participation.

Table 15-2 reveals that counties with a relatively small proportion of blacks (less than 30 percent) on the average received less than their expected share of the AFDC benefits obtained by the poor within the state. Since more of the poor within these counties are white, this finding is consistent with the anti-welfare, individualistic ethos often associated with Southern whites. Within the middle category of counties from 30 to 49.9 percent black, there is a mean score greater than unity for 1964, indicating that these counties received benefits greater than their need relative to the other counties within the state, which suggests that as the black proportion of the poor increases, the poverty community becomes less enamored of individualistic attitudes and more receptive to the benefits offered by the welfare system.

Yet when the black-majority counties are considered for 1964, the mean *E* score falls below unity, indicating that in these counties where traditionally the most rigid discrimination has occurred, the incipient mobilization of the black poor was impeded by the discriminatory practices of the white establishment. Thus the rather weak 1964 correlation between racial composition and county *E* scores obscures the discrimination in black-majority counties which is suggested by interpretation of the nonlinear distribution of mean *E* scores in table 15-2.

If it is assumed that the civil rights movement weakened white resistance to the needs of the black poor in the South, then the preceding interpretation of the 1964 column of table 15-2 is consistent with the distribution appearing in the 1972 column. Rather than the curvilinear relationship found for 1964, the mean *E* score increases monotonically within categories of percentage of blacks. The predominantly white counties receive approximately half their share of the state's AFDC benefits, while the counties with proportionately more blacks tend to receive larger portions, with the black-majority counties receiving more than should be due them on the basis of their need relative to the rest of the state. With the constraints of black access to the welfare system now largely removed by the black mobilization and federal interventions engendered by the civil rights upheavals of the 1960s, the relatively mobilized black poor are able to obtain an equitable share of the welfare relief dispensed within the state in 1972. Such relief was less accessible in 1964, when the black-majority counties—those with the greatest need—received less than their equitable share of state AFDC expenditures.

Concluding Comments

It would be unwarranted to draw general conclusions about the distribution of welfare benefits within the states on the basis of this limited case study of a rather distinctive state welfare system. However, the analysis of the Mississippi AFDC distribution has served to demonstrate the feasibility and illustrate the utility of studies which focus on the distribution of policy benefits to the constituent units of a government system. The development and employment of a measure of the ratio of benefits to need not only have provided the foundation for identifying the factors associated with the relative success of units in securing policy benefits within a larger system, but also have permitted, as in this case, the description of changes in distributional patterns during a period of substantial political change within a state political system. Since the study on which this report is based was primarily exploratory in nature, the results are merely suggestive of the theoretical and descriptive potentials of distributional analyses, leaving unexploited its full potential as an approach to the study of public policy.

Several points which relate to the descriptive results of the study are, however, worthy of concluding emphasis. The study indicates a substantial increase in the benefits paid to the state's Black Belt counties in the aftermath of civil rights struggles of the 1960s and a redressing of the policy discrimination which was seemingly applied to the black-majority counties in 1964. The decomposition of the variance in E among Mississippi counties clearly establishes that the crucial factor determining the relative success of the poor within counties in obtaining benefits commensurate with their aggregate need is the rate at which potential welfare constituents take advantage of benefit opportunities. Thus if it is to examine the more crucial component of the relationship between the welfare system and the poor, future research should concentrate less on average payment levels and instead pay greater attention to variation in the mobilization levels of welfare constituencies. Mobilization levels are especially critical for understanding welfare policies *within* states, where both eligibility requirements and average payment levels are more uniform than they are from state to state.

The ultimate utility of the redirection of welfare policy research toward the mobilization of the poor lies in the opportunity it offers to identify the conditions under which deprived policy constituencies are activated to take advantage of, and ultimately to influence, public policies which directly affect them. Considerable work beyond that underlying this chapter needs to be done before reasonably satisfactory solutions can be provided for this important research problem. This chapter leaves unexplained an embarrassingly large proportion of the intercounty variance in the rate at which Mississippi welfare constituents actually take advantage of the welfare system's benefits. Moreover, the generalization to other states of the results of this study would be unwise because of the dominant role played by differences in the racial composition of counties in the explanation of mobilization levels in Mississippi. The results indicated, as expected, that the black poor are mobilized to more frequently take advantage of the welfare system in Mississippi. But because of the vast differences in mobilization between counties of different racial composition, we are unable to draw generalizable inferences about the effects of other variables on mobilization in sysems not characterized by the distinctive racial polarization of the South. Moreover, because of the South's unique one-partyism, the study did not permit examination of the effect of interparty, as distinguished from factional, competition on the mobilization of the poor.

Because of the limitations of the foregoing analysis as a basis for generalization, broader studies of intercounty differences in poverty constituency mobilization within several states need to be conducted in order to identify more general conditions under which the aggregate poor are likely to take advantage of and influence policies designed for their relief. Such investigations should cnable political scientists to better understand the conditions under which the poor are likely to achieve relatively high levels of awareness and mobilization. To the extent that U.S. governments are classically pluralist systems predisposed toward making policies in response to the demands of those groups whom policies most directly affect, the mobilization of the poor is a necessary condition for effective participation by the poor in the making of public policy.

Notes

1. Michael Parenti, "Power and Pluralism: A View from the Bottom," *Journal of Politics* 32 (August 1970): 501-530. See also Michael Lipsky, "Protest as a Political Resource," *American Political Science Review* 62 (December 1968): 1144-1158.

2. Robert Dahl, *Who Governs* (New Haven, Conn.: Yale University Press, 1961). Also see Nelson Polsby, *Community Power and Political Theory* (New Haven, Conn.: Yale University Press, 1963).

3. William Keech, *The Impact of Negro Voting: The Role of the Vote in the Quest for Equality* (Chicago: Rand McNally, 1968).

4. Otis Dudley Duncan, "Path Analysis: Sociological Examples," *American Journal of Sociology* 72 (July 1966): 1-16.

5. Joe R. Feagin and Harlan Hahn, "The Second Reconstruction: Black

Political Strength in the South," *Social Science Quarterly* 60 (June 1970): 42–56.

6. U.S. Department of Health, Education, and Welfare, *Recipients of Public Assistance Money Payments and Accounts of Such Payments, by Program, State, and County,* February 1972 (Washington: Government Printing Office, 1972).

7. The number of county families with incomes below poverty was obtained from the 1970 census. The number of families receiving AFDC assistance was taken from the publication cited in note 6.

8. Ira Sharkansky, "Economic Theories of Public Policy: Resource-Policy and Need Policy Linkages between Income and Welfare Benefits," *Midwest Journal of Political Science* 15 (November 1971): 722–740.

9. V.O. Key, *Southern Politics in State and Nation* (New York: Alfred Knopf, 1949); and Donald R. Mathews and James W. Prothro, *Negroes and the New Southern Politics* (New York: Harcourt, Brace and World, 1966).

10. Feagin and Hahn, "The Second Reconstruction."

11. In 1970, 59.2 percent of Mississippi's black families had incomes below poverty, comprising 60.4 percent of all poverty-income families in the state. Mississippi's population is 37.2 percent black according to the 1970 census.

12. Thomas P. Dye, *Politics, Economics and the Public* (Chicago: Rand McNally, 1966); Richard Hofferbert, "The Relation between Public Policy and Some Structural and Environmental Variables in the American States," *American Political Science Review* 60 (March 1966): 73–82; and Richard Dawson and James Robinson, "Inter-Party Competition, Economic Variables, and Welfare Policies in the American States," *Journal of Politics* 21 (May 1963): 265–289.

13. Sharkansky, "Economic Theories of Public Policy," related average family income to county variation in average welfare payments as a means of interferring resource-policy linkages and need-policy linkages in welfare benefit distributions within thirty-six states. It is being suggested here that the relationship between proportionate size of the welfare constituency and liberality of payments would be a more appropriate basis for drawing inferences about the extent to which welfare distributions are based on need.

14. Key, *Southern Politics in State and Nation;* Duane Lockard, *New England State Politics* (Princeton, N.J.: Princeton University Press, 1959).

15. Key, ibid., p. 523.

16. The elections used were those in 1963, 1967, and 1971.

17. The path estimates are standardized beta coefficients. Separate regression analyses for each endogenous variable were performed to estimate all the paths depicted in figure 15-1. Insignificant paths resulting from this procedure were eliminated from the final model.

18. See Key, *Southern Politics in State and Nation,* p. 562; and Mathews and Prothro, *Negroes and the New Southern Politics,* p. 131.

16 Styles and Priorities of Marginality: Women State Legislators

Marianne Githens and
Jewel L. Prestage

In 1928 Park first introduced the concept of the marginal man. Nine years later, Stonequist expanded the original concept and further developed it as a personality type. For both Park and Stonequist, the definition of *the marginal* was basically the same. The marginal individual was "on the margin of two societies";[1] "condemned to live in two worlds in neither of which he ever quite belonged";[2] "poised in psychological uncertainty between two or more social worlds; reflecting in his soul the discord and harmonies, repulsions and attractions of these worlds, one of which is often 'dominant' over the other; within which membership is implicitly if not explicitly based on birth and ancestry; and where exlusion removes the individual from a system of group relationships."[3]

While the marginal man concept has gained wide acceptance among social scientists since its introduction by Park and Stonequist, numerous critiques, qualifications, and modifications of this original concept have been offered. Goldberg contended that a person may belong to a racial or nationality group considered marginal without himself being marginal. Instead, he might be a "participant member of a marginal culture every bit as real and complete to him as is the non-marginal culture to the non-marginal man."[4] Within the framework of this marginal culture, reaction patterns are provided and defined by the marginal group rather than by the individual. In such circumstances, an individual may show none of the personality signs of the marginal person, but rather those of a "stable and normal person participating in an integrated manner in the activities of a unitary culture."[5] Green has suggested that the personality characteristics of the marginal person arise from group antagonisms, rather than cultural conflict.[6] Kerckhoff and McCormick basically accepted Green's position and went on to argue that the marginal man is "one who has internalized the norms of a particular group, (thus it is his reference group) but he is not completely recognized by others as being a legitimate member of that group (thus it

We wish to thank Southern University and Goucher College, especially Dean James Billet of Goucher, for the encouragement and financial support that allowed this research project to be undertaken. Thanks are also due Professor James Prothro of the University of North Carolina at Chapel Hill for helpful advice and suggestions.

is not his membership group)."[7] They further suggested that not all individuals in a marginal situation would respond in the same way. Additionally, they contended that the greatest incidence of marginality occurs in those who identify with the dominant group but encounter a relatively impermeable barrier. Conversely, as long as members in a subordinate group remain members of that group, contradictions in expectations and aspirations would not arise. Merton and Rossi saw the concept of marginality as a special instance of reference group theory. For them, marginality entailed abandoning the values of one group in favor of those of another to which the marginal individual is socially forbidden access. This results in the individual becoming the victim of aspirations he cannot achieve and hopes he cannot satisfy.[8] Gist and Dworkin believed that there are at least three separate dimensions of marginality: cultural, social, and political. Cultural marginality involves the sharing of cultural values and behavior patterns of the dominant group and one or more other groups, whereas social marginality means that the individual is refused full participation in groups and institutions of the dominant culture. In a situation of the political marginality, the discrimination and prejudices of social marginality are enforced by laws rather than informal group pressures. Further, they believed that the personality characteristics described by Park and Stonequist are most likely to manifest themselves when all three forms of marginality are present.[9]

A fusion of a number of these themes appears in Turner's interpretation of marginality. Turner describes the marginal man as one

> who seeks to change his identification from one stratum to another, but is unable to resolve the related choices between value systems and between organized group ties. The choices are necessary because the strata have incompatible value systems and because it is difficult to maintain ties across stratum boundaries.[10]

He identifies marginality as objective—the position occupied; experiential—the experience of conflicting demands; and symptomatic—the observable characteristics which point to the existence of experiential marginality.[11]

From the literature on marginality, then, the marginal man emerges as one who experiences stress as a result of the unique position he occupies. However, the intensity of the marginal experience and the consequent effects of personality will vary depending on the existence of a marginal culture; the extent to which marginality entails a cultural, social, and political dimension; the existence of group antagonisms; and the degree to which the barriers between the marginal's reference and membership groups are permeable. This composite is essentially the backdrop against which the present study is launched.

In the great volume of literature which has developed in the discipline of political science, very little focuses on women in politics. That limited attention which has been directed to the subject is of very recent origin and consists mostly of autobiographies and biographies of selected women politicians.[12]

Women in Congress and state legislatures have been studied by Werner who found that women lawmakers were well educated, had combined a mutiplicity of roles, and were most interested in those public policy areas that related to social welfare, education, and family life. Mobility patterns for the earlier congresswomen entailed appointments to fill seats of deceased husbands while the more recent ones involved service in state legislatures and political party organizations.[13] Virtually the same patterns emerge from a study of Bullock and Heys.[14]

Perhaps the single most comprehensive study of women in politics to date is Kirkpatrick's *Political Woman.* She examines four hypothetical constraints in an efffort to account for the dearth of women in politics. She found that differences between female and male legislators were primarily in regard to economic role, work experience, and age of entry into the legislature.[15] In a more recently published study Diamond, contending that sex differentiation decreases as competition for political office increases, examined the place of gender role in state legislatures.[16]

While the Kirkpatrick study represents a major contribution in the study of women in politics and Diamond's provides some interesting insights, they also raise several important questions and point to other possibilities for the examination of the configuration of social and cultural complexities that have categorized and constrained female politicians. One such possibility is the theory of marginality. In an earlier work, *A Portrait of Marginality: The Political Behavior of the American Woman,* we contended that women in politics, like the marginal man, are intensely involved with two groups—women and politicians. Each represents a way of life and provides an identity and strong social ties. Inherent in the woman's decision to seek political office is the rejection of some of the values and norms of most women. At the same time, the political group with which she wishes to affiliate is reluctant to accept her. Thus, the woman politician experiences isolation from both groups.[17]

The case studies included in *A Portrait of Marginality* seemed to support our belief that the behavior and performance of female politicians could best be explained and understood within the context of marginality; but a more direct testing of our thesis was clearly required. The findings reported here represent an initial effort to examine whether elected female state legislators are, indeed, marginal.

Our research, as reported here, was predicated on two specific hypotheses. The first was that the women legislators were objectively marginal. This, we believed, would be manifested by (1) the upward mobility of the woman legislators, a situation that Turner thought might possibly contribute to marginality; (2) the assignment of women to committees dealing with more stereotypic female concerns, such as health, education, and welfare, despite the legislators' more diverse interests and expertise; (3) the sponsoring of more legislation in the area of health, education, and welfare regardless of the legislators' committee assignments and expertise; (4) greater consultation by interest groups dealing with public policies such as health, education, and welfare; and (5) minimal representation of the women in legislative and party leadership positions. The second hypothesis was that the women would be experientially marginal in terms of (1) their feelings of influence and success, (2) the importance they attached to family attitudes, and (3) the factors influencing them to run for public office.

In February 1978 a questionnaire consisting of 122 items was mailed to the 703 women state legislators in all fifty states. The overall response was 42 percent—not as large as the response to some mail surveys, but more than adequate for a study of this type. The questionnaires were subsequently coded, tabulated, and analyzed.

Findings

The Survey Population

The bulk of the respondents to the questionnaire were over 40 years of age (73 percent); married (76 percent); and, of those who were married, widowed, or divorced, 86 percent had children. The average number of children was 2.6, and of the respondents with children 76 percent had children over the age of 18. Almost two-thirds of the women were Democrats; 55 percent gave their religion as Protestant, 24 percent as Catholic, and 11 percent as Jewish. The remainder indicated no preference or stated their religion as other or did not answer the question. A little less than 5 percent of the respondents were black. Those demographic characteristics are essentially the same as those reported in earlier studies.[18]

Objective Marginality

Objective marginality essentially involves the placing of an individual in that unique situation where he is on the margin of two cultures, two worlds. The small number of women sitting in state legislatures (9.3 percent) already suggests the uniqueness of their situation, but number alone is probably not enough to confirm objective marginality. Therefore, an effort is made to explore other indications of female legislators' marginal situation. Several areas were examined: upward social mobility; area of expertise, committee assignment and area in which most legislation is sponsored; patterns of consultation by interest groups, chamber leadership, and executive and department heads; and leadership positions in the legislature. It was hoped that these factors would give a more definitive indication of whether women legislators were objectively marginal.

Upward Social Mobility

The first finding is that the female legislators are an upwardly mobile group. In terms of educational achievement, the legislators had, as a group, more schooling than their parents. Among the legislators, 70 percent had at least a bachelor's degree, whereas only 20 percent of their mothers and 35 percent of their fathers had similar levels of education. Given the patterns of education of their parents' generation, it was expected that the fathers would be better educated than the mothers. One curious pattern did emerge, however. Almost twice as many fathers as mothers had eight years of schooling or less.[19]

Intergenerational changes in occupational prestige are another factor in determining upward mobility. Since traditionally occupational prestige for women is determined by the male head of family, prestige scores of fathers were compared with those of husbands. The occupational prestige scores of the legislators' husbands are higher than those of their fathers. In an effort to explore the upward mobility of the legislators compared to their mothers, comparisons were made of occupational prestige of mothers and daughters. There were problems in accomplishing the latter though.[20] The occupation of a majority of the mothers was homemaker (63 percent), and many of the legislators indicated that their occupation was homemaker. Since there presently exists no accepted procedure for assigning occupational prestige to women whose occupation is homemaker, other than giving them the prestige score of husband, an effort was made to assign occupation prestige to the women legislators and their mothers whose occupation was homemaker. The assignment was based on (1) education, (2) husband and father's occupational prestige, and (3) in the case of the legislators, their mother's education and occupation.[21] Although at this point only minimal confidence can be placed in this formula for computing a homemaker's occupational prestige, the resulting scores seem to suggest the same pattern of upward mobility as the scores of father and husband.

It appears, then, that the present women state legislators are not only well educated, but also a genuinely upwardly mobile group in terms of educational achievement, husband's occupational prestige, and the legislators' prestige as compared with that of their mothers. This upward mobility may very well contribute to the legislators' overall marginality. However, this connection between upward mobility and the marginality of the legislators needs further exploration before any definite relationship can by asserted.

**Area of Expertise, Committee Assignment
and Legislation Sponsored**

The second aspect of objective marginality examined was the relationship of area of expertise, committee assignment, and the area in which most legislation is sponsored. As might be expected, the area of expertise cited frequently is health, education, and welfare (31 percent), although the largest percentage of legislators (38 percent) indicated expertise in a broad range of concerns ranging from inter-governmental relations and constitutional reform at one end of the spectrum to animal protection and the Panama Canal at the other. These were categorized and coded as other. The next largest category of expertise mentioned by the respondents (12 percent) is fiscal affairs. Also, 7 percent of the women indicated the judiciary as their area of expertise; 5 percent women's issues; 3 percent agriculture and business; and a little less than 2 percent highways and public works. Just over 1 percent mentioned minority issues. This distribution seems to support earlier studies that showed women legislators to be primarily concerned with public policy areas involving stereotypic concerns of women.[22]

When area of expertise is compared with assignment to standing committees, some interesting findings emerge. Slightly more women sit on committees dealing with health, education, and welfare than their self-identified areas of expertise would warrant; and slightly fewer sit on committees dealing with concerns coded as other. These discrepancies between area of expertise and committee assignment are too small to be considered significant. In marked contrast, 12 percent of the legislators claimed fiscal affairs as their area of expertise, but only 3 percent of them sit on standing committees dealing with fiscal matters. This is especially striking in light of the fact that almost all the women reported multiple committee assignments and that there was a real mesh between all other areas of expertise and committee assignment. Since the majority of the respondents had served in their respective legislatures for at least one term, their absence from fiscal committees can not be easily attributed to their lack of seniority.

There is one very important implication of this minimal representation of women legislators on committees dealing with fiscal affairs. Primary among the functions of a state legislature are the enactment of a budget for the state and the establishment of taxation policies. Fiscal committees are critical in the budgetary process and help, in large measure, in determining priorities for spending in other policy areas such as health, education, and welfare. It can be argued that the imbalance between the small number of women sitting on fiscal committees and the relatively large number who claim fiscal affairs as their area of expertise virtually excludes female legislators from one of the most important tasks performed by a state legislature.

Area of expertise and committee assignment seem to mean little when it comes to the area in which most legislation is sponsored. By far the most frequently cited policy area in which most legislation is sponsored is health, education, and welfare. Just over 41 percent of the respondents identified this as the area in which they sponsored the most legislation. Moreover, the percentage of women sponsoring most legislation in this area exceeds by 10 percent the number of women claiming health, education, and welfare as their area of expertise.

This discrepancy, coupled with the general correspondence between area of expertise and committee assignment, prompted an examination of the relationship between committee assignment and legislation sponsored most. When committee assignment is considered, only 43 percent of the respondents reported sponsoring the most legislation in the area coming within the scope of their committee. If health, education, and welfare committee members are omitted, the percentage of those sponsoring legislation in their area of committee assignment drops to 22 percent. The women sitting on standing committees dealing with agriculture and business, for example, are as likely to sponsor most legislation in health, education, and welfare as they are legislation dealing with business or agriculture. Women sitting on highways and public works committees are twice as likely to sponsor most legislation in the area of their committee assignment. Of the women sitting on fiscal committees 43 percent sponsor most legislation in the area of fiscal affairs, and 53 percent of the women on judiciary committees sponsor most legislation in the area of judicial affairs. However, even they are less likely to sponsor most legislation coming within the scope of their committees, where 67 percent report that most legislation sponsored falls within the scope of their committee.

These data seem to suggest that despite the general correspondence of area of expertise and committee assignment for all except those claiming fiscal affairs as their area of expertise, a situation of objective marginality does exist for women state legislators. They do, indeed, appear to be on the margin. Only 25 percent of the women who claim fiscal affairs as their area of expertise sit on fiscal committees, while somewhat more women sit on health, education, and welfare committees than claim it as their area of expertise. Fiscal committees, furthermore, are critical in setting budget priorities, and the virtual exclusion of women legislators from fiscal committees diminishes the role and influence which these women can have in policy making. Also, although women sit on a broad spectrum of committees, they still tend to sponsor legislation in one area stereotypic to women—health, education, and welfare. Apparently, there are some conditions in the legislative environment which encourage the women to be more concerned with stereotypic female concerns than with concerns in their area of expertise or assigned committees. This situation would seem to fulfill the definition of objective marginality.

Patterns of Consultation

Next the pattern of consultation by executive and department heads, legislative leadership, and interest groups was examined. The percentage of respondents who claimed to be frequently consulted by public utilities was only 8 percent, by labor only 12 percent, by their chamber's leadership 15 percent, and by executive and department heads 15 percent. On the other hand, public service and voluntary groups, such as the Red Cross and United Way, consulted very frequently with 20 percent of the female legislators, and consumer groups with 21 percent. At the same time, the percentage of women stating that they were rarely or never consulted by public utilities was 32 percent, by labor 30 percent, by their chamber's leadership 27 percent, and by executive and department heads 23 percent. Only 17 percent of the legislators said that they were rarely or never consulted by public service and voluntary groups, and 10 percent rarely or never by consumer groups.[23]

The pattern of consultation does not seem to particularly support the prmise of objective marginality. Despite the fact that almost 10 percent of the women claim never to be consulted by public utilities, 8 percent never by labor, a little over 6 percent never by the leadership of their chamber, and almost 4 percent never by executive and department heads, and although these groups are generally considered more powerful in terms of their impact on public policy, the responses still do not clearly indicate objective marginality. Further investigation is needed to determine whether the absence of consultation with between one-fourth and one-third of the women legislators by the most powerful lobby interests results from their relative absence from formal positions of power in their political party's legislative organization and in their chamber's organization or from other factors. This would seem to be particularly interesting in that the face-to-face "contact man" orientation is more pervasive among state-level lobbyists than among those at the national level.[24]

Leadership Positions

The somewhat ambiguous findings on consultation by interest groups are in marked contrast to the data on the women's formal leadership position in their legislative chambers. Only 14 percent of the respondents held any position of leadership. Five women serve as speaker or president of their chamber. Nine are majority or minority leaders. Five are deputy majority or minority leaders. Four are whips. One woman is a deputy whip. Ten women serve as committee chairpersons, and one woman is a deputy committee chairperson. Table 16–1 illustrates the meager representation of women in leadership positions.

The smaller number of leadership positions among women state legislators is most often attributed to recency of election. This contention does not seem to be borne out by the data, however. In the first place, if the absence of women was due to their more recent election, then one could expect fewer women to hold positions such as speaker, majority or minority leader, or committee chairperson. By the same token, more women should hold positions such as deputy whip or deputy committee chairperson. However, the reverse is true. In the second place, the average age of the women legislators at the time of their first election is 38, and 61 percent stated that the first office to which they were

Table 16-1
Women in Political and Chamber Leadership Positions

Leadership Position	Total Number of Women Respondents Holding Position	Percentage of Women Respondents Holding Position	Total Number of Such Positions Available[b]	Percentage of Total of Such Positions Available Held by Women
Speaker/presiding officer	5	2	99	5
Majority/minority leader	9	4	177	5
Assistant deputy majority/ minority leader and other party positions	5	2	317	1.57
Majority/minority whips	4	2	131	3
Standing committee chair-personships in 1977	10[a]	4	1,615	0.006
Other positions	2	1	—	—
Total	35 (N = 247)	14	N = 2,339	1.49

[a]Includes both Standing and Special Committee Chairpersonships held by women.
[b]Source of figures on positions available is *The Book of the States 1978–79*, vol. 22 (Lexington, Ky.: The Council of State Governments, 1978).

elected was the state legislature. Since 31 percent of the respondents were between the ages of 51 and 60, and 31 percent between the ages of 41 and 50, it is
strongly suggested that the majority of the respondents are not first-year legislators. There seems little, then, to substantiate the position that the absence of
women from legislative leadership positions is attributable to their recent election. Rather, the data seem to confirm the hypothesis of objective marginality.

Experiential Marginality

The experientially marginal individual is thought to be one "who experiences
conflicting demands which converge upon those in his marginal position."[25]
Several different factors were examined in order to test for experiential marginality. They included motivation to run for elective office, the importance of
family attitudes in deciding to run for public office, perceptions of influence
and success, and attitudes on the assessments of their success by their legislative peers.

Motivation to Run for Office

About 47 percent of the women legislators said that they themselves were the
most influential factor in their decision to run for the state legislature. Only 19
percent claimed that their friends were the most influential, 11 percent cited
their families, 11 percent their political party, 5 percent civic and community
groups, and less than 1 percent mentioned labor organizations. While the majority of the respondents (52 percent) said that both men and women urged them
to run, 31 percent answered that only men urged them to run. Only 13 percent
said only females urged them to run. At the same time, a somewhat higher percentage of women (79 percent) claimed that white women were very helpful in
their campaigns than those who mentioned white men (72 percent). Black
women were also cited as being very helpful slightly more often (21 percent)
than were black men (19 percent).
    These data may be interpreted as representing the conflicting values typical
of experiential marginality. The importance that almost half of the women
legislators attributed to themselves in their decision to run for the state legislature seems to suggest the isolation characteristic of the marginal person. The
somewhat larger percentage who mentioned women as very helpful than those
who cited men combined with the relatively meager percentage who said they
were urged to run only by females is illustrative of the conflicting pressures and
values of the experientially marginal person.

Family Attitudes

Given the relatively high percentage of women who indicated self-motivation as the most important factor in their decision to run for public office and the small percentage who mentioned family, one would expect family attitudes to be considered irrelevant or unimportant. This is not the case at all since 54 percent of the women said that husband's attitude toward their running for public office was enthusiastic, and 29 percent claimed that husband's attitude was generally favorable. Only 4 percent said that husband's attitude as neutral, unfavorable, or hostile. Moreover, 74 percent said that they considered husband's attitude about their political career very important, and 21 percent asserted that husband's attitude was somewhat important. Only 5 percent of the respondents claimed that husband's attitude was not very important, unimportant, or irrelevant. In fact, only one woman said husband's attitude was unimportant, and one women that it was irrelevant.[26] Similarly, 79 percent of the women said that their children's attitude was either very important or somewhat important while only 4 percent said that their children's attitude was unimportant or irrelevant.

The importance of children's attitude is particularly interesting in light of the fact that only 24 percent of the women legislators had children under the age of 18, and of that 24 percent the overwhelming majority had children who were between the ages of 12 and 18. At the time of their first campaign the data suggest that in most instances the children were at least teenagers. Thus, concern about children's attitudes would not seem to be tied to the necessity of physically caring for young children, but rather to cultural norms about a mother's responsibility toward and self fulfillment through her children.

The pattern of self-motivation to seek a career in elective politics and the importance attached to husband's and children's attitude may be interpreted as typical of the contradictory pressures of experiential marginality. These conflicting pressures are confirmed elsewhere in the questionnaire. For example, 65 percent of the respondents described themselves as someone priding herself on doing things on her own without asking anyone else for help or advice, and 54 percent said that they felt strongly and quite sure of that choice. While this confirms their assertion of self-motivation to pursue a political career, it is clearly at odds with the importance that the legislators attach to husband's attitude and children's as well. This "apparent" inconsistency is perhaps best explained by the theory of marginality.

Perceptions of Influence and Success

Over four-fifths of the legislators (81 percent) felt at least somewhat influential, with 16 percent describing themselves as very influential and another 65 percent asserting that they were somewhat influential. Less than 1 percent said that they were not at all influential, and the remainder claimed that they were either not very influential or influential on one or two issues only. An even larger number (92 percent) said that they were either very successful (37 percent) or somewhat successful (55 percent). Approximately 8 percent saw themselves as mostly unsuccessful or as having only a few successes. In response to the question "How successful do you feel your fellow legislators think you have been as a legislator?" 93 percent responded either very successful (38 percent) or somewhat successful (55 percent). Not a single respondent thought her fellow legislators considered her mostly unsuccessful; and 7 percent felt that their legislative colleagues thought that they had only a few successes.

At first glance these responses about influence and success would seem to reject the hypothesis of experiential marginality categorically. The existence of objective marginality but the absence of experiential marginality might be seen as an example of what Goldberg had described. That is to say, a marginal culture exists in which the marginal individual no longer exhibits the characteristics that Park and Stonequist associated with marginality. Rather, the marginal legislators have created a new cultural environment in which they feel comfortable, influential, and successful, just as second- and third-generation Jews had in Goldberg's study.

This explanation would seem to be substantiated by the discrepancy noted between responses to the question dealing with influence and the questions dealing with success. Whereas only 16 percent of the women legislators described themselves as very influential, 37 percent thought that they were very successful, and 38 percent thought that their fellow legislators considered them very successful. On the face of it, this would seem to suggest that the women have developed a new set of norms for success that is only partially related to influence. In other words, a cultural environment with realistic goals has emerged that allows the women to consider themselves as successful, both in their own eyes and in the eyes of their fellow legislators.

As tempting as this explanation is, however, there are certain problems with it. When asked to choose the kind of person that would describe you best—someone who has the reputation of being conceited but is also respected for her real abilities or someone who has the reputation of being quite modest and not at all conceited but whose acquaintances don't know their real abilities—57 percent felt that they were modest persons whose acquaintances don't know their real abilities and 51 percent said that they felt strongly and quite sure of their choice. In response to another question, 77 percent described themselves as someone who often loses out because she is too kind to take advantage of anyone who isn't as smart as she is. Also, 62 percent claimed that they were a real family woman who wasn't very successful in her career. These responses, it is true, do not negate absolutely the explanation of a marginal culture; but they certainly do raise serious questions about consistency between avowals of influence and success, on the one hand, and feelings that abilities are not recognized, that they lose out because they are too kind, and that they are not very successful in their career, on the other. Indeed, when the responses to questions about what kind of person a woman is are compared with responses to questions about influence and success, the evidence seems to support the hypothesis of experiential marginality, rather than the existence of a marginal culture which insulates the legislators from conflicting pressures.

Conclusions

Overall, the data seem to support the hypothesis that women state legislators are objectively marginal. Given the low representation of women in state legislatures, one must conclude that they are a very small, elite group of women, quite different from women as a group. Despite their very different aspirations as manifested by a very nonstereotypic female career choice, their integration into the group of state legislators is incomplete. While generally no clear-cut pattern of discrimination in committee assignments exists, except appointment to fiscal committees, pressures of some sort obviously encourage women to sponsor most legislation in the area of health, education, and welfare, in spite of their more diverse areas of interest and committee assignments. Furthermore, the women's minimal representation in positions of leadership suggests that the women may well be considered different and as nonequals by their male peers in the legislature.

Some of the data clearly suggest that the women legislators are experientially marginal. Most notable are their high level of self-motivation, on the one hand, and the importance they attach to family's attitude about their involvement in elective politics, on the other. However, when it comes to perceptions of influence and success, the evidence is not as strong. Although it appears as if the women are conflicted about how successful they really are, their assertion of success and influence may reflect the existence of a marginal culture that reduces the conflicting demands and value choices of those who may be described as experientially marginal. Further exploration of the existence of a marginal culture is not required.

One further comment needs to be made. Those studies that have described women legislators as benchwarmers or spectators and branded them as generally ineffectual have failed to understand the unique and difficult position of these women. Perjorative epithets and negative evaluations of the work of these women are obvious examples of blaming the victim. What needs to be said instead is something about how well they have survived and operated within the legislative environment. Regarding additional research on women legislators, particularly needed is some exploration of the inherent potential for creativity attributed to marginal status by the same writers.[27]

Notes

1. Robert E. Park, "Human Migration and the Marginal Man," *American Journal of Sociology* 33 (May 1928): 892.

2. Ibid., p. 893.

3. Everett Stonequist, *The Marginal Man: A Study in Personality and Culture Conflict* (New York: C. Scribner's Sons, 1937), p. 8.

4. Milton Goldberg, "A Qualification of the Marginal Man Theory." *American Sociological Reviews* 6, no. 1 (1941): 53.

5. Ibid.

6. Arnold W. Green, "A Reexamination of the Marginal Man Concept," *Social Forces* 26 (December 1947): 167-68.

7. Alan C. Kerckhoff and Thomas C. McCormick, "Marginal Status and Marginal Personality," *Social Forces* 34 (October 1955): 50.

8. Robert K. Merton and Alice Rossi, "Contributions to the Theory of Reference Group Behavior," in Robert K. Merton, *Social Theory and Social Structure* (New York: The Free Press, 1968), pp. 279-334.

9. Noel P. Gist and Anthony Gary Dworkin, eds., *The Blending of Races: Marginality and Identity in World Perspective* (New York: Wiley-Interscience, 1972), pp. 16-17.

10. Ralph Turner, *The Social Context of Ambition* (San Francisco: Chandler Publishing Company, 1964), p. 109.

11. Ibid., p. 5.

12. For example, see Peggy Lamson, *Few are Chosen* (Boston: Houghton Mifflin, 1968); Hope Chamberlain, *A Minority of Members* (New York: Praeger, 1973); Maurice Duverger, *The Political Role of Women* (Paris: UNESCO, 1955); Martin Gruberg, *Women in American Politics* (Oshkosh, Wis.: Academia, 1968).

13. Emmy Werner, "Women in Congress: 1917-1964," *Western Political Quarterly* 19 (1966): 16-30; and Emmy E. Werner, "Women in State Legislatures," *Western Political Quarterly* 21 (1968): 40-50.

14. Charles S. Bullock, III, and Patricia Lee Findley Heys, "Recruitment of Women for Congress: A Research Note," *Western Political Quarterly* 25 (September 1972): 416-23.

15. Jeane Kirkpatrick, *Political Woman* (New York: Basic Books, 1974).

16. Irene Diamond, *Sex Roles in the State House* (New Haven, Conn.: Yale University Press, 1977), pp. 4-5.

17. Marianne Githens and Jewel L. Prestage, *A Portrait of Marginality: The Political Behavior of the American Woman* (New York: David McKay Company, 1977).

18. Werner, "Women in State Legislatures."

19. While we are concerned here with the upward mobility of the legislators, this finding is a most interesting one. The impact of mother's education on the

woman legislator's career choice of elected official undoubtedly warrants further investigation.

20. For discussion of occupational prestige see Otis D. Duncan, David Featherman, and Beverly Duncan, *Socio-Economic Background and Achievement* (New York: Seminar Press, 1972). Great liberty was taken by the authors of this chapter, however, in the utilization of this source as a basis for the method used in arriving at occupational prestige scores for purposes of this chapter.

21. There is no generally accepted method for computing a full-time home-maker's occupational prestige. In our assignment of occupational prestige equal weighting was given to all the factors mentioned. The reliability of this weighting requires further analysis and evaluation.

22. Werner, "Women in Congress: 1917–1964" and "Women in State Legis-latures."

23. One interesting and unexpected finding was the small number of legis-lators who claimed to be consulted very frequently by religious and racial minorities. Only 13 percent claimed to be consulted very frequently by these groups. Why the women should be consulted so infrequently by these groups is difficult to explain.

24. See Malcolm E. Jewell and Samuel C. Patterson, *The Legislative Process in the United States* (New York: Random House, 1966), pp. 285–289.

25. Turner, *The Social Context of Ambition,* p. 5.

26. Emily Stoper, "Wife and Politician: Role Strain among Women in Pub-lic Office," in Githens and Prestage, *A Portrait of Marginality,* pp. 320–337.

27. See Robert E. Park's introduction in Stonequist, *The Marginal Man,* and Charles V. Willie, "Marginality and Social Change," *Society* 12 (July/August 1975): 12. Also, Melvin Seeman, "Intellectual Perspective and Adjustment to Minority Status," *Social Problems* 3 (January 1956): 442–453.

Part VI
A Comparative Perspective

17

Abortion in Israel; Social Demands and Political Responses

Yael Yishai

The question of abortion is loaded with paradoxes: although universally practised, it is not universally accepted;[1] while ostensibly a medical issue, it involves economic interests and ideological orientations. Abortion is regarded in many countries as a criminal offense, yet the law is hardly enforced since no evidence can be obtained and no complaint is presented.[2] Abortion is a private matter, arousing the deepest human feelings, yet it is largely an issue of public political bargaining and compromising.[3] Moreover, despite its ubiquitous practice, abortion has been a "dead secret of our society";[4] as one Israeli columnist has put it, "Mankind's war on abortion has raged throughout the long history of mankind's hypocrisy."[5]

Israel is numbered among those countries in which abortion has been practised and not accepted. It was widespread, and generally illegal; at the same time it was not dealt with by political authorities and only recently has it emerged as a negotiable political issue.

The purpose of this chapter, which will focus on the politics of abortion in Israel, is fourfold: (1) to reveal the factors that made abortion a nondecision issue, preventing its appearance on the public agenda; (2) to explore the factors that have successfully pushed forward abortion to the point that it became a public issue; (3) to study the process that made abortion a subject of legislative public policy; and (4) to examine the implementation (or lack thereof) of this policy.

When an issue based on grievance or social demand is neither debated nor decided openly in political institutions, it is regarded as a "nondecision issue." This may happen when the dominant values, the accepted rules of the game, the existing power relations among groups and the instruments of force, singly or in combination, effectively prevent certain grievances from developing into full-fledged issues which call for decisions."[6] Abortion in Israel has been a nondecision issue. For more than twenty years after the founding of the state, political authorities hardly dealt with abortion, which was an illegal action, though widely practised. It is assumed here that the dominant values upheld by power relations sustained nondecision politics with regard to abortion.

There seem to be three phases through which a nascent issue needs to pass if it is to enter onto and then remain on the public agenda for debate and decision. First, it should command attention, by being linked to particular occurrences or events. Second, the issue should be able to claim legitimacy, which means a change has occurred in the dominant value systems. Third, it should be able to invoke action taken both by supporting groups and decision-making elites.[7]

The purpose of this chapter is to find out whether the emergence of abortion as a public issue in Israeli politics indeed fits this scheme.

Abortion in Israel is a case study and regarded as such; however, its study might contribute to the understanding of policy-making processes within a political system. While recognizing that the emergence of any public policy is a highly complex process is which there is no beginning or end and the boundaries of which are most uncertain,[8] specific sources of power and influence affecting this policy can nevertheless be discerned.

Power is concerned with the role played by social groups and organizations, supported by values and ideologies, in influencing decisionmakers. According to the structural-functional model, the interest groups aggregate public demands and transmit them to political parties which articulate these demands as policy alternatives.[9] There is thus a two-step process of policy formation which turns a public demand (that is, input) into authoritative decisions (that is, output). This theory has been criticized on two grounds. First, it is widely suggested that political parties are not as salient as assumed and that interest groups alone may perform the function of transmitting demands to decisionmakers.[10] Second, interest groups, instead of influencing government policies, are manipulated by elites for purposes of promoting a recognized social objective.[11] Thus there are three hypothetical sources for initiation of public policy which may or may not be mutually exclusive: political parties, interest groups, and state organs, namely, government and legislature. These sources are scrutinized in the course of analyzing the politics of abortion in Israel.

The underlying assumption of this chapter is that a combination of social changes and group pressures turned relative freedom of choice regarding abortion into a public policy alternative which then was formulated into a bill. However, this bill, rather than reflecting a radical change of attitude toward abortion was rather a manifestation of incremental policy.

Incremental solutions, argue Lindblom, appear within a highly pluralistic environment dominated by interdependent interest groups. These groups operate in an open system which accepts the necessity for compromise for the production of policies in a process which is characterized by "partisan mutual adjustment."[12] Thus when values and policies clash, as they obviously have in the case of abortion, "one chooses among values and among policies at one and the same time,"[13] invoking only marginal changes with regard to both rule making and rule application.

The incremental feature of the politics of abortion in Israel is manifest in its implementation which reflects (1) the countervailing forces that played a decisive role in its formulation, (2) the need to compromise on a highly controversial issue, and (3) the unfinished process of social change which is underway in the Israeli political system.

Abortion in Israel: The Non-Decision-Making Stage

Up to 1977, Israeli abortion laws were still reminiscent of those of the British Mandate in Palestine, derived from the English Offence against the Person Act of 1861. The regulations were extremely rigid. Both the person procuring a miscarriage and the aborted woman were liable to imprisonment (for fourteen and five years, respectively). However, this law was rarely implemented, since very few cases of abortion were brought before the court.[14]

Throughout the years some changes in the legal situation occurred. In 1952 the District Court of Haifa declared that induced abortion for bona fide medical reasons was permissible if done openly. Instructions issued by the attorney general clearly supported the legality of abortions performed in accordance with the standards laid down by this case. Advocates were advised to refrain from initiating criminal charges except in cases deemed deleterious to the life and health of a woman. In 1963 these instructions were repealed because of doubts as to their legality. Three years later penalties imposed on the woman were abolished, and the term of imprisonment for the person performing the abortion was reduced to five years.

Table 16-1 presents the rate of legal abortions in Israel in selected years. These obviously were only part of the total sum, most of which were illegal and thus not tabulated.

The "legal" (or rather the quasi-legal) abortions were provided by the largest Sick Fund, a suborganization of the Jewish Labor Movement (Histodrut), upon the approval, usually on medical grounds, of a committee consisting of two physicians. This method had a number of deficiencies: the committee's existence was not publicized, thus minimizing its services; its decisions were hasty and arbitrary; and the husband's consent was required. As a result, most of the woman resorted to private abortions which were either costly or unsafe.[15]

Table 17-1
Rate of Abortions in Israel (per 100,000) in Selected Years

Year	1950	1955	1960	1965	1970	1974
Number of abortions	897	654	686	591	567	622

Source: *Statistical Abstract of Israel*, no. 29 (1977), p. 103.

There are no accurate figures on the frequency of private abortions in Israel. The estimates ran from 45,000 to 60,000 in 1976. Data published in 1970 indicated that 46.7 percent of women aged 40 and over had at least one induced abortion. The maximum was found among Jewish women of European origin (52 percent in comparison to 25 percent and 30 percent, respectively, among Afro-Asian and Israeli women), who were highly educated, secularized, and residing in large towns and settlements. The lowest frequency was found among new immigrants of Asian and African origin, who were less educated and living in small, remote settlements.[16] These findings proved later to be the major trigger for inducing changes in the politics of abortion.

The reasons for the discrepancy between the legal regulation of abortion and its daily practice were grounded both in the value system and in the power relations.

The Dominant Values: Religious and National Attitudes

Though Israel is largely a secular society inasmuch as most Israelis consider themselves nonreligious, religious issues are of far-reaching significance in that they constitute one of the basic determining factors of national sovereignty.[17] It has been noted that "an intrinsically secular movement [the Zionist Movement] arrogated to itself the fulfillment of a mission which religious belief alone had to keep alive."[18] The fact that Judaism is a monoethnic religion has made the relationship between state and religion in Israel a complicated issue laden with both deep emotions and political pressures, part of which were focused on the issue of abortion.

The predominant (and almost exclusive) congregation in Israeli society is orthodox, whose views reflect traditional attitudes. Jewish religion regards life as sacred, and the duty of saving life overrides all other commandments. This rule applies also to abortion, the question being *whose* life? The Jewish answer is explicit: the fetus becomes a living soul only when it detaches itself from its mother, and only then is it deemed to be a human life that may not be pushed aside for another. On the other hand, the unborn child has a right to life which cannot be denied him even if it is the product of incest or rape or if an abnormality of any kind is foreseen. The only condition under which this right may be denied is when it threatens the *life* of another, namely the mother. Under the principle which permits taking the life of a human being in defense of another who is being attacked by the first, an abortion can be permitted if the mother's life is endangered. It is for a confident religious authority, on consultation with medical sources, to determine whether the danger to a mother's well-being is sufficient to warrant an abortion.[19]

The orthodox view, permitting an abortion only in the event of a clear

Table 17-2
Fertility Rates in Israel by Religion and Place of Birth

	1955	1960	1965	1970	1973	1976
Non-Jews	7.29	7.99	8.42	7.65	7.34	6.86
Jews	3.64	3.49	3.47	3.41	3.15	3.20
Mother's Place of Birth						
Israel	2.83	2.76	2.88	3.12	2.94	3.11
Afro-Asia	5.68	5.10	4.58	4.07	3.78	3.66
Europe/America	2.63	2.38	2.60	2.84	2.74	2.96

Source: *Statistical Abstract of Israel*, no. 29 (1977), pp. 80–81.

and immediate danger to the mother's life, is supported by another tenet which is grounded in national ideologies: "Thou shall be fruitful and multiply and replenish the earth." This tenet has become a national imperative, not confined to religious people. For decades one of the more important aspects of Zionist ideology has been to maximize population growth, by both immigration and increased natality. This need has been both political and emotional.

Politically, population increase has been considered an important issue in determining the country's political future since conflicting political ambitions of the two major communities in Israel, Jews and Arabs, deemed it necessary.[20] Table 17-2 presents comparative data on fertility rates among Jews and non-Jews in selected years. Evidently the Jews (of all origins) have a lower rate of fertility than the non-Jews. While all fertility rates have decreased since 1960, Jewish fertility is less than half of that of the non-Jewish. Since immigration is also tending to decline, Israel might become a country with an Arab majority. This poses a grave threat to the Zionist idea, aimed at creating a Jewish homeland and sovereignty in Israel, and raises serious political apprehensions. The "demographic danger" is regarded as one of the major arguments for retreat from heavily populated Arab zones in the West Bank and the Gaza Strip. Since abortion is correlated, perhaps unjustly, with population control and decreased fertility,[21] it was not regarded as a desired political objective.

The emotional aspect of population control is less conspicuous, though not less prevalent. Emotions have bearing on two domains: social status and individual security. Fertility is linked with social status mainly among Jews of Afro-Asian origin for whom childbearing is a symbol of success and a source of social esteem. Lack thereof may cause shame and disgrace. As one man has put it: "If my wife does not bear a child every year, I'll be ridiculed and blamed for not being a man."

Individual security has a different basis: memories of the holocaust coupled with the continuous state of war produced a myth of childbearing although, as evident from table 16-2, this myth was not always followed by action. The small size of the country and the sense of living on the brink of a never-ending war have created an antiabortion atmosphere. For many Jewish people bearing children became a symbol of survival and existence. This feeling was translated into a political demand when Ben Gurion, Israel's first premier, called on parents to fulfill their "demographic duty" toward the nation and bear children. This, obviously, has not illicited a favorable climate for the liberalization of abortion. Not only was the climate antiabortionist, but also political authorities became concerned about the low rate of fertility among Jewish women and took measures aimed at increasing natality. In 1949, on Ben Gurion's initiative, the Israeli government decided to pay a cash prize of (of 100 I£) to every woman bearing her tenth child. This prize was abolished ten years later when it became apparent that the main beneficiaries were Arab women.

Power Relations

Israel is a multiparty system in which not even the former dominant party, Mapai, secured a majority enabling it to control the government without partners. Multiplicity led inevitably to coalition government in which the largest religious party, the National Religious Party (NRP), was almost a permanent member.

The NRP has been described as "the main proponent of the 'Judaisation' (so to say) of Israeli public life."[22] It has been a most convenient coalition partner for the Labor Party, since the concessions it had to make were in an area it considered secondary to its primary goals. These concessions, which were mostly on religious matters, were viewed as secondary to the support which the Labor Party derived in return for its foreign defense, and, to a minor extent, its domestic politics.

Abortion was one of those secondary issues which the Labor Party could, and did, ignore for the sake of gaining the NRP's support. In contrast to the U.S. situation, religious power was not confined to the ballot,[23] but could have threatened the stability of the coalition. Students of Israeli politics have noted the consociational spirit in which controversial issues are settled.[24] In the name of this consociationalism the abortion issue was set aside, not being considered worth the breakup of the coalition, a government crisis, or even a deep friction between its partners.

Thus, the abortion issue was in a "prepolitical or at least predecisional" stage[25] because of cultural values which leaders and citizens shared, socialization patterns, and the political history of the Israeli government.

The Emergence of Abortion as a Public Issue

Abortion as a political issue commanded attention only indirectly, since the major political concern was the decreasing fertility rates of Israeli Jewish women.

In the early 1960s, after it had become evident that government efforts to encourage fertility were in vain, a Natality Committee was appointed for the purpose of dealing with various aspects of the demographic issue. One of the committee's major recommendations was related to abortions. It was unanimously agreed that abortion was a serious problem in view of its possible effects on health; there was also the demographic point of view to be considered. The views were divided, however, on solutions to these problems. The majority contended that abortions should be permitted if performed in authorized public hospitals, conditioned on the approval of a committee whose considerations not only would be medical but also would be based on sociopsychological grounds.[26] This recommendation resulted in part from the perceived relationship between large families and deprivation, which, as a rule, was not openly acknowledged in Israeli society.

The Natality Committee's report had one definite result—the establishment of a Demographic Center whose major purpose was to encourage childbirth, especially among those women who resorted heavily to abortions. The recommendations on this issue were not translated into political demands, nor were they crystallized as policy alternatives.

The changes that made possible the emergence of abortion as a public issue became apparent only in the early 1970s. Though no precise date can be discerned, the Six Day War and its aftermath are regarded as a turning point in the Israeli social and political system. The changes occurred both on the level of norms and values and in power relations. With regard to values two processes may be discerned. On the one hand, with increased military strength, territories, and immigration came massive foreign investment and "easy money" which resulted in disintegration of the older pioneering, egalitarian values. On the other hand, the changes in the political constellation generated new processes and aided in the diffusion of ideas which were previously submerged or unfamiliar. Two of these ideas were the increasing social gap within Israeli society and the liberation of women. These ideas were promoted by groups that resorted to pressure politics in order to obtain their objectives.

The Black Panthers

In 1971 the prospect of the emergence of "two nations" within the Israeli society was widely accepted as the crucial problem of the era. These two nations consisted of people originating from Afro-Asian and from European countries.

The first were less affluent and less educated. Their average income (per capita) was much lower than that of the European Jews, and their housing was poorer. Moreover, they suffered from a deep feeling of deprivation and discrimination which led eventually to the formation of the protest group the Black Panthers. This group held violent street demonstrations demanding employment, improvement in educational opportunities, and better housing arrangements. Evidently there was a social "gap" which could become explosive since it differentiated between two parts of the Israeli nation on the basis of origin.[27]

The Black Panthers succeeded in capturing the attention of the political elite to an unprecedented degree. The government reacted by appointing various committees to look into the problems of underprivileged groups. Chief among these was the Prime Minister's Committee for Youth in Distress. The committee's report indicated that again there was a clear correspondence between the size of the family and distress since 75 percent of the children who grew up in economic deprivation were from large families (four children or more). These comprised 38.6 percent of all Israeli children. The committee recommended that immediate measures be taken to prevent unwanted pregnancies and to limit the size of those families whose fertility had been proved to be a social burden by resorting to legal abortions.[28]

Thus, the Black Panthers made the Israeli public and political authorities aware of two facts: (1) multiplicity of children may be (and statistically is) a source of serious deprivation; (2) abortion may be considered as a method for birth control, although as a last resort.

The Israeli Feminist Movement (IFM)

The IFM was established officially in March 1972 although it had started its activities two years earlier. It consisted of women who were mostly from English-speaking countries, from which they had imported ideas of feminism.

Israeli feminism is a milder version of the universal one. Bras were not burned in the streets, and violent demonstrations were not held. The movement had a small appeal to Israeli women who are mostly conservative in outlook and of whom only one-third are employed out of their homes—mostly in traditional feminine occupations. Even the national element incorporated into Israeli feminism—"a country of only three million people, whose history has been characterized by war and economic crisis, cannot afford to neglect the potential of one half of its population"[29]—has not aided in spreading the feminist notion.

Abortion has been an ideal issue for the IFM to submit political demands. It was not a controversial issue among feminists who were widely divided over other subjects. Moreover, the campaign for abortion was in line with similar movements abroad, especially in the United States,[30] and thus legitimized the

Israeli organization in the eyes of its counterparts. The IFM pressures toward abortion on demand culminated in presenting a petition to the Knesset demanding legislation in this spirit.

In conclusion, the role played by the Black Panthers and the IFM in promoting abortion as a public issue was both a result of and a stimuli for changes. Abortion did claim legitimacy since it was evident that its legal denial resulted in serious damage to the social web of the community. What was still needed was political support that would translate this legitimacy into state action.

The Legislative Process

Once abortion had become a publicly debated issue, social pressures were exerted that demanded political responses. As has been contended earlier, public policy may be initiated by three organs: parties, interest groups, and government. The case of abortion politics in Israel demonstrates that:

1. There was a blurring of lines among interest groups, political parties, and government with regard to initiation.
2. There was no linear process of transmitting demands from interest groups to political parties and then to authoritative decisionmakers; rather the issue was articulated simultaneously while the solutions provided differed.
3. The distinction was not between interest groups, political parties, and state organs but within all three on the basis of ideological orientations. That is, those who were proabortion cooperated against their counterparts on the other side of the ideological fence.
4. The process of formulating policies on abortion was characterized by a bandwagon effect. Once the political wheels started to turn, various groups and individuals followed suit.

In June 1971, a Member of Knesset submitted a private member's bill aimed at allowing the Minister of Health to gazette regulations governing abortions which would be elective.[31] The initiator was a single delegate of a marginal radical party who was famous for his unconventional proposals.

The Minister of Health responded by reporting that a public committee had been appointed (in 1972) to study the issue of abortion.[32] Actually "study" was not the sole purpose for this appointment, since by choosing people of various backgrounds whose views were publicly known, the Minister anticipated its conclusions, which would have cleared the way for appropriate legislation.

The crucial question is, What induced the Minister of Health to set up this committee? The answer demonstrated the complexity of the decision-making process, the multiplicity of factors having an influence on the political elite, and the impact of the social environment. The setting up of the committee resulted from the following factors:

1. The Minister of Health was a liberal-minded member of a left-wing party that had joined the coalition a short time before the appointment of the abortion committee. He realized that this issue had become a public grievance in need of a political remedy which could be provided by his office.
2. Interest groups such as the IFM and troubled individuals pressured the Minister of Health to legitimize abortion.
3. In 1971 the Sick Fund's dissatisfaction with abortion politics had increased as a result of two major factors. First, two of its physicians were prosecuted for performing illegal abortions, one of whom committed suicide in the course of the trial. Although the case was dropped, the situation called for legal clarification. Second, studies of causes of interruption of pregnancies in the Sick Fund's hospitals revealed that only in a few cases were medical reasons the source of application.[33] These findings were followed by a demand to add a psychiatrist and a social worker to the committee deciding on abortions. While the Sick Fund's authorities declared that the expansion of the committees was intended not to increase the number of abortions but, on the contrary, to encourage the applicant to bear her child, the decision created a favorable atmosphere to induce changes in the politics of abortion.

The involvement of the Sick Fund is a clear manifestation of the blurring of lines between interest groups and political parties. The Sick Fund is an integral part of the Labor Movement which is controlled by the Labor Party. Its institutions are compounded on the basis of the relative power distribution within the mother organization, thus ensuring the party's control over health services. Although formally an interest group, the Sick Fund has been (and to a large extent still is) the most powerful hold that the *Histadrut* has over its members since, as a rule, one cannot enjoy the Sick Fund's benefits without being a union member, nor can one be a union member without having to pay the health service.[34]

While the committee was pursuing its work, various other interest groups and parties joined the campaign for abortion legislation.

Women's Organizations

The major women's organization that joined the pressures to liberalize abortion was Naa'mat (Pioneer Women), which is also affiliated with the *Histadrut.* Naa'mat, like the Sick Fund, is politicized to a large extent. Although it comprises women of various parties, its leaders are prominent members of the Labor Party and Members of the Knesset (MKs). Thus it is difficult to distinguish, in this context, between initiative originating in a party or group.

In both capacities Naa'mat demanded legalization of elective abortion. The demand was included as an item in the Labor Party's platform and was brought, after the elections to the 8th Knesset (1974), as an issue at the party's institutions in the Knesset.

The Civil Rights Movement (CRM)

The CRM is a party led by Shulamit Aloni, a former Labor Party MK, who was one of the major proponents of civil rights in Israeli society. Aloni advocated separation between state and religion and has been deeply involved in various struggles aimed at supporting individuals who have suffered injustices resulting from religious rulings. Prior to the 1973 elections the CRM incorporated the IFM, presenting its leader on its list to the Knesset. The feminist representative was most active in promoting abortion and pushing it forward within and outside the Knesset, clearing the way for the legislative process.

In 1973 the Committee on the Study of Abortion submitted its report to the Minister of Health. In its conclusions it reiterated the Natality Committee's recommendations, namely that abortions be performed by qualified physicians in authorized medical institutions. It laid down five conditions under which abortion should be performed after the approval of a committee: when a women's physical or emotional health is endangered; when pregnancy endangers her life; when pregnancy results from rape or incest; when there is fear for the unborn child's physical or mental health; and last and most important, when there is a possibility of serious disruption of the life of the woman or other members of her family, such as would be the case in large families.

The recommendations were not revolutionary. Actually some of them were already practised to a limited extent by the Sick Fund. At the same time, however, they did represent a radical change since the issue was openly debated and was about to be regulated by a state law.

The problem was how to avoid a government crisis in view of the anticipated religious opposition to the proposed bill. The solution was found in a Knesset procedure according to which party discipline is not imposed when a case is declared to be a matter of conscience and is initiated by a private member rather than by the government. This tactic was pursued with regard to abortion.

On January 1975 two private member bills were submitted to the Knesset: one by a member of the Alignment,[35] the other by a feminist member of the CRM. The first set down seven conditions under which abortion could be performed without prosecution, adding two more to the Committee's recommendations, namely, pregnancy out of wedlock and the woman's age being under 17 or over 45. The second proposal promoted an elective abortion within the first twelve weeks of pregnancy. Both draft laws required the operation to be performed in a recognized medical institution. There was no mention of a committee of any sort on whose approval abortion would be contingent.

The reasoning behind the two proposals was not similar: the first clarified the role of abortion in family planning,[36] thus emphasizing its social aspect. While admitting it was not the ideal way of controlling family size, it was perceived as the "only way for women who would not use contraceptive devices for religious reasons."[37] This policy was opposed by those who demanded to encourage natality by changing national priorities and allocating large resources to those who are "blessed" with children.[38] It should be noted that although a voluntary association,[39] the Sick Fund as well as the Ministry of Health has set up special services for family planning. These services to date lag behind public needs. The idea of family planning based on modern contraceptives is not easily inculcated in large sectors of Israeli society.[40]

The proposal submitted by the CRM had a different reasoning, based on the sheer right of a woman to be master of her own fate and body. As to family planning, this, the CRM leadership believes, should be dealt with separately.

The Minister of Health favored the first proposal, agreeing that the real problem was not abortion but family planning. He added, though, the desirability of prior consultation with a medical-sociological committee before a woman could proceed with a legal abortion.[41] In a later interview[42] he admitted that this attitude was based on a realistic perception—the Israeli Knesset, regardless of party affiliation, could not go further; perhaps it would not have gone that far unless an extreme measure had been proposed since "the more extreme or controversial proposals tend to legitimate more moderate advances by shifting the boundaries of discourse."[43]

The religious parties protested passionately against the proposed bill. Quoting Jewish sources, religious MKs claimed that preventing the live birth of a child was tantamount to murder. Opposition was grounded also in nationalistic arguments. However, the bill was passed to the Public Services Committee for further deliberation.[44]

While abortion legislation was being discussed by the committee the following developments occurred:

1. The committee voted down the CRM proposal because of the power relations within that committee; the CRM had the support of only one of the committee's twelve members.

2. The committee decided on the makeup of a two-member abortion committee consisting of a gynoecologist and any one of the following: a general practitioner, social worker, or public health nurse. This further retreat from the concept of abortion on demand rendered a necessary compromise in

view of the strong pressures within the committee, five of whose members opposed the proposed bills.[45]

In February 1976 the abortion bill was brought to the Knesset for the first hearing. The scenario of the preliminary hearing repeated itself when the chairperson of the committee explained that the bill was not aimed at encouraging abortions. The vigorous opposition was upheld by the NRP, which had to prove its adherance to religious principles despite (or perhaps due to) its partnership in the coalition. This opposition generated political response—the Knesset, although approving the proposed bill, decided to pass it to a joint committee in which (1) small parties such as the CRM had no representation and (2) the religious MKs had more numerical weight and influence.

While the bill was elaborated in the joint committee, interest groups exerted pressure by presenting their views directly to the committee or through the mass media. The major proponents of the bill remained the women's organizations; they were joined, however, by the Social Workers Organization (SWO) who insisted on the inclusion of both the social clause in the bill and a professional social worker on the abortion committee.

Objection was elicited mainly by religious groups, who employed violent means in order to terminate the process of legislation, which was well underway. The chairperson of the committee was accused of being the incarnation of Hitler; in addition, street demonstrations were held and manifestos were distributed against the "bill of murder." The protest against the bill was not confined to small religious zealot groups but was joined by figures such as the chief Rabbis of Israel who demanded that it be abolished altogether.

Opposition emerged from another direction, namely the Society of Gynecologists and Obstetricians, which declared it would not cooperate with health authorities in implementing the law. It has been noted that the medical profession has played a key role in sustaining community opposition to abortion, since doctors have exploited their expertise to restrict the availability of the procedure.[46] The doctors justified their objection by their concern for the women's health; they were accused, however, of making large sums of "black money" out of illegal abortions.[47] The gynecologists finally consented to support the bill after some changes had been inserted, the chief of which enlarged the approval committee to three members: one gynecologist, one general practitioner, and a social worker.

In January 1977 the bill was finally approved by the Knesset, only after the clause regarding "large family" as a reason for abortion was eliminated, at the last minute, from the bill. When the vote took place, religious MKs left the chamber to join a protest being held outside the house.[48] The law on abortion was scheduled to go into effect in 1978.

Thus, by law, abortion in Israel is legal within the framework which permits a doctor to perform the operation in a recognized hospital upon the approval of a committee, which must find justification in either the mental or physical conditions of mother or expected child, or in social environmental factors.[49]

The bill became a law because of the following factors:

1. The Minister of Health and the Knesset committee's chairperson were of the same party and supported each other in pushing the bill.
2. The bill had not been a subject for imposing party discipline, thus enabling MKs of both coalition and opposition to coalesce on its behalf.
3. The Knesset committee's chairperson handled the issue well. Had this not been the case, the legislation could well have been pushed into a corner.[50]
4. The extensive pressures that were exerted on decisionmakers were too strong to be ignored. On the other hand, the Knesset responded to the opposition's objections by compromising among various demands.

In conclusion, two questions are pending. First, what is the relative role played by interest groups, parties, and government in initiating policies? Second, are groups manipulated by political elites for the sake of national objectives? The answers to both questions are not clear-cut. Evidently, only the interaction between various groupings has rendered possible changes in the policy of abortion. Second, the final legislative outcome reflects, no doubt, national imperatives more than the other, radical proposal; however, one can hardly consider manipulation as the major strategy in decision making. Unless public opinion was ripe and even calling for change, the Minister's initiative would have fallen on deaf ears and would not have matured into legislation.

Implementation of the Law

In analyzing the implementation of the abortion law, two aspects are discerned—political-legal and empirical. From a political point of view, the process of legislation has not ended since changes are due owing to the turnover in the Israeli government. The winning Likud was dependent on the support of the religious parties in order to form the cabinet, thus making it susceptible to pressure for concessions on religious matters, such as the conscription of girls to the army and the abortion law. The Likud undertook, in the coalition agreement, to strike out the social clause, which permits abortion on social grounds. It has been reported that the amendment deleting the section is already in the legislative process.[51]

The intention to repeal the social clause was attacked on the grounds the Likud won the elections by securing the votes of the underprivileged, many of whom obtain abortions because of social circumstances. Data compiled by the

SWO indicate that since the law came into effect 50 percent of the requests for abortion have been based on social reasons. The government's move has evoked protests and pressure from various groups—women and professional and voluntary organizations. These groups have been campaigning against the amendment by trying to influence MKs and cabinet ministers (a few of whom are declared opponents to the amendment), either directly or by resorting to mass media techniques. In this case, however, public opinion is bound to have a meager influence since the government is tied by its coalition commitment and is bound to prevent a crisis over an issue which is not regarded as salient.

The implementation of the abortion law has also encountered practical problems relating to both the providers of the service and its clients. As to the provision of abortion services, although a "steering committee" consisting of members of the Sick Fund and the Ministry of Health was appointed, progress has not been impressive. Moreover, since the amendment is expected to go into effect, the Minister of Health has not rushed to gazette regulations nor to provide the budgets or workforce necessary to take care of a large volume of abortions. This was the case especially with regard to state hospitals whose Association of Physicians threatened to paralyze the abortion committee as a protest against the absence of adequate facilities. On the other hand, the physicians were accused of taking advantage of the abortion law for obtaining after-duty medical services, for which they would be additionally paid. Statistical data support the physician's claims since the average hospital bed occupancy in the obstetric departments of state hospitals in February–March 1978 has been 97.3 percent.

With regard to clients the underlying question is, Who are the aborted women? Does the law reach those who most need it in accordance with the intention of the lawmakers? As a rule, it has been argued that even when abortion law is liberalized, the poor are slow to take advantage of it.[52] So far the only source of data on abortions in Israel is the Sick Fund's files covering the period from 1972 to 1976.[53] While data were gathered in the period preceding the law and they cover only those who applied to the Sick Fund for abortion (having in mind that the majority secured private services), they nevertheless present a picture of those who resort to public health institutions to obtain abortion.

In contrast to earlier findings, currently Israel seems to deviate from the practice of abortion for the affluent, since many of the aborted are of Afro-Asian origin (37 percent) with low educational attainments (only 14 percent with postsecondary education). Medical indications were given in only 26.9 percent of the cases; the rest were based on social-psychological grounds. Moreover, over half of the applicants (50.2 percent) had three or more children, which is not a common practice among affluent Israeli women.[54]

Thus, apparently, despite the fact that abortion is not free of charge,[55] it is a technique used by women of lower economic status groups.

In conclusion, the period since the law came into effect is too short to evaluate its implementation. But despite present and foreseen difficulties, political solutions are being provided as follows:

1. The Sick Fund, whose insurance covers 71.8 percent of the Israeli population, provides abortion services to most women who request it. Table 16-3 demonstrates that approximately 90 percent of the appeals lodged between the years 1972 and 1977 were approved.

   The different rates of approval in the table are related to committees rather than to specific years. Apparently approval depends, to a large extent, on the attitudes of the individuals who staff the committee. According to authorized information, those who obtain the approval are aborted without delay in the Sick Fund's hospitals. Thus although the law is likely to be amended, it seems likely that the Sick Fund will continue to provide abortion services especially to those who, according to social priorities, need it most.

2. The Minister of Health, in a meeting with the SWO, declared that approval of the committee would be granted on the basis of psychological impairment, which would mask those requested on social grounds.[56] This proposal (which was later denied) has been a source of deep public concern, and the Minister was blamed for recommending a procedure to circumvent the law.

3. The army also responded to the new law by referring pregnant soldiers to abortion committees (no data are available on their numbers).[57] Previously a woman who became pregnant while serving in the army was immediately released from military duty. At present, she is permitted to continue with her military service after the abortion, if she wishes to do so.

The implementation of the abortion law highlights the dynamics of change in Israeli society. Evidently the law produced only incremental changes since abortions were previously available and the administration is not eager to provide the service. In this respect, the process of change, which made possible the formulation of abortion policy, is yet unfinished. At the same time, while there are political and other impediments to the implementation of the abortion law, it is unlikely that the clock will be turned back and abortion would once again become an illegal practice, risky to health or reserved only to affluent women.

Conclusions

Israel is at present numbered among the thirty-one countries with liberal abortion laws and policies.[58] It was argued that these policies developed in three phases: emergence of abortion from nondecision stage, legislation, and imple-

Table 17-3
Applications to the Sick Fund's Abortion Committee, 1972–1977

	1972	%	1973	%	1974	%	1975	%	1976	%	1977	%
Applications	5,836	100	5,609	100	7,066	100	7,542	100	7,724	100	7,256	100
Approvals	5,157	88.4	5,024	89.6	6,302	8.78	6,545	86.8	6,876	89.0	6,512	89.8
Rejections	679	11.6	585	10.4	863	12.2	997	13.2	848	11.0	744	10.2

Source: The Sick Fund of the General Labor Union in Israel, "Applications to the Sick Fund's Abortion Committees," 1976, publication no. 4.1.77.
The figures for 1977 are unofficial, to be published in a forthcoming report.

mentation. Each of these phases was a product of interaction among socio-economic, cultural, and political factors.

The crystallization of abortion as a public issue developed in two stages. First, it was brought to the public's attention by linking it with social problems of distress and deprivation. One has to remember that Israel, in contrast to many other countries, does not face the problem of population explosion. Quite the contrary, one of its major national objectives has been to increase the Jewish people's fertility. Abortion was perceived as a method of curtailing child-birth, thus only a critical event (such as the Black Panthers' riots) made possible a change in attitude. Without the occurrence of these events, it is doubtful whether proponents of change, such as the IFM, would have succeeded in pushing forward the issue of abortion.

Second, abortion claimed legitimacy by all actors involved—government, parliament, parties, and interested groups. The government could take action since abortion was defined in terms of *national* objectives, rather than in terms of individual liberty, which is not yet deeply rooted in Israel's society. In this capacity abortion has been a form of social engineering—to aid those whose fertility is not geared to national needs.

The process of legislation was advanced as a result of the following factors:

1. *The personal factor.* Without the vigorous support of leading political figures (such as the Minister of Health and the Committee's chairperson) the right to an abortion might have not become law.
2. *The political factor.* Interest groups and political parties, the lines between which were often not clear, played a decisive role both in bringing the issue of abortion to public attention and in articulating it on the political level. However, most of these organs have not been pioneers. Rather they joined the campaign after it was already underway.
3. *The normative factor.* Unless the liberalization of the right to abortion was legitimized and agreed on by both citizens and leaders, legislation would not have materialized. Cocurrence was high, especially on the moderate proposal, which deviated only slightly from existing practices.

Although it is difficult to assess the relative importance of each of these factors in the process of legislation, one conclusion is evident: there has been established an effective link between public interest groups and elites which sustained changes in abortion politics.[59]

The stage of implementation reveals the incremental pattern of abortion politics. On the one hand, changes were marginal; on the other hand, pragmatic solutions were provided to problems which encountered difficulties. Incrementalism was described as an "idological reinforcement of the pro intertia and anti innovation forces."[60] Admittedly, Israeli politics of abortion, as of now, do not manifest an ultimate change either in norms or in practices. Rather, it is one of the cases in which almost sheer inertia drove political elites to respond to social demands and pressures.

In conclusion, if one may generalize on the Israeli political system on the basis of one case study, apparently four conditions are essential in order to advance an issue from the subtle phase of nondecision to its implementation as a public policy:

1. It must be sustained by elites searching for political rewards.
2. It must be supported by political mediators both in the center and in the periphery of power.
3. It must be congruent with national objectives, as perceived and defined by decisionmakers.
4. Anticipated changes must not be unbearable to large segments of the public.

The fulfillment of these conditions has made Israel, which is loaded with national emotions with religious overtones, a country in which abortion is both legalized and liberalized.

Notes

1. One of the newest and best descriptions of abortion practices around the world is found in Malcolm Potts, Peter Diggory, and John Peel, *Abortion* (London: Cambridge University Press, 1977).

2. This point is elaborated by Edwin M. Schur, *Crimes without Victims* (Englewood Cliffs, N.J.: Prentice-Hall, 1965), p. 39.

3. See Harriet F. Pilpel, Ruth Jane Zuckerman, and Elizabeth Ogg, "Abortion, Public Issue, Private Decision" *Public Affair Pamphlet* no. 527 (September 1975).

4. Lawrence Lader, *Abortion* (Boston: Allyn and Bacon, 1966), p. 1.

5. Ephraim Kishon, "The Knitting-Needle Law," *Jerusalem Post,* March 10, 1978.

6. Peter Bachrach and Morton Baratz, "Decisions and Nondecisions, An Analytical Framework," *American Political Science Review* 57 (September 1963): 642. See also Raymond E. Wolfinger, "Non-decisions and the Study of Local Politics," *American Political Science Review* 65 (December 1971): 1063–80.

7. These arguments are presented by William Solesbury, "The Environmental Agenda," *Public Administration,* Winter 1976, pp. 379–97.

8. Charles E. Lindblom, *The Policy Making Process* (Englewood Cliffs, N.J.: Prentice-Hall, 1968), p. 4.

9. See especially Gabriel A. Almond and G. Bingham Powell, *Comparative Politics* (Boston: Little, Brown, 1966).

10. This view is held, among others, by Nils Elvander, "The Politics of Taxation in Sweden 1945-1970: A Study of the Functions of Parties and Organizations," *Scandinavian Political Studies* 7 (1972): 63-82; Robert B. Kravik, *Interest Groups in Norwegian Politics* (Oslo: Universitetsforlaget, 1976); F.G. Castler, "The Political Functions of Organized Groups: The Swedish Case," *Political Studies* 21 (1973): 26-34.

11. See Kravik, *Interest Groups in Norwegian Politics*, p. 48.

12. Charles E. Lindblom, "The Science of Muddling Through," *Public Administration Review,* Spring 1959, pp. 79-88.

13. Ibid, p. 82.

14. This information is derived from Roberto Bachi, "Abortion in Israel," in ed. Robert E. Hall, *Abortion in a Changing World,* vol. 1 (New York: Columbia University Press, 1970), pp. 274-83.

15. "Report of the Committee Appointed to Examine the Restrictions Applying to Induced Abortions," *Public Health* 17 (November 1974) (Hebrew).

16. Bachi, "Abortion in Israel," p. 276.

17. On the special relation between state and religion in Israeli politics see Emanuel Gutmann, "Religion in Israeli Politics," in ed. Jacob M. Landau, *Man, State and Society in the Contemporary Middle East* (London: Pall Mall, 1972), pp. 122-134.

18. Martin Seliger, "Positions and Dispositions in Israeli Politics," *Government and Opposition* 3 (Autumn 1968): 470.

19. For more details on the Jewish orthodox attitude see Fred Rasher, "The Jewish Attitude toward Abortion" *Tradition* 10 (1968): 48-71. The more moderate reform attitude is found in Israel R. Margolis, "A Reform Rabbi's View," in Hall, *Abortion in a Changing World,* pp. 30-33.

20. A comprehensive account of the demographic problem in Israel is found in Dov Friedlander, "Israel," in ed. Bernard Berelson, *Population Policy in Developed Countries* (New York: McGraw-Hill, 1974), pp. 42-97.

21. On the relation between abortion and fertility see Jean Van der Tak, *Abortion, Fertility and Changing Legislation: An International Review* (Lexington, Mass.: Lexington Books, D.C. Heath, 1974).

22. Gutmann, "Religion in Israeli Politics," p. 131.

23. On abortion as an issue of election campaign see "Abortion Politics," in Editorial Research Report, *The Women's Movement: Achievements and Effects* (Washington: Congressional Quarterly, 1977), pp. 103-22.

24. Kaim Z. Paltiel, "The Israeli Coalition System," *Government and Opposition* 10 (1975): 397-414.

25. Roger W. Cobb and Charles D. Elder, *Participation in American Politics: The Dynamics of Agenda-Building* (Boston: Allyn and Bacon, 1972), p. 12.

26. Israel, *"Report of the Committee for Natality Problems,"* presented to the Prime Minister, 1966 (Hebrew).

27. A comprehensive description of the Black Panthers is found in Erik

Cohen, "The Black Panthers and Israeli Society," *Jewish Journal of Sociology* 65 (June 1972): 93-109.

28. Israel, "Report of the Prime Minister's Committee on Children and Youth in Distress," presented to the Prime Minister, 1974 (Hebrew).

29. Quoted from a letter of the IFM to potential contributors abroad, n.d.

30. The campaign for liberalizing abortion that took place in the United States at that period is described by Lawrence Lader, *Abortion II: Making the Revolution* (Boston: Beacon Press, 1973).

31. *Minutes of the Knesset,* vol. 61, p. 3038, June 30, 1971.

32. Ibid., vol. 68, pp. 3876-7, July 11, 1973. See also *Jerusalem Post,* July 12, 1973.

33. Tova Yeshurun-Berman, "Causes of Interruption of Pregnancy," *Harefug* 76 (May 1969): 452-56.

34. On the politicization of the Sick Fund see Amitai Etzioni, "The Decline of Neo-Feudalism: The Case of Israel," in Ferrel Heady and Sybil L. Stokes, *Papers in Comparative Public Administration* (Michigan: The University of Michigan Press, 1962), pp. 229-243.

35. The bill was deliberately presented by a man in order to demonstrate that abortion is not a "feminine" issue.

36. On the policy of abortion as a method of birth control see Germain G. Grisez, *Abortion* (New York: Corpus Books, 1970), pp. 261-3.

37. *Minutes of the Knesset,* vol. 72, p. 1319, January 15, 1975.

38. In 1972 a voluntary association was established in order to secure legislation benefiting large families. The association's title demonstrates that having many children is God's blessing.

39. Family Planning Association, also established in 1972 by gynecologists and public figures.

40. On methods of birth control in Israel see Dov Friedlander, "Family Planning in Israel: Irrationality and Ignorance," *Journal of Marriage and Family* 35 (February 1973): 117-123.

41. *Minutes of the Knesset,* vol. 72, p. 1323, January 15, 1975.

42. The interview with the ex-Minister of Health was held on June 21, 1978.

43. Bernard Berelson, "Beyond Family Planning," *Studies in Family Planning* 38 (February 1969).

44. *Jerusalem Post,* July 10, 1975.

45. One of the proposals of a nonreligious member was that a rabbi be added to the committee and the doctor and social worker would be married people themselves. Ibid., July 16, 1975.

46. On the role of the medical profession in politics of abortion see D.A. Pond, "Therapeutic Abortion in Great Britain," in ed. R. Bruce Sloane, *Abortion, Changing Views and Practice* (New York: Grune and Straton, 1971), pp. 126-130. See also Potts, Diggory, and Peel, *Abortion,* p. 532.

47. It was estimated there were approximately 45,000 illegal abortions, each of which cost the patient 2,000 I£, thus providing the 600 gynecologists with an annual profit of 90 million I£.

48. See *Jerusalem Post,* January 28, 1977.

49. For the English version of the abortion law see Zeev W. Falk, "The New Abortion Law of Israel," *Israel Law Review* 13 (1978): 109-110.

50. This has been the case with regard to the Human Rights' Bill which was not favored by the religious chairperson of the Committee on Constitution, Law, and Justice.

51. *Jerusalem Post,* April 5, 1978.

52. Sloane, *Abortion, Changing Views and Practice,* p. 5.

53. The data were derived from the Sick Fund of the General Labor Union in Israel, *Applications to the Sick Fund's Abortion Committees 1976,* publication no. 4.1.77.

54. If education is correlated with affluence, those who had thirteen or more years of schooling have had an average of 3.2 births, in comparison to 5.9 or 4.5 to those of zero and one to eight years of schooling, respectively. *Statistical Abstract of Israel* 1977, p. 87.

55. At present, unless there is a clear medical indication, abortion costs the sum of one day's hospitalization (1,100 I£).

56. *Haaretz,* June 12, 1978 (Hebrew).

57. *Maariv,* May 30, 1978 (Hebrew).

58. See "Abortion," *People* 5 (1978): 4-20.

59. On the ambiguity of this link see Russell W. Getter and Paul D. Schumaker, "Contextual Bases of Responsiveness to Citizen Preferences and Group Demands," *Policy and Politics* 6 (March 1978): 249-78.

60. Yehezkel Dror, "Muddling Through—'Science' or Inertia!" *Public Administration Review* 24, no. 3 (1964).

Conclusion

The demands made by minorities and women to eliminate racial and sexual discrimination are now becoming institutionalized. New legislation and judicial decisions have been passed to eliminate, or at least reduce discrimination in such policy areas as education, employment, housing, credit, reproductive choice, and sex bias in the issuing of federal awards and contracts. It is important to note that the actions taken by political and judicial officials have had the effect of legitimizing the demands made by these groups. The legitimation of these demands by political and judicial officials is important because their agreement is often a prerequisite to changing the traditional attitude held by government bureaucrats and the U.S. public in general.

In many cases, legislation to reduce racial and sexual discrimination has been preceded by executive orders and judicial decisions. Yet, as students of public policy are aware, the passage of legislation and court orders do not ensure implementation. Indeed, if there is one central theme that emerges from this book, it is that success in the legislative process does not ensure success in the corridors of the bureaucracy. And it is equally true that policies passed by Congress at one time may be modified by congressional action at another. That is to say that public policy decisions are not static; this is true not only of Congress but of the judiciary as well (as was observed in the case of the Burger Court's stand on abortion policy).

There are two important lessons to be learned from the findings presented in this book. First, if the legislative victories are not to become hollow prizes, minorities and women must form political alliances that are capable of sustained action in pursuit of their objectives. To do less is to see victories won during the earlier stages lost in the later process of legislative and administrative rule making. The second lesson is that bureaucratic intransigence is to be expected after new legislation has been passed. Bureaucrats tend to delay implementation. Thus, their delay may be considered a rational response to conflicting demands made by powerful, competing groups. If minorities and women are to stimulate positive bureaucratic action, they must become either valued allies or feared opponents. The more that minorities and women come to be perceived as strong allies of a particular policy, the more likely it is that legislative victories will result in effective policy implementation.

Another theme of this book is that policy impact is constrained by lack of enforcement by federal and state agencies. Indeed, this is one of the central criticisms made of federal agencies by the Civil Rights Commission in its 1977 report to the President. For example, they found, along with some of the authors of this book, that lack of enforcement of desegregation guidelines, especially in the South, has led to the firing and demotion of minority faculty and a high suspension and expulsion rate among black youngsters. In employment, failure to enforce antidiscrimination laws has had the effect of minorities and women being hired by federal and state officials, only to see them excluded from most policy-making jobs. Indeed, it is interesting to note that even in states that have favorable political climates toward women and minorities (New Mexico), there is a lack of women and minorities in policy-making positions. It may well be that states with a more favorable policy environment toward women and minorities may not lead to greater impact in hiring for several reasons: (1) minorities and women can find better jobs in private industry; (2) representativeness does not equal responsiveness; and (3) the time lag needed to assess hiring improvements is too short, or a residue of institutional sexism and racism remains.

This book also points out that some states still maintain practices which discriminate against minorities and women as individuals or as a class. Women, for example, tend to be discriminated against in state legislatures because they are women. They are relegated to certain committees and kept out of leadership positions. Blacks, on the other hand, are denied credit if they live in certain areas or neighborhoods. Blacks also tend to be discriminated against in some public unions that have collective-bargaining agreements which are unrepresentative of minority interests.

What, then, has been the impact of the policies discussed in this book on the rights of minorities and women? The chapters suggest that some of these policies have been successful in reducing discrimination based on race and sex. However, they also point out that the impacts of some policies are less positive because of the lack of enforcement by federal and state officials. From one point of view, then, these policies may be said to have provided "incremental equalitarianism" for women and minorities. It may well be that the most important victory for minorities and women has been the legitimation of their demands by top policy-makers, for while the policies are incremental, in the long run they may educate and prepare the U.S. public for the inevitable expansion and eventually eradication of racism and sexism in the United States.

Index of Names

Index of Subjects

About the Contributors

Glenn T. Broach is associate professor of political science at East Tennessee State University. He has contributed to professional journals in the areas of legislative politics, state policy, judicial policy making, and public perceptions of policy problems.

Charles S. Bullock, III, is professor of political science at the University of Georgia. His primary areas of research are legislative politics and policy analysis, where he focuses on civil rights policies. He has authored or coauthored numerous books and articles in political science, education, and sociology journals. He is coauthor of *Public Policy and Politics in America* (Duxbury, 1978).

Cal Clark is a visiting associate professor of government at New Mexico State University. His research interests include political participation and representation, East European politics, and local policy making. He is coauthor of a book and a monograph and has published in such journals as *American Political Science Review, International Studies Quarterly, Journal of Conflict Resolution, Political Methodology,* and *Publius.*

Janet Clark is an associate professor of government at New Mexico State University. Her research interests include local policy making, state parties and legislatures, and women's political participation. She has published articles in such journals as *American Politics Quarterly, East European Quarterly, Journal of Political Science,* and *Western Political Quarterly.*

M. Margaret Conway is associate professor of government and politics at the University of Maryland, College Park. She is a coauthor of *Parties and Politics in America* and *Political Analysis,* and she has published articles on local political party organization, voting behavior in local elections, and political socialization.

Anne N. Costain is an assistant professor of political science at the University of Colorado at Boulder. She received the Ph.D. from The Johns Hopkins University. In addition to her research on lobbying for women's rights, she has published work on U.S. national nominating conventions.

Jose Z. Garcia is an assistant professor of government at New Mexico State University. He received the doctorate from the University of New Mexico and is a specialist on military regimes in Latin America as well as an observer of the political scene in New Mexico. He has published in the *Western Political Quarterly, Policy Studies Journal,* and several books of collected works.

Marianne Githens has a Ph.D. from the London School of Economics and is professor and former chairperson of the Department of Political Science at Goucher College. Having served as chairperson of the Committee on the Status of Women and as a member of the Executive Council of the Southern Political Science Association, she is currently the recording secretary. With Jewel L. Prestage she is coauthor of *A Portrait of Marginality: The Political Behavior of the American Women,* published in 1977. She has taught at Catholic University, St. John's University and the University of Florida.

Leslie F. Goldstein is an associate professor at the University of Delaware. She has written several articles that address problems of minorities, and she is the author of *The Constitutional Rights of Women* (1979).

Diane Levitt Gottheil is an assistant professor in the Department of Criminal Justice at Illinois State University in Normal, Illinois. Formerly director of the Adult Diversion Program of Champaign County, she has published in *Crime and Delinquency* and has research interests in alternatives to prosecution.

Richard J. Hardy is an assistant professor of political science at the University of Missouri-Columbia. He will obtain the Ph.D. from the University of Iowa in 1979. His dissertation is on the impact of civil rights policies in the post-World War II period. He has published research in the *American Journal of Political Science.*

Edward R. Jackson is an associate professor of political science at Howard University. He received his Ph.D. from the University of Iowa. He has published several articles on blacks in political science, politics in the black community and affirmative action.

Donald J. McCrone is professor of political science at the University of Washington. He obtained the Ph.D. from the University of North Carolina. He was a Fullbright Lecturer at the University of Strathclyde, Scotland, in 1974-1975. He has published research in the *American Political Science Review, American Journal of Political Science,* and the *British Journal of Political Science.*

Kenneth J. Meier is assistant director of the Bureau of Government Research and assistant professor of political science at the University of Oklahoma. He is the author of *Politics and the Bureaucracy* as well as articles in the *American Political Science Review, Public Administration Review, Western Political Quarterly, Administration and Society,* and *Human Relations.* His current research focuses on the impact of bureaucracy on public policy.

H. Brinton Milward is an assistant professor of political science at the University of Kansas. He has recently authored "Politics, Personnel and Public Policy" in the *Public Administration Review* (1978). His main research and teaching interest centers on the impact of bureaucratic and organization variables on public policy outcomes.

Howard A. Palley is professor of social welfare policy at the School of Social Work and Community Planning of the University of Maryland. He is coauthor of *Urban America and Public Policies* (1977), and he has written numerous articles on both U.S. and British health and welfare policy.

Jewel L. Prestage, professor and chairperson in the Department of Political Science at Southern University, has a Ph.D. from the University of Iowa. She has served as a vice president of the American Political Science Association, president of the Southern Political Science Association, president of the National Conference of Black Political Scientists, and president of the Southwestern Social Science Association. Her research interests include minority politics, political socialization, and women in politics. With Marianne Githens she is co-author of *A Portrait of Marginality: The Political Behavior of the American Women.*

Sarah Slavin Schramm is an author, scholar, and community activist. She has published articles about the presidency, national policy making, and women in politics. She has written *Plow Women rather than Reapers: An Intellectual History of Feminism in the United States.*

Joseph Stewart, Jr., is assistant professor of Political Science at the University of New Orleans. His research in policy evaluation focuses on equal educational opportunity and school desegregation. He is the coauthor of recent articles in *Integrated Education* and the *Journal of Politics* in this area.

Cheryl Swanson is an assistant professor of political science at the University of Kansas. She has written for *Urban Affairs Quarterly* and the *Journal of Police Administration* in the area of criminal justice and has recently coauthored an article on women in administration for a forthcoming issue of *Public Administration Review.*

Toni-Michelle C. Travis is a graduate student in the political science department at the University of Chicago.

Susan Welch is professor and chairperson of the Department of Political Science, University of Nebraska-Lincoln. She is currently completing (with Albert Karnig) a manuscript on black elected officials and urban politics, and she has published recent articles on women in politics in the *American Journal of Political Science* and the *Western Political Quarterly.*

Maurice C. Woodard is a professor of political science at Howard University and staff associate at the American Political Science Association. He received the Ph.D. from the University of Kansas. He has published many articles in the areas of equal employment opportunity, affirmative action, and poverty programs. He recently edited a book on blacks in political science.

Yael Yishai is an assistant professor in the Department of Political Science at Haifa University.

About the Editors

Marian Lief Palley is professor and chairperson of the Department of Political Science at the University of Delaware. She is coauthor of *Urban America and Public Policies* (1977), *Tradition and Change in American Party Politics* (1975), and *The Politics of Social Change* (1971). In addition, she has written articles addressing problems of national welfare policy and urban policy as well as articles relating to the role of women in politics.

Michael B. Preston is an assistant professor of political science at the University of Illinois-Urbana. His primary areas of research are bureaucratic politics, black and urban politics, and public policy. His policy research focuses on minority and manpower policies. He has written for *Public Administration Review, Policy Studies Journal,* and *Urban Affairs Quarterly.*